BY GEORGE
A Kaufman Collection

BY GEORGE S. KAUFMAN

Compiled and Edited by
Donald Oliver

ST. MARTIN'S PRESS
New York

Copyright © 1979 by Anne Kaufman Schneider
All rights reserved. For information, write:
St. Martin's Press, Inc., 175 Fifth Avenue, New York, N.Y. 10010.
Manufactured in the United States of America
Library of Congress Cataloging in Publication Data
Kaufman, George Simon, 1889–1961.
By George: The collected Kaufman.
I. Oliver, Donald. II. Title.
PS3521.A727B9   812'.5'2   79–16346
ISBN 0–312–11101–0

CONTENTS

CONTENTS

CONTENTS

Foreword

Of all the people who lived well into my lifetime that I wish I had met, George S. Kaufman leads the list.

Groucho Marx unashamedly referred to Kaufman as "my personal god," and the fact that I got to be friends with Groucho eased some of my frustration. Reading these collected miscellaneous writings redoubles my sense of loss.

I became an ardent fan of Kaufman's through his appearances on the long-gone TV program "This Is Show Business." The premise of the program was that an entertainer came on and, before singing, dancing or whatever, laid his "problem" before the panel —on which Kaufman was a regular. After the entertainer performed, his problem was discussed.

One particular incident I recall vividly. It endeared Kaufman to me for life. The very young Eddie Fisher revealed that due to his youth the girls in the chorus at the Latin Quarter, where he was appearing, would not go out with him. He then did his song. Kaufman, when his turn came to discuss and advise, took a long moment, his head leaning wearily against his hand, and finally spoke. This is how I remember what he said:

Mr. Fisher, on Mount Wilson there is a telescope that can magnify the most distant stars to twenty-four times the magnification of any previous telescope. This remarkable instrument was unsurpassed in the world of astronomy until the development and construction of the Mount Palomar telescope. The Mount Palomar telescope is an even more remarkable instrument of magnification. Owing to advances and improvements in optical technology, it is capable of magnifying the stars to four times the magnification and resolution of the Mount Wilson telescope. [Pause, while tension builds as to whether Kaufman has lost his mind] Mr. Fisher, if you could somehow put the Mount Wilson telescope *inside* the Mount Palomar telescope, you *still* wouldn't be able to see my interest in your problem. [Laughter, continuing almost into the following program]

Alas, Kaufman was later bounced from that program by the cowards-that-be because a few boobs complained when he made an offhand remark about the excessive use of "Silent Night" at Christmastime. I went into an angry mourning. Fred Allen's comment was, "There were only two wits on television, Groucho Marx and George S. Kaufman. Without Kaufman, television has reverted to being half-witted."

Once, while walking past a Broadway opening, I got my only in-person glimpse of "the gloomy dean of comedy" as he entered the theater. I stood rooted to the spot for a time. I had laid eyes on the man who said, when a play of his got tepid reviews, "All we have to worry about now is word of mouth," and who, while shopping with his wife at Bloomingdale's drapery department, asked a clerk, "Have you got any good second-act curtains?"

I resumed walking up Broadway, rolling my favorite sayings of his over and over in my mind. Like the one prompted by a stage doorman who failed to recognize the famous forlorn countenance when Kaufman arrived for a rehearsal. "Are you with the show?" the doorman asked. My hero replied, "Let's just say I'm not against it."

In recent years the fates have conspired to tantalize me even further about Kaufman. My wife and Leueen MacGrath, who was once married to Kaufman, became close friends while acting together. Whenever Leueen says to us, "George would've enjoyed you so much," the pangs return.

But enough of this self-pity. I suppose the "This Is Show Business" appearances have been lost or dumped in the East River. The appearances that Kaufman made with Jack Paar on "The Tonight Show" are probably gone. Only Kaufman's writings, remembered witticisms and legend remain.

Among my mentally noted pet projects that never got done was a plan to someday go to the New York Public Library and track down Kaufman's magazine pieces and other miscellaneous writings. Now, happily, someone has done the job for me. The Gilbert and Sullivan parody, the piece about the Waiters' School (where waiters are trained, among other things, to interrupt Kaufman anecdotes just before the punch line) and just about everything else here fills me with delight. The sketch "If Men

Played Cards As Women Do" is alone worth the price of the book. In the phrase of an unknown blurb-writer on a book of old Jewish folk songs, "This collection fills a long-needed want."

Because of Kaufman's well-known obsession with cutting, reading these pieces makes me wonder what gems he may have eliminated. He once said plays are not written, they're rewritten. Some years ago, in a New York autograph dealer's shop, I ran across a letter Kaufman had written on the stationery of Boston's Ritz Hotel. It was lesson in epistolary brevity: "Dear Sir, I don't want any German plays. George S. Kaufman." When asked to write an appreciation of S. J. Perelman for a dust jacket, he wrote, "I appreciate S. J. Perelman—George S. Kaufman."

Despite the master's edict about brevity, the only way I could enjoy this book more would be if it were longer.

Dick Cavett
New York City
July, 1979

Preface

During my formative years, my passion for theatre heightened by reading every theatre book I could get my hands on. It did not take me too long to realize that there was a common link between many of the plays I admired: George S. Kaufman. For many years I felt secure in the knowledge that, after endless trips to libraries, I had read all of Mr. Kaufman's published works, that is to say, his plays. Recently, a biography of Kaufman appeared and made me aware that I was wrong—the author brought to light a substantial amount of Kaufman's prose writing that had appeared only in newspapers and magazines. So off I went again to the libraries, and the idea for this book was born.

Contained within these covers is the first comprehensive collection of George S. Kaufman's short pieces and sketches. Those readers who only know of Kaufman's work in conjunction with at least one other writer will be pleased to find so much material written by Kaufman alone.

By George is by no means a complete compilation. The famous plays (written with Moss Hart, Marc Connelly, Edna Ferber, Ring Lardner, Morrie Ryskind, Howard Teichmann, and many others) are readily available elsewhere and therefore aren't reprinted here, and for various reasons a handful of the magazine and newspaper articles aren't included either. However, the following selections are being published in this book for the first time: *Hollywood Pinafore*, *Meet The Audience*, *On The American Plan*, *The Cocoanuts*, and *The Great Warburton Mystery*.

All of the selections in *By George* appear as written by George S. Kaufman with the exception of *Hollywood Pinafore*, the text of which I have condensed.

A special thanks is given to Anne Kaufman Schneider for her gracious cooperation, and I truly appreciate the efforts of my editor, Rebecca Martin, and her assistant, Karen Johnsen, in the preparation of this book.

I am much obliged to David Grossberg, Bill Gile, Annette Harper, Henry Machtay, Lucinda Ballard Dietz, Elliott Sirkin and Michael Odza for their initial and continued support and enthusiasm for *By George*. My gratitude is also extended to the following people who contributed much needed information and assistance: Hector Baez, Ken Bloom, Malcolm Goldstein, Terry Miller, Scott Robertson, Deirdre Shaw, Mary Ann Jensen (curator of the Theatre Collection of the Princeton University Library), Louis Rachow (librarian of the Walter Hampden–Edwin Booth Theatre Collection and Library at the Players Club), and the staff of the New York Public Library's Theatre Collection at Lincoln Center.

Donald Oliver
New York City
June, 1979

BY GEORGE

ADVICE TO WORRIERS

Life, *July 27, 1922*

Pray list to me a modest while;
    I fain would spill an earful:
Don't worry—cultivate a smile—
    Be always bright and cheerful.

When things are looking dour and black,
    Then *you* be blithe and hearty;
Just slap me gaily on the back—
    The life of every party.

Let naught your cheery nature spoil;
    Be always gay and chipper . . .
And I'll supply the boiling oil,
    If someone has a dipper.

SCHOOL FOR WAITERS

THE NEW YORKER, *August 2, 1947*

In a vague sort of way, I had felt for a long time that the place existed. Several times, I had tried to pin them down about it, but invariably they denied it—just didn't know what I was driving at, they said. And then, about ten days ago, I happened to be talking to Pierre, who bows to customers in and out at the Alabaster Room. Suddenly, I felt the moment was ripe.

"Pierre," I said, "I've been going to restaurants for many years. And I've noticed that the waiters all have certain little tricks—little ways and means of doing things that generally can be counted on to drive the customer crazy. It seems to me that these little tricks have a certain similarity. They follow a definite pattern, and it's hard to believe that it's accidental. There must be someplace where they are taught these things. They couldn't just blunder into them, every one of them. Come on, Pierre—I've known you a long time. Tell me."

He hesitated a few seconds, looked around cautiously, then came a step nearer. "Meet me outside the restaurant at midnight," he whispered. "Wear a plain dark suit."

Needless to say, I was at the rendezvous on time. Pierre appeared almost instantly; with a nod he beckoned me to follow him. At the corner, he motioned me into a cab; the driver started off with no word of instruction. Pierre produced a blindfold and fastened it around my head. "I am sorry to do this, " he said, "but you will understand."

We rode for about ten minutes, in silence. Then we stopped. Pierre helped me out of the cab, and we crossed the sidewalk and went down three or four steps. There was the clank of chains and the sound of a heavy door opening; then a coarse voice said, "Well?" Pierre gave what was evidently the password. *"Sauce maison, "* he said.

Then he took off my blindfold. For a moment, I could see nothing. I heard the sound of the chains again as they dropped back into place, and then, vaguely, I discerned another door in front of me.

"Do not speak," said Pierre. "Just watch."

The door opened. What met my eyes was merely a restaurant, or at least it seemed to be a restaurant—gleaming tables, waiters and captains, velvet rope. Outside the rope, about a dozen men and women in evening clothes were standing, although the restaurant itself was empty.

"Why don't they let them sit down?" I whispered to Pierre.

"Sh-h-h! They are not customers. They are merely hired for the waiters to practice on." Suddenly, he pointed to a tall, distinguished figure who was just emerging from a side door. "Professor Ziegler," he whispered. "Head of the school. Trained abroad."

I looked at Ziegler with interest. He was handsome, impassive, and had eyes that could look through one to the wall. He snapped his fingers. Immediately, a couple in evening clothes detached themselves from the group and were admitted inside the rope. A captain came forward to meet them.

"Yes, sir," said the captain to the man in evening clothes.

Ziegler winced. "No, no!" he cried. " 'Yes, sir' is never used at this point—it would make too much sense. 'Yes, sir' is said only when filling the water glass or putting down a plate. That is the time to say 'Yes, sir'—when it can't possibly mean anything at all. Right now, you look carefully at the lady and gentleman for about five seconds. Then you say, 'Two?' "

"But I can see that there are two," said the captain. "Why do I ask them such a silly question?"

"Idiot!" spluttered Ziegler. "The single word 'Two?,' used at this moment, has several possible meanings, all designed to aggravate the customer. It can mean, for example, 'You piker, you! If you were anybody of consequence, anybody with money, you would certainly bring six or eight people along, not just a lousy one. Phooey!' Or it can mean 'Just two, eh? I know what you're after, you little sneak. Just you and that girl. What are you up to with her, anyhow?'

"See what I mean? Or else it can imply that although there are only two people standing there, the customer is planning to smuggle three or four more in behind your back. So this is by way of warning him that we are on guard against any chicanery—he'd better not try anything.

"The customer may accept any one of these meanings; it does not matter, because all of them are calculated to unsettle him just a trifle upon entering. That is the purpose."

Ziegler paused for a moment and waited for this to sink in.

"All right! The couple is seated. I will now show you how to get the order wrong. Of course, it would be a simple thing for the waiter to take the order and personally tell the man who is going to prepare it. But with that method it would come out right entirely too often. We have a different system. Let me have a captain, an assistant captain, a waiter, a chef, and an assistant chef. Line up!"

In a few seconds, the five men were in line.

"These men have worked with me before," said Ziegler, "and understand the system. Let the lady order a dish. Anything! Don't worry—you won't get it."

"Breast of guinea hen under glass," said the lady.

"Good!" said Ziegler. "Now, each of the men will pass the order on to the next man, and we will see what it becomes. Remember to speak rapidly and unintelligibly."

"Breast of guinea hen under glass," said the first man.

"Quick!" commanded Ziegler.

"Breast of glass under guinea hen," said the second man.

"Best glasses should be brought in again," murmured the third man.

There was a pause.

"Quick! What did he say?" called the impatient Ziegler.

"I couldn't understand him," said the fourth man.

"Of course you couldn't. Make something up! Quick!"

"A hamburger!"

"Next man!"

"A ham sandwich!"

"Good!" This from Ziegler again. "The lady orders breast of guinea hen under glass and receives a ham sandwich. Exceptionally good!"

He actually smiled for a moment, then immediately turned businesslike again.

"Class in Point Killing!" he called. "I will dispense with the little things, such as moving a glass one-tenth of an inch for no reason at all. Point Killing, please! The gentleman will tell the lady a story! Any story!"

The man at the table picked up at once. He was obviously experienced. "It seems that out at the race track the other day, a horse came up to the two-dollar window and said, 'I want to bet on myself in the third race.' The man at the window was pretty surprised. 'What's that you said?' he asked. 'What's the matter?' asked the horse. 'Are you surprised I can talk?' 'No,' said the man. 'I'm surprised that—'"

Instantly, the waiter cut in. "Oysters for Madame?" he asked.

"Fine!" said Ziegler. "Not only does he kill the story, but the oysters are not for Madame at all. They are for the gentleman, who ordered clams."

He stopped for a second and took a breath.

"I do not want to give you too much in one session," he said, "but I would like to say just a few words about Vision Blocking. This is a science that really cannot be taught to you; it requires an instinct, and you either have it or you haven't. Let me have a beautiful girl and a homely woman!"

They were provided at once. Ziegler crossed with them to the other side of the room.

"Sit here," he said to the girl, "You wait a moment" to the woman. Then he came back to the diners at the first table. "All right," he said to the man. "You know what to do."

The man turned to his companion. "Look at that girl sitting over there. Isn't she pretty? Right over there."

With the first spoken word, Ziegler made a quick move. In an instant, he was standing squarely in front of the pretty girl.

"Oh, dear!" said the man. "That waiter's right in front of her. He'll move in a second."

Ziegler made a lightning gesture toward the homely woman. In a flash, the pretty girl was out of the seat and the other woman had taken her place.

"You see?" said Ziegler. *"Now* I move!"

The entire room burst into applause. Ziegler bowed.

"Now, then!" he said. "Class in Avoiding the Diner's Eye!"

HOW I BECAME A GREAT ACTOR*

THEATRE, *December, 1930*

If I live to be a hundred—and in that event the Union Central Life Insurance Company will do practically all the cheering—I shall never forget how I jumped into the cast of *Once in a Lifetime* and saved the day. Things were pretty desperate, I tell you that. It was already late in January, and we were due to open at the Music Box the following September. The part which a strange Fate was to call upon me to fill—into which I was destined to leap overnight, as you might say, or over winter and summer, if you want to quibble—was as empty as a thrush. (That may not be just the right simile, but the editor of this magazine has been on the phone twice today, and I'm in a hurry.)

Sam H. Harris, the play's producer, was at his wits' end. (He generally goes out there every Friday and then doesn't come to his office again till Monday morning.) Aside from fifty or sixty actors, he was at a complete loss as to how to fill the part. I remember one actor who seemed to fit the part perfectly—in fact, he would have been engaged for it if he had not suffered a rather unfortunate accident on leaving the office. He had just had an interview with Mr. Harris, who said he liked him enormously, and was starting down the stairs when he tripped over something right on the top step. It was really a very funny fall—it happened that I had a good view of it, because I was standing right on the top step.

It was shortly after this that Mr. Harris and Moss Hart, desperate, sought me out. Now I am aware that there are several stories abroad about this meeting, so I would like to set down here exactly what was said. My memory for things of this sort is excellent, and I am willing to swear that what they said to me was: "Good God, man! Can't you jump in?" That was it exactly—"Good God, man! Can't you jump in?"

*When *Once in a Lifetime,* written by Moss Hart and Kaufman, opened at the Music Box Theatre in New York on September 24, 1930, Kaufman played the role of Lawrence Vail, a playwright.—*ed.*

Subsequently even Moss Hart admitted that these were the precise words spoken, but made the absurd claim that the interview took place *after* I had gone into the part, and that the line was uttered upon their being informed that there was a building burning down in the next block. . . . I am willing to leave it to any fair-minded person.

Of course it was a herculean task. The part was a long one, and I had only until September to learn it. Many a night I sat alone in my room until the wee hours, gulping down cup after cup of strong black coffee, pounding the words into a brain already wearied by the long grind. But I kept on, and when the opening night arrived walked onto the stage of the Music Box and spoke every "if," "and," and "but." And if it had not been for a certain pardonable nervousness I would have spoken some of the other words, too.

The rest is history, of course, but in the interest of fair play there are two or three points that I would like to set straight. It has been said in some quarters that I could not have been so *terribly* good, or else people would have taken the horses out of my carriage and hauled me to my home, the way they did with Jenny Lind. As a matter of fact every effort was made to do this, and the plan was defeated only because they were unable to get the right horses.

It seems that the horses who do this work were on another job that night—I believe some star was opening down on the East Side, although it would not surprise me if certain people deliberately arranged for the horses to be elsewhere. (There is a good deal of jealousy in the theatre—I've found that out.) At the last minute there was talk of taking the gasoline out of a taxicab, but it was realized that that wouldn't be the same thing.

Now about the bomb that came to the theatre. I examined the paper closely after the explosion, and I am willing to swear that it was not meant for me at all. It was addressed to "George S. Kaufmann," with two n's, and we have always spelled our name with only one. There are some Kaufmanns in Pittsburgh who spell it with two n's, and I suppose it was meant for one of them. I think one of them is named George, too—or Adrian, or something. I am sorry, of course, about the three actors who were killed, but we had a pretty large cast and were thinking of letting some people out anyway.

As for the poisoned candy, I have a theory about that, and I'll bet you I'm right. I think it was that actor who tripped on the stairs.

ANNOY KAUFMAN, INC.

The New Yorker, *December 21, 1957*

For some time now, I have suspected the existence of an organization whose scope and energies are so enormous that they stagger the imagination. I am not prepared to say with certainty that such an organization exists, but there are various recurrent phenomena in my life that can be explained only by the theory that a major plan is in operation—a plan so vast and expensive that it is almost impossible to envision it.

The organization that carries out this plan must spend millions of dollars annually to achieve its object. It has—it must have—great suites of offices, and thousands upon thousands of employees. On a guess, I would put its running cost at ten million dollars a year; if anything, the figure may be higher. With some presumption, I have christened it Annoy Kaufman, Inc., though I will admit that I cannot find that title in any lists of corporations.

But the facts are incontrovertible:

First there is the matter of going to the bank. Let us say that I have run out of money and am required to cash a small check. Now, no one knows that I am going to the bank on that particular morning. There is nothing about it in the papers. I am not immodest, and I know that, at best, such an announcement would get only a few lines on a back page: "George S. Kaufman is going to the bank this morning to cash a check. We wish him all success"—something like that.

But not a word is printed. No one knows about it. As a matter of fact, I have probably not made up my mind to go until about eleven o'clock. Yet the organization is prepared. It immediately arranges that half a dozen big companies should be drawing their payroll money that morning, and that each of them should send a clerk to the bank with a list of payroll requirements—so many five-dollar bills, so many dollar bills, so many quarters, dimes, nickels, pennies. Next it is arranged that all these people should get to the tellers' windows just a few seconds ahead of me.

Now, this takes doing. Remember, the organization has not known just which morning I was planning to go to the bank, so for weeks and weeks these clerks have been held in readiness somewhere. And suppose I stop to talk to a friend and arrive five minutes later than expected. Obviously, several relays of clerks must be kept in reserve in a corner of the bank, awaiting a signal.

Moreover, these are not people who are just pretending to be cashing payrolls; the bank would never stand for that. No, they are people from real companies—companies founded by the organization and kept in business for years and years, probably at an enormous loss, just so that their representatives can get to the bank windows ahead of me. And it is not always the same people who stand in front of me; it is different ones. This, in turn, means a large number of separate companies to maintain. These companies run factories, keep books, pay income taxes, hold board meetings, advertise on television, pension their employees. Surely this side of the enterprise alone must run to a pretty figure.

My next example may sound like a simple and inexpensive thing to manage, but it isn't. It has to do with the engineer's little boy, Danny. Danny is six years old. In fact, he has been six years old for the thirty-five years that I have been making overnight train journeys. (I suppose that, actually, they keep on having an engineer's little boy born every year, but even that takes planning.) Anyhow, for years and years Danny has been begging his father to let him run the locomotive some night. For years and years, his father has been saying no. Then, finally, the night comes. "Can I run the engine tonight, Daddy?" asks Danny, who is too young to know about "can" and "may." And his father says, "Yes, Danny, boy. We have just got word that Kaufman will be on the train tonight, and he is very tired and needs a good night's sleep, so you can run the engine." So Danny runs the engine, the result being the neck-breaking stops and starts that keep me awake all night.

The organization has, of course, the incidental expense of maintaining Danny in Chicago or Pittsburgh or Cleveland, as the case may be, until I am ready to make the return trip. (Danny's father obviously cannot wait over to take care of him; he must go back to running the engine properly on the nights when I am not travelling.) So the organization must keep branch offices in Chicago and Pittsburgh and Cleveland (and wherever else I may go), and provide someone else to take care of Danny, and schools for him to go to, and somebody to make sure that he doesn't practice, and so learn how to run the engine better, before I make my return trip. This seemingly small part of the business can run to fantastic sums over the years.

But the bank and Danny are, after all, relatively minor matters. Once done with, they are over till the next time. I come now to the major opus—the basic activity for which Annoy Kaufman, Inc., was founded.

Years ago, when I moved to New York, I noticed that a little man in a gray overcoat was watching me closely as I took the ferry from Jersey City to Twenty-third Street. I don't know why, but I think his name was Mr. Moffat. At all events, Mr. Moffat was the first person off the ferryboat when it docked. Hurriedly joining his pals in a midtown office, Mr. Moffat reported as follows: "Boys, he's here. We can take out incorporation papers in Albany tomorrow and go to work. In a day or two, I'll have all the dope for you."

Now you may think it arrogant of me to claim that the entire rebuilding of New York City, at present in full bloom, came about solely as a result of my arrival here, but I can only cite the facts. No sooner did I move to a given neighborhood than the wreckers were at work on the adjoining building, generally at eight o'clock in the morning. The pneumatic asphalt-ripper, with which we are all now familiar, was first used early one morning as a weapon against the slumber of none other than myself. The first automatic rivet came into existence to be the destroyer of my sleep. (All dates and names of streets are on file in the office of my attorney.) Naturally, I kept moving to new neighborhoods in quest of peace, but the boys were always ready and waiting. Can you blame me for feeling that it was I, and I alone, who unwittingly charted the course of the city's onward sweep?

Only once, in all these years, did they slip up. Acting without sufficient research, they put up Lever House just to the south of me, unaware that my bedroom was on the other side of my apartment. Discovering their error, they, of course, bought the property to the north and went quickly to work. Well, sir, heads rolled in the office that morning, I can tell you. Mr. Moffat, I like to think, shot himself, but I suspect he was immediately succeeded by his son, and since then the organization has functioned so efficiently that I am now exactly thirty-seven years behind on sleep, with only an outside chance of making it up.

With all that on their hands, you wouldn't think they'd have time for Congressional lobbying, too, would you? This ultimate move came to light during a visit of mine to Washington a few weeks ago. Having been made suspicious, over the years, by my dealings with the Internal Revenue people, I went to the trouble of looking up the original text of the income-tax law, as filed in the Library of Congress. Sure enough, there it was—Paragraph D, Clause 18—just as I had suspected: "The taxpayer, in computing the amount of tax due to the Government, may deduct from his taxable income all legitimate expenses incurred in the course of conducting his business or profession—except," it added, "in the case of George S. Kaufman."

BARBER SHOP "WHY'S"

LIFE, *December 22, 1921*

Why does a haircut always cost the same no matter how much hair you have?

Why does a barber always ask you if you shave yourself?

Why is no barber ever satisfied with the weather?

Why does no barber ever have a good word for the last fellow that cut your hair?

Why does a barber always try to persuade you to buy out the shop when all you want is a shave?

Why does a barber, when drying your face, always overlook that little corner of your ear?

Why does your nose always begin to tickle just as soon as your hands are tucked under the covering?

Why is the foot-rest on the shine-stand always too small for your feet?

Why does the shine boy always have a vigorous argument with the other shine boy right in the middle of polishing your shoes?

AND

Why is the best-looking manicure girl always working down at the other end of the room?

DEPARTMENT OF AMPLIFICATION

THE NEW YORKER, *June 29, 1946*

Holicong, PA.
June 20, 1946

To the Editors of *The New Yorker,*
Dear Sirs:

I noticed in John McCarten's review of the motion picture *Henry V,* in this week's *New Yorker,* the reappearance of my old friend "judicious pruning" after a lapse of several years, and used in a sense that I believe is unique in the field of criticism. As a long-time student of judicious pruning, I trust you will not think it out of place if I clarify this statement for the record.

The definitive work on the subject is, of course, the elder Bergmeister's monumental *Pruning,* published in 1873, and now, I believe, out of print. Bergmeister listed many different varieties of pruning, including even *in*judicious pruning, of which there had been but one known case up to that time. Far in the lead, of course, and always a great favorite of critics, was judicious pruning, the origin of which was traced to a review of *The Canterbury Tales* in the Canterbury *Daily News* (circa 1389).

In every instance, however, the particular work under criticism always *needed* judicious pruning; never had it received it. This became so definitely the custom that it was acknowledged by Weinstock in his *Dictionary of Dramatic Criticism,* in which judicious pruning is defined simply as "what the play needs." This is what makes Mr. McCarten's use of the phrase so unusual; he does not say that *Henry V needs* judicious pruning but that "judicious pruning . . . has served to keep it uncluttered." It is an interesting use of the phrase and should not go by unnoticed.

It is also interesting to note, by the way, that Bergmeister cites a review by a sixteenth-century critic which reads, in part, "Many prunings remain in the play." This, of course, is the origin of the phrase "full of prunes."

Sincerely yours,
George S. Kaufman

LIFE'S CALENDAR FOR
DECEMBER 1921*

by George S. Kaufman and Marc Connelly

1 Th Baltimore, Md., lighted by gas, 1816. Mayor Hylan tries the same thing in New York, 1921. Christopher Sholes invents typewriter, 1867.

2 F Battle of Austerlitz, 1805. Christopher Sholes gets his hands covered with ink changing typewriter ribbon, 1867. John Brown hanged; popular songwriters get busy, 1854. Monroe Doctrine born, 1823. First Pullman car bed patented, 1856. First Pullman car joke, 1856.

3 Sa Illinois admitted to Union; Chicago celebrates with 87 murders, 1818. First cases of ante-Christmas politeness among elevator men and apartment telephone operators noticed in New York, Utah and parts of southern Connecticut, 1921.

4 Su Washington bids farewell to his officers, 1783. Citizen of Duluth, Minn., loses mind trying to fish short spoon out of mustard bottle, 1919. Three hundred and fourteen British novelists, playwrights, war correspondents and poets arrive in America for lecture tours, 1920.

5 M Martin Van Buren, eighth President, born 1782. Female lawyer breaks into newspaper without being referred to as Portia, 1906. Christopher Sholes calls in man to change typewriter ribbon, 1867.

6 Tu Delaware, with consent of DuPonts, ratifies Constitution, 1787. Chinese labor exclusion act passed; China takes it coolie, 1894. Three hundred and fourteen British novelists, playwrights, war correspondents and poets complete books on conditions in America, 1920.

*All installments of *Life's Calendar* (from December 1921 through November 1922) were written by both Kaufman and Marc Connelly.

7 W Congress declared war on Austria-Hungary, 1917. Austria-Hungary doesn't much care by this time, 1917. One-thousandth book on South Seas completed by Harold L. Pleevey, of South Bend, Ind., 1921. Ten-year-old boy reads entire inscription on street car transfer, New York, 1919. Christopher Sholes sells the typewriter, 1921.

8 Th President Jefferson sends first message to Congress, 1801. Green and red glass jars for drug store windows invented, 1743. Six million, eight hundred and fifty thousand people still wonder what that stuff is that's in them, 1921.

9 F Three men light cigarettes from same match and are immediately struck dead by lightning, 1889. Judge Gary predicts era of prosperity, 1908, '10, '11, '12, '13, '14, '15, '16, '17, '18, '19, '20, '21. New York telephone directory issued in four volumes, 1924.

10 Sa Mississippi admitted to Union, 1817. Frances White learns to spell, 1917. Spanish War ends, 1898.

11 Su Plato begins lecture course, 399 B.C. Husbands bring home something new in explanations, 399 B.C. Indiana admitted to Union, 1816.

12 M First National Republican convention; Elihu Root refuses to see reporters, 1831. Record for output of Christmas cigars smashed by Ajax Portland Cement Co., 1920.

13 Tu Battle of Fredricksburg, 1862. Mean temperature grows meaner, 1921.

14 W First number of Boston, Mass., *Gazette* published, 1719. Constant Reader makes a complaint, 1719. First banquet photograph taken, forty diners coming out on the bias, 1871. George Washington dies, 1799. Alabama admitted to Union, 1819. South Pole discovered, 1911.

15 Th Battle of Nashville, 1864. Hotels stop starching towels, 1956.

16 F Boston Tea Party; British guests arrive late, 1773.

Managers pronounce it the worst theatrical season in years, 1912, '13, '14, '15, '16, '17, '18, '19, '20, '21. Great fire in New York, 1835. Janitors celebrate it by turning off heat, 1921.

17 Sa Eighteenth Amendment passed, 1917. Eighteenth Amendment passed up, 1918, '19, '20, '21. First successful flight of aeroplane, 1903. Six million, four hundred and thirteen thousand persons say it will never work, 1903.

18 Su Thirteenth Amendment, abolishing slavery, passed, 1865. *Monah,* new Arrow collar, invented, 1922. Motion picture magnate sends representatives to see D. Alighieri about film rights to *Inferno,* 1919.

19 M Library at Alexandria opened to public; first sixteen patrons asking for Harold Bell Wright, 283 B.C. Elephant in circus winter quarters at Bridgeport, Conn., kills great-grandson of man who gave him bad peanut in Salt Lake City, Utah, 67 years before, 1899.

20 Tu S. Carolina secedes from Union, 1860. Seventy-five extra beds put in New York hospitals to take care of Christmas card buyers, 1920, '21.

21 W Cambridge, Mass., founded, 1630. Yale men take steps, 1630. Man checks hat and coat with management of Childs' restaurant, 1916. First optimist-pessimist joke, 1453.

22 Th Pilgrims land at Plymouth, 1620. Shuberts build Plymouth Theatre, 1917.

23 F Dolls for telephones invented, 1916. Shopping rush breaks all records; manufacturers hurriedly make 100,000 more art calendars, 1921.

24 Sa Treaty of Ghent ends war with England, 1812. Hearst resumes same, 1812. Seventeen thousand parodies on " 'Twas the night before Christmas and all through the house, etc.," appear in newspapers, 1890-1921, incl.

25 Su CHRISTMAS DAY; extra matinées.

26 M George Dewey born, 1837. Ground broken for first

transcontinental railway; Pathé news scooped, 1863. Apartment house attendants resume normal manners, 1921.

27 Tu John C. Calhoun, Vice-President of U.S., resigns, probably to seek fame and fortune, 1832. Six hundred thousand Christmas neckties worn for last time, 1921.

28 W Iowa admitted to Union, 1846. Woodrow Wilson born, 1856. Government takes control of railroads, 1917. Complaints on food begin, 1917. Thousands of homes gladdened by return of relatives—to their own homes, 1921.

29 Th Texas admitted to Union, 1845. East Liverpool, O., woman claims to have seen entire 22 installments of 22-installment movie serial, 1918.

30 F King George III succeeds to English throne; Brisbane editorial demands recount, 1760. Gadsden Purchase, 1853. Twenty-two million-dollar movie theatres erected on same, 1920.

31 Sa Assault on Quebec, 1775. Thirsty Americans resume attack, 1919. Ring out, Wild Bells! In one Year and out the other!

EINSTEIN IN HOLLYWOOD

THE NATION, *August 6, 1938*

Warner Brothers have cabled Sigmund Freud, in London, asking him to come to Hollywood to assist in the preparation of the new Bette Davis picture, *Dark Victory.—News item*

Sigmund Freud had been in Hollywood about a year, and was engaged to marry Merle Oberon, when the studio got another great idea. Louella Parsons broke the story, and her papers gave it a two-column head:

WARNER BROS. TO FILM
THEORY OF RELATIVITY

Prof. Einstein Signed to Write Screen Treatment of Own Story—Arrives in Hollywood Next Month

Einstein's arrival in Hollywood, of course, was the signal for a gay round of dinners and cocktail parties. The Basil Rathbones, who had given a party in Freud's honor to which everyone came as his favorite neurosis, gave one for Einstein in which the guests were got up as their favorite numbers. Needless to say, there were some pretty hot numbers.

The climax, however, was a dinner at the Trocadero, given by the film colony as a whole, at which Will H. Hays was the principal speaker. "The signing of Professor Einstein for pictures," said Mr. Hays, "is the greatest forward step that the industry has ever taken. American motion pictures appeal to people all over the world. I will be happy to okay Professor Einstein's contract just as soon as we get permission from Germany."

Next morning, on the Warner lot, Professor Einstein was assigned an office in the writers' building and a stenographer named Goldie. Promptly at twelve o'clock he was summoned to a conference. The producer received him with a flourish.

"Professor," he said, "allow me to introduce Sol Bergen and Al Jenkins, who are going to work with you on the picture. Now, I've been thinking this thing over and we want this to be absolutely *your* picture. What you say goes. But of course we all want a hit, and I'm sure you're willing to play ball with us. Now, I've got some great news for you. I've decided to put Joan Blondell in it."

Sol Bergen let out a war whoop. "Gee, Boss, that's great. Her name alone will put it over."

"I want the Professor to have the best," said the producer, "because I'm sure he's going to give us a great picture. Now, Professor, here's the problem: how can we treat this theory of yours so as to keep it just as you wrote it—because this has got to be *your* picture—and still make it entertainment? Because first and foremost a motion picture has got to be entertainment. But of course we want your theory in it too."

"I'm not sure that I've got the Professor's theory exactly straight," said Al Jenkins. "Would you mind, Professor, giving me just a quick summary of it, in a sort of non-technical way?"

"I don't think we have to bother the Professor about that," said the producer. "I've been thinking it over, and I've got a great way to work it in. And here it is." He leaned back and looked at them. "The scene is a college where they *teach* this theory of the Professor's. Only it's a very *tough* theory, and there's never been a *girl* that's been able to understand it. Of course it's a co-ed college. And finally along comes a girl, attractive, of course, and says, '*I* am going to understand it.' "

"Blondell!" said Sol Bergen.

"Right!" said the producer. "So she pitches in and goes to work. She won't go to parties or dances or anything, and she wears horn-rimmed glasses, and the boys think she's a grind and hasn't got any sex appeal. Underneath, of course, she's a regular girl."

"There's got to be one guy in particular that falls for her," said Jenkins.

"Sure!" said the producer, "and I'll tell you who'd be great in the part. Wayne Morris. How's that, Professor? How'd you like to have Wayne Morris in your picture?"

"Let's make him the captain of the football team," said Bergen. "It'll give us a great finale."

"Fine," said the producer. "Now, Blondell has got a girl friend that goes to college with her, only she's a different type. Flighty, and never does any studying, but a smart little kid when it comes to handling the boys. Knows 'em from A to Z. Now, there's a millionaire, an old grad that's just presented the college with a stadium, and his son is going to the college. Lots of money, and a racing car, and this kid sets her cap for him. We could have a crack-up on his way back from the roadhouse."

"Or he could lead the college band," said Bergen. "That way you could get your music in."

"Great! And we have a kid playing the girl that can handle a couple of numbers. Here's an idea, Professor. How about Warren and Dubin for the score? How would you like that, huh?"

"And how's this?" asked Jenkins. "She has another girl friend that sort of likes the older boys—with dough, see? And she sets out after the rich father."

"I've got it!" said the producer. "I've got the title! *Gold Diggers at College.* Yes, sir, *Gold Diggers at College,* by Albert Einstein, Sol Bergen, and Al Jenkins, based on the Theory of Relativity, by Albert Einstein. Professor, you've done a great picture!"

MEET THE AUDIENCE*

SCENE: *A living room. Very little furniture necessary. A divan, a chair, a desk. At the rise the* MAID *is putting the room in order. Her mistress enters.*

SHE: What time is it, Lilith?

MAID: You mean now?

SHE: No, no—not now. Just give me any time at all. Half past —quarter to. Thursday.

MAID: Yes, Miss.

SHE: The room looks beautiful, Lilith. What there is of it.

MAID: Thank you, Miss.

SHE: Now remember—when Mr. Winterbottom gets here you are *not* to interrupt us. *Not* to interrupt us—do you understand?

MAID: Yes, Miss.

SHE: Because he has telephoned, Lilith. What do you think of *that?* He has telephoned that he has something *very important* to say. *(She grows very arch)* I wonder what it could be.

MAID: I think I know, Miss.

SHE: You needn't tell me, Lilith. I've known for twenty years. Twenty years, come Mickey Mouse.

MAID: Oh, I'm sure he'll propose tonight, Miss.

SHE: I'm sure he will, too. Or else get a clip on the jaw.

MAID: Oh, I wouldn't do that, Miss. I don't think he'd like it.

SHE: Like it or not like it, twenty years is—*(The doorbell rings)* Let Mr. Winterbottom in, Lilith.

(The MAID *goes off. Her mistress meanwhile further arranges the cushions on the divan. Puts one at the foot and one at the head; then changes her mind and puts them both at the head, side by side.* MR. WINTERBOTTOM *enters)*

---

*Because *Meet the Audience* has not been performed to date, a cast list and production notes are not included.—*ed.*

21

SHE: Mr. Winterbottom!

HE: Miss Teitelbaum!

SHE: Mr. Teitelbottom!

HE: Miss Winterbaum!

SHE: *(As she sits on the chair)* Take a divan.

HE: *(Seating himself)* Thank you. . . . Miss Teitelbaum, do you remember the night we first met?

SHE: *(Coyly)* Yes, Mr. Winterbottom.

HE: We—went for a buggy ride.

SHE: Yes. Automobiles had not been invented yet.

HE: That very night, I felt that I wanted to say something to you. But—I haven't. All these years, I haven't. *(She laughs a little, passing it off)* But today—today I was made general manager of Feingarten and Cassidy.

SHE: Mr. Winterbottom!

HE: At last I can speak. At last I can say something that I have waited twenty years to say.

SHE: *(Meekly)* Yes, Mr. Winterbottom. *(A change of manner)* Only for God's sake, *say* it!

HE: Very well. I will. Are you ready?

SHE: I've been ready for—twenty years.

HE: Miss Teitelbaum, will you—

(The rest of his declaration is lost in a hearty cough from the audience. He waits a moment, then starts to speak again)

Miss Teitelbaum, will you—

(A still bigger cough. Mildly annoyed, he waits again)

Miss Teitelbaum—

(The cough comes even earlier this time. And louder. He waits for quite an interval; perhaps even takes a turn around the room)

Miss—

(The cough)

SHE: Perhaps, Mr. Winterbottom, perhaps I can guess. Shall I tell you?

HE: Yes, Miss Teitelbaum.

SHE: Is it—

(A hell of a cough. She bites her lip. Tries again)

I said, is it—

(More coughing)

HE: No, no. At a time like this, it is the man who should speak.

SHE: Yes, but the girl should at least hear him.

HE: Miss Teitelbaum—

(Cough)

SHE: Or how the hell will she know what to answer?

HE: Miss Teit—

(Cough. He looks out at the audience this time, and in not too friendly fashion, either. He tries to beat the game by wheeling quickly toward MISS TEITELBAUM and speaking very rapidly)

Miss Tei—

(Cough)

SHE: Mr. Win—

(Cough. They wait a second. Then they start to speak right together. A cough, of course. A great hacking cough. They walk around the stage, eyeing the audience, sparring for an opening. As the coughing stops he makes another quick try.)

HE: MissTeitelbaumwillyou—

(Terrific coughing. Then he gets an idea. Awaiting his opportunity, he tries one syllable at a time)

Miss—

(A cough, but the "Miss" was heard)

Tei—

(More coughing, but he got over the "Tei")

Tel—

(Cough)

Baum—

(Cough)

Will—

(Cough)

You—

(Prolonged coughing. He cannot go further. He lies down and takes a rest. It seems the only thing to do. She eyes the audience as the coughing continues. Cowed by her, the audience actually becomes still. He sits up, in wonder. She is a genius. Feeling that victory is his)

Miss Teitelbaum, will you—

(And she *coughs. He sinks back again)*

SHE: I'm—I'm very sorry. What were you saying?

(He sits slowly up. A pretty sick man by this time)

You were about to—

(And he *begins to cough. Then* she *starts. The audience joins in. It becomes a free-for-all. They turn and cough right* at *the audience. Gradually they all become quiet again)*

SHE: *(Calling off)* Lilith! Lilith! *(The* MAID *appears)*

Lilith, will you—

(But LILITH *starts coughing.* MISS TEITELBAUM *picks up a paperweight from the desk and throws it at her; the* MAID *quickly goes. The audience starts coughing furiously.* MISS TEITELBAUM *and* MR. WINTERBOTTOM *stand looking at them for a decent interval, but the coughing only becomes louder. It is now absolutely deafening. Simultaneously they turn to the wings and beckon. From each side* THREE SOLDIERS *walk on stage. They meet centre, level their guns at the audience, and fire.)*

BLACKOUT

BY THE WAY

SATURDAY REVIEW, *August 11, 1945*

Noel Coward, on his opening nights, togs himself out in white tie and tails and plants himself prominently in a stage box, where he joins happily in the applause and the laughter. Jerome Kern, in his pre-Hollywood days, used to sit fifth row on the aisle at his own openings, and enjoyed himself vastly. Herbert and Dorothy Fields, at the premieres of their musical shows, always sit second row on the aisle, and have a whale of a time.

But they are the great exceptions—most playwrights of my acquaintance run screaming from the theatre as soon as the curtain goes up and bury themselves in a double feature somewhere on Forty-second Street. Me, I stay there and suffer, nor can all my advance resolutions stay me from those appointed rounds. As each opening night approaches I swear a solemn oath that I will spend the evening seeing a movie or playing bridge, but eight o'clock always finds me pacing the rear of the auditorium, cursing the audience for its failure to arrive half an hour ahead of time. At eight-eleven word is brought that Lucius Beebe has just ordered a second bottle of Chablis '27 at the Colony, and at eight-twenty a courier brings news that Jules Broulatour, or someone who looked like Jules Broulatour, has just been seen at Fifth Avenue and Fifty-Sixth Street, going *north.* At eight-twenty-five it begins to rain. . . .

I spend the first act hiding behind the curtains at the rear of the boxes, peeping out occasionally at the audience. Kelcey Allen is laughing! But Kelcey Allen is a good soul, and has not given anything a bad notice since *Ben Hur.* At the end of the first act I keep tryst with the producer at some isolated spot, and thereto, by arrangement, come emissaries with bulletins, all favorable. No matter how badly the play may be going, the bulletins are favorable. They're crazy about it. Everybody! Robert Coleman, who arrived at nine-twenty, told someone it was the best first act of the season.

And so it goes, right through the evening. Yet, be the play good or bad, it never goes well enough to please the author. It is an evening of acute agony, from beginning to end. Some day, perhaps I will really summon up a little strength of character and not go near the theatre, and that will be the evening that the audience laughs its head off, unreservedly. So maybe I'd better not take a chance. I'll be there.

In the matter of reviews I have grown a little calmer. Time was when I always sat up for the morning papers. I would even sit up for *Time* and *Newsweek,* and once, I think, I sat up for Burns Mantle's *Year Book.* But nowadays I go home and go to bed. You can be panned just as well in the morning.

* * *

It is about time, I think, that someone laid to rest the myth of the Algonquin Round Table. The legend persists that here was a tight little group of critics, playwrights, and novelists, all intent upon praising each other to the skies and rigidly damning the work of any upstart outsider. Just recently I read intimations to this effect in the columns of John Mason Brown and George Jean Nathan, among others. Perhaps there is some mild excuse in the case of Mr. Brown, for he rose to fame in the post-Algonquin days, and inherited the legend. But Mr. Nathan is old enough to know better. Older.

The truth is, of course, that the Round Table was made up of a motley and nondescript group of people who wanted to eat lunch, and that's about all. They had no power at all over the literature of the day, and it seems to me that the least thought on the part of their accusers would convince them of that fact. How in God's name could they wield any such power? How could any group wield such power in the critical world as it is made up today, and as it was made up then?

The Round Table members ate at the Algonquin because Frank Case was good enough to hold a table for them, and because it was fun. The jokes, as I recall, were rather good, but completely unimportant. I cannot recall that a serious literary note was ever injected, and anyone who tried to inject one would have had a piece of lemon chiffon pie crammed down his throat.

Perhaps one anecdote will suffice to show the high literary quality of those luncheons. There was among us, in those days, one John Peter Toohey, who was and is a theatrical press agent, and a good one. I believe that John had read several books at that time, but I am sure he will agree with me that he was not a literary giant. John's main luncheon interest was in the food—and the prices. Mr. Case asked thirty-five cents for a slab of pie and about thirty cents for coffee, and John was Irish and a rebel, and he felt that this was too much.

So we hatched a little plan. With the connivance of Frank Case and his staff, a whole new menu was printed, on which the prices of everything were just about tripled. It was arranged that on the following Monday this menu should be solemnly handed to the lunchers at the Round Table. All of the waiters, of course, were carefully rehearsed in these shenanigans, and it need hardly be added that we had a record attendance that day.

I was about the third to arrive, but John was already there. He gave me a rather tight little nod, and his eye followed me eagerly as I took my seat. Then he reached over and tapped my arm. "You've got a little surprise in store for you," he whispered. "Just wait!" He followed me closely as I picked up the menu. "Well?" he inquired, leaning back to enjoy my outburst. But I took it rather calmly. "Things are going up all over town," I told him. "I suppose Frank just found it necessary to raise prices." "Raise prices!" he snorted. "Just wait till Alex gets here! He'll have something to say!"

But Woollcott also took it calmly, and so did the succeeding lunchers, although John, almost bursting, followed each one intently as he picked up the card. We all ordered as usual, but John, in protest, ordered only tea and toast, which, as I recall, came to two dollars and forty cents. Then he took charge of the plan of procedure. Frank Case must be brought to his senses. On the following day we were to scatter over the city—each was to lunch at a different hotel and each must bring back a menu to show Frank the absurdity of his prices. Marc Connelly was to go to the Ritz, Benchley to the St. Regis, John himself to the Plaza, and so on.

On the following day, of course, John went to the Plaza—and the rest of us went to the Algonquin. John carried a Plaza menu back to Frank Case, and won his point—Frank broke down and admitted that his prices were too high.

And that, boys and girls, was the Algonquin Round Table. Just that and nothing more.

* * *

This is a story about books, in a way. About books and the law, and the fact that the latter is a good deal more profitable, at least on occasions. For where is the writer who receives $166.67 a word?

A few years ago Moss Hart and I faced a plagiarism suit on *The Man Who Came to Dinner*. It seems that the plaintiff had written a play about Harold Ross and *The New Yorker*, and, as everyone knows, that is exactly what *The Man Who Came to Dinner* was about. So he sued us. In fact, he sued everyone in sight. Not only Moss and me, but the Estate of Sam H. Harris, Mr. Harris having been the producer; Warner Brothers, who had made a movie of it, and even Random House, which had published the play.

The trial lasted two or three days, during which counsel for all of the accused parties sat solemnly in the courtroom. Occasionally the man from Warner Brothers or the Harris Estate would put in a word, but in the main the proceedings were in the hands of Moss's lawyer and my own. The arguments raged back and forth, the lawyers objected and argued—only the lawyer from Random House sat in dignified silence.

Finally, on the third day, all buttal and rebuttal were over. Our lawyer rose and uttered the solemn words, "Moss Hart and George S. Kaufman rest." Up sprang the attorney for Sam H. Harris. "The Estate of Sam H. Harris rests," he intoned. Then the Warner Brothers man. "Warner Brothers rest," he pronounced.

And then up rose the lawyer for Random House. He adjusted his pince-nez, looked the judge squarely in the eye, and spoke up for the first time since the case began. "Random House rests," he said—and sent a bill to his clients for five hundred dollars.

As I said, the writer doesn't do as well as that.

* * *

One more book story and I'll get the hell out of here.

As I believe every playwright knows, one does not exactly get rich from the publication of plays in book form. Checks for three and four dollars fairly rain in every six months, and it is not unusual to receive no dollars and about fifty-six cents. But I think I reached a new low a few years ago.

True, it was a pretty old play, but the six-months statement was still something of a disappointment. It came, as I recall, from Scribner's and it ran as follows:

Sold in the U.S.A. . . . . None
Sold in Canada . . . . None
Returned . . . . Three

Of course what had happened was very clear. Some smart bird was printing that play and selling it back to Scribner's.

THAT MORNING MAIL

THE NEW YORK TIMES, *April 18, 1948*

The steaming coffee is in the cup,
      And another day's a-borning—
(I'm even thinking of getting up;
    It's eleven o'clock in the morning)—
        Then, buoyant, happy, even hale,
    I gaze upon the Morning Mail.
        And dream, with beatific smile,
        Of golden treasure in that pile:

A letter from a man named Jones:
His client in Kentucky,
Has left me twenty million bones
    (No reason—I'm just lucky).

From someone else I get a prize
Because I have such pretty eyes;
Two Presidents, and seven Kings,
Are sending me just LOTS of things.

A girl that I don't know at all
    (She lives right up above me)
Has seen me walking in the hall
    And writes that she could love me.
        Those are the dreams that my palate whet;
        This, my hearties, is what I get:

A note from a cousin in Lansing, Mich.
(The one that borrowed a hundred fish)—
He's coming to visit Manhattan soon,
And how about passes for *Brigadoon*?

My landlord, bless his little face,
Has been declared a Hardship Case . . .

"You'll kindly notice that the rent
Has been increased fifteen percent."
       (Or find another place.)

The winter coat that I stored in May
Is in a most *distressing* way;
"It needs to be re-lined"—I quote—
"And two more sleeves, and another coat."

And bills and bills and bills and BILLS—
       (The butcher's is a beauty)—
My dentist has some lovely drills;
       I'm called for jury duty.

Will I come to a dinner on May the third
To hear a *terribly* private word
On the awful state of the woofle bird?
       (NO!)
Will I kindly purchase the cheaper cuts?
Will I rid the city of smokers' butts?
Will I go definitely NUTS?
       (YES!)

Will I buy tickets for a fete?
Vote for some stupid candidate?
Call Plaza three, one-three one-eight,
And pay a higher insurance rate!
Have just a thirty-minute chat
With someone-or-other's gifted brat,
Adopt a little Persian cat,
And sponsor THIS and sponsor THAT! . . .

                *   *   *

Oracle, deep in thy sylvan vale,
       Gaze in thy mystic glass:
Tell me, why is my first-class mail
       Not even near first-class?

WRINGING IN THE NEW YEAR

Harper's Weekly, *January 1, 1916*

Hold on, New York! The rules of civilized warfare have got to be observed this year. No poisonous gases. No dumdum bullets. No battle-axes. No butcher knives—unless obtained from thoroughly reliable butchers. It is time that this business of celebrating New Year's Eve was standardized—time that it was run along conservative business lines. Laxness in the past has resulted in the springing up of various techniques. South of Forty-second Street it has been considered quite all right to strike a fellow-celebrant over the right ear; north of it the left is favored. The need for standardization is pressing.

Right from the jump it must be admitted that the annual celebration is aptly enough named. Wringing in the New Year, it is called, and the latest five-star sporting extra of the Funkandwagnalls defines Wring as follows: "To cause torture to; to distress; to force a way; to squeeze." If you doubt the pertinence of the definition go thou into Broadway this year and mingle with the bunch— mingle and be mingled, mangle and be mangled. Suffer the great horned night owls to blow blasts on their great horns an inch or thereabouts from your ear; suffer the clanging of cowbells and the raucous rasping of a dozen demoniac devices; suffer the featherduster humorists to waylay you; suffer the confetti hurlers, with infinite speed and control, to throw packages of the stuff down your throat; suffer the bladder swingers to swat you; suffer the onslaughts of the flying wedge of hilarious stewedants of Screechumbia, '19; suffer and support the Fraternal Order of Metropolitan Pickpockets; suffer to move only north on the east side of Broadway and only south on the west; suffer the trampling under foot of a six-dollar derby (yours); suffer the renting of your garments; suffer to be pushed and pulled; suffer.

New York's first step toward a safeandsane New Year's Eve

must be the abolition of the mass formation. Germany has discarded it on the western front, and there is no reason why Broadway should be less safe than the Battle of Ypres. Also, it might be a good idea to make confetti a bit more palatable. It could be published, for example, in chocolate, strawberry and vanilla flavors.

Yes, New York's New Year's Eve could be celebrated in accordance with the principles of humanity—but it won't. For the Gothamite and the man from Des Moines or Rutherford want a high old time, and they have been raised in the belief that the only way to get it is to be nearly murdered and entirely fleeced. As usual, there are indications along the Incandescent Avenue that those who start out for a high time this year will be rewarded. The stress should be put upon the "high."

LIFE'S CALENDAR FOR JANUARY 1922

1 Su NEW YEAR'S DAY: 14,276 recipients of unexpected New Year's cards send out 14,276 New Year's cards dated Dec. 29. Betsy Ross born, 1752. Emancipation Act in effect, 1863. Parcel Post inaugurated, 1913; all parcels mailed on opening day safely delivered to addressees, 1914.

2 M Twenty-five million persons, before throwing away New Year's cards, rub fingers over them to see if they are really engraved, 1922. First Olympic games; Norwegians break ski jumping records, 1453, B.C. Robbers raid post office at Limerick, Ireland, presumably in attempt to get correct version of the one about the pelican, 1920.

3 Tu Battle of Princeton, 1877; Yale still favored in betting, 1922. Half a million persons crack jokes about still writing it 1921, 1922. Balm salesman driven out of Gilead, 3627 B.C.

4 W Utah admitted to Union; called a Smoot operation, 1896. Publication of statistics for 1921 show that 14,826 shines ruined by hostesses stepping on guests' feet while searching for buzzers under dinner tables, 1922. David W. Griffith opens negotiations for film rights to Wells's *Outline of History* for the Gish sisters, 1922.

5 Th Indians capture John Smith; Pocahontas realizes it is Leap Year, 1608. "Battle of Kegs"; first use of American floating mines, 1777. Maine reports heavy snowstorm; Delaware peach crop gets ready to be ruined, 1922.

6 F First telegraph instrument, 1838; first messenger boy joke, 1838. New Mexico admitted to Union, 1912.

7 Sa First Presidential election; Ohio not only doubtful but not even present, 1789. Millard Fillmore, thirteenth

President, born, 1800. Bootleggers' Chamber of Commerce predicts bumper year, 1922.

8   Su   First annual Presidential message; average citizen reads a fifth of it, 1790. Battle of New Orleans, 1815. Tea discovered, 342 B.C. Seven million cups ruined by too much water, 1922.

9   M   First shot fired in Civil War, 1861. J.W. Schloss, New York architect, wins competition for new Gloria Swanson coiffure, 1922. Patron consults soda fountain menu card before ordering his drink, 1987.

10   Tu   Ethan Allen dies, 1789. Standard Oil Co. incorporated, 1870. Standard Oil Co. attacked as trust, 1870. Harvey invents steel armor plate; dairy lunches served on it, 1888. Villa killed by own men, 1916, 1917, 1918.

11   W   A. Hamilton born, 1804. Coshocton, Ohio, man discovers that new shoes are too tight before leaving store, 1891. Piece of ham accidentally falls into frying pan with egg, and ham and eggs are invented, Byzantium, 390 B.C.

12   Th   John Hancock born; personally signs birth certificate, 1737. Eli Whitney invents cotton gin, 1793. Ten million other inventors leave out the cotton, 1922.

13   F   Sam'l Woodsworth, author of *The Old Oaken Bucket,* born, 1785; parodies became moss covered, 1856. Baseball magnates hold annual meeting in New York; real news item gets onto sporting page, 1922.

14   Sa   British burn Capital at Washington; business goes on as usual, 1801. Machine for eating toast in bed without getting crumbs under the covers invented, 1937.

15   Su   First American locomotive, 1831. First engineer photographed with watch for magazine advertisements, 1831. Federals capture Fort Fisher, 1865. F. Scott Fitzgerald discovers the next generation, 1919.

16   M   Garfield issues Heatless-Monday proclamation, 1918. Queen Laliuokalani of Hawaii deposed; 50,000 Americans have tongues ironed out, 1893. Eighteenth Amendment proclaimed in effect, 1920. Who cares? 1922.

17 Tu Benjamin Franklin, famous magazine publisher, born, 1706. Cain married; first mother-in-law joke, 8625 B.C. Rupert Hughes defends the movies, 1922.

18 W Daniel Webster born, 1782. Electric signs on Broadway begin burning at noon, 1921. Season's first hurdy-gurdys appear; same tunes as last year, 1922. Electric trolley system patented; receiverships invented, 1892.

19 Th Robert E. Lee, godfather of famous steamboat, born, 1807. Edgar Allan Poe born, 1809. First Crusade started; Isadore Einstein arrested as spy, 1096.

20 F Robert Morris, financier of American Revolution, born, 1734. Little Wonder Dynamite Company patents apparatus for loosening salt in restaurant salt cellars, 1922.

21 Sa Stonewall Jackson born, 1824. Pullman Porter really shines a pair of shoes, 1906.

22 Su Queen Victoria dies, 1901. President Wilson coins "Peace without victory" in address to Senate, 1917. Everybody knows what he meant, 1922.

23 M Congress appoints first Tuesday after the first Monday in November as national election day; those who wanted it to be the third Wednesday after the second Friday want to know if there is any justice, 1845.

24 Tu Samuel Morse first demonstrates his telegraph code, 1838. James Wilson Marshall discovers gold in California, 1848. So do the movie men, 1910.

25 W Philadelphia man breaks shoe lace while not in a hurry to keep important engagement, 1918. World's record established when initials pasted in derby hat remain in place for three days, 1920.

26 Th Thirty-two fashion magazines begin annual Palm Beach photographic season, thus greatly increasing the chances of the Socialist party, 1922. First settlement in Australia; kangaroos begin getting boxing lessons, 1788.

27 F Edison patents incandescent lamp, 1880. Ten thousand persons discover they make a fine noise when they're smashed, 1880.

28 Sa   Panama railroad completed; hatless passengers drive conductors frantic looking for a place to stock ticket receipts, 1855. Shoehorn invented, 782.

29 Su   William McKinley born, 1843. Kansas admitted to Union, 1861. First California Redwood used as public thoroughfare, 1853.

30 M   James G. Blaine born, 1830. Hours of collection printed on mail box in Tallahassee, Florida, turn out to be correct, 1906. Theatre ticket speculation stopped, 1901-1922, incl.

31 Tu   Thirteenth Amendment adopted, 1865. One school child in Reading, Pa. is able to say what the Thirteenth Amendment is all about, 1922. Actor takes a full three seconds to write a check during the action of a play, 1971.

MUSIC TO MY EARS

STAGE, *August, 1938*

You must not be surprised at anything these days, of course, but I am at least mildly stunned to find myself writing an article about music. It is as though you turned the pages of the *Atlantic Monthly* and stumbled suddenly on a piece entitled "Chaucer: An Inquiry Into His Style," by Samuel Goldwyn.

Mind you, I like music. If the Society of Ascaps or whatever it is wants to take a small ad in the *Times* and quote me, that's fine with me. "Music is all right."—George S. Kaufman. But I'm not what you'd call an expert at it. To be sure, I have been known to go walking along the street, in broad daylight, singing at the top of my voice. In a single block, once, I had thirty-five cents tossed to me out of windows. And I have one or two solid convictions about music, chief of which is that the unbelievable invention known as "swing" is strictly for mental defectives.

But I have had no musical training, and I don't pretend to know. Berlin, Kern, Herbert, anybody else with a good tune—that's music to me. It is a choice, I am afraid, that does more than mark my musical limitations. It also betrays my years.

When it comes to lyrics I am a shade closer to familiar ground, but no more than that. In my newspaper youth I wrote a good deal of light verse, and to this day my ear rejects the breaking of the rhythm of a line. While I admire enormously the acrobatic ingenuity of the modern lyric-writer—Larry Hart and Ira Gershwin, for example—my idea of a lyricist is still Sir William Gilbert. Middle-age again, of course, but at least Sir William never advanced the theory that trouble is just a bubble, after all. Some day, in a memorable test case, the Supreme Court will decide that trouble is *not* just a bubble after all, and ten thousand lyric-writers will be thrown on relief.

And now back to composers. In the course of some eight or ten musical shows I have worked with four of the best of them—Berlin, Gershwin, Rodgers, Schwartz. Without exception they have been delightful and considerate collaborators—fond of their music, of course, but keenly sympathetic to the problems of the book writer. In the main, I should say that their concern over the book has been far greater than mine over the music. To be sure, there comes a point in musical-comedy collaboration when both composer and librettist are pretty impatient with the departmental worries of the other fellow. Once a show has reached the tryout stage, this feeling expresses itself very simply. As a musical number gets under way the librettist strolls out into the lobby, passing the composer on the way in. And vice versa.

As a matter of fact, the composers with whom I have worked must obviously have been lovely and gentle fellows, or I would have been killed long ago. In one important respect I fail them miserably, and I would not have blamed any one of them for taking a shot at me. I refer to my inadequacy as an audience. As I have already said, I don't know a great deal about music. I have not, for example, the gift of knowing a good song when I hear it. I know people who can listen to a song halfway through and at once pronounce it the hit of the year. Most of the time, to be sure, they have turned out to be wrong. But in the interim they have made the composer very, very happy.

I am sure it is not my excessive honesty that makes it impossible for me to do that—it must be some less admirable trait. At all events, I am a highly unpopular fellow at such times. The first playing of the score of a musical comedy is, of course, an auspicious occasion. The composer is highly anxious that his melodies shall have their full value, and to this end he not infrequently causes another grand piano to be moved into his study. At no little expense, a piano player has been hired for the evening, and all through the afternoon he and the composer have been rehearsing diligently. Trays of drinks have been scattered here and there, and there is a white-coated butler who talks to you at just the wrong moments.

Then, while you sit with a drink in one hand and a copy of the lyrics in the other, the composer and his assistant play the score. At the same time the lyric-writer sings the lyrics in an extremely bad voice, making a particular botch of the soprano portions. In the middle of the big love song the telephone rings, and the composer has a carefully worded conversation with some over-eager young lady, while everybody pretends not to listen. He then starts the song again, and the vibrations from the piano cause the tray of drinks to do a merry tinkly dance, not planned in the orchestrations.

When it is all over you are expected to come through in a big way, and I just can't. As a rule I simply say "That's nice," and it doesn't go well at all. Broadly speaking, I should say that I never like a song the first time I hear it. It is not until it has been played again and again that I begin to see its possibilities. By the time a show is ready to open, for example, I am convinced that every tune in it is a knockout—by then the melodies have been so dinned into me that they all have that pleasant familiarity that is to me a substitute for musical merit. At this point, I am again *persona grata* with the composer, but generally it is too late. The damage was done at that first hearing.

Looking back, I should say that I have done something less than meet the composer half-way—both in the matter of appreciation and in the general planning of the show. No composer ever has been given real musical opportunity in any show in which I have had a hand—the shows never have been primarily romantic, and the composer has thus been psychologically handicapped from the beginning. It is probably the reason that there never has been a real song hit in any show with which I have been connected, although there have been some good songs. Arthur Schwartz's "Dancing in the Dark," from *The Band Wagon,* seems to have advanced into the hit class in recent years, if I may judge from the number of times that I hear it over the radio. I might add that it is my idea of a great number, and never fails to give me a thrill of pleasure when I hear it.

If I had to name what I consider the best song in any show of mine, it would be George Gershwin's magnificent march at the end of the first act of *Strike Up the Band*—that was the name of the song, too. I have always regretted that I failed to provide a better book on that occasion—a composer of musical comedy is so horribly dependent on the quality of the book.

Incidentally, I did have a moment of pleasure out of the failure of that show. Edgar Selwyn, who produced it, was wisely unwilling to hazard too much of his own money, and had persuaded a rich Kentuckian (I think his name was Levy) to help back the show. This turned out to be nothing less than genius on Mr. Selwyn's part, because in a single tryout week in Philadelphia *Strike Up the Band* hung up a record which, to the best of my knowledge, never has been equalled to this day. It lost $22,000. In one week, I mean.

I am not sure just how much Mr. Levy dropped in all, but it was considerable. At all events, it was some four or five years after the debacle that I encountered him again. He came up to me in the lobby of a theatre, full of pleasure at seeing me. "Well!" he cried. *"Here* you are!" And with that he ushered forth his wife. "My dear, here is the man that you have been wanting to meet all these years. George Gershwin!"

Then before I could even give him an argument, he plunged on. "Tell me," he said—"tell me one thing. With all the magnificent music that you have written, all the money that your shows have made, why is it that *I* had to invest in the only one that was a failure? Why wasn't *Strike Up the Band* a big success?"

I have always flattered myself that I made the only possible answer. I said, "Kaufman gave me a lousy book."

But if there never has been a real song hit in a show of mine, at least I once came close. Back in 1925 Irving Berlin and I teamed up on a deep study of psychology called *The Cocoanuts,* for the Marx Brothers. Most of the work was done in a hotel suite in Atlantic City, and long after I went to bed each night Irving would be busy at the piano. At exactly five o'clock one morning he woke me up.

"I've got it!" he cried. "Come on out to the piano!"

Business was business, even at that hour, so I pulled myself together and obeyed. Once at the piano, Irving played and sang for me a little number entitled "Always." "When the things you've planned need a helping hand, I will understand, always."

Even *my* deficient musical sense recognized that here was a song that was going to be popular. I listened to it two or three times, then took a stab at it myself, and as dawn came up over the Atlantic Irving and I were happily singing "Always" together—its first performance on any stage.

I went back to bed a happy man, and stayed happy until rehearsals started, when it turned out that "Always" had not been written for our show at all, but purely for Irving's music-publishing house. In its place in *The Cocoanuts* was a song called "A Little Bungalow," which we never could reprise in Act Two because the actors couldn't remember it that long . . . Ah, me!

CAN YOU FINISH IT?

Saturday Review, *November 21, 1959*

"And that's the latest edition of *'News Around the Clock,'* brought to you by the New York *Daily News,* the paper that reads faster and livelier."

That comes over the radio every half hour or so, and it seems to me that there is an unfinished sentence hanging around there somewhere. Faster and livelier than *what?*

In an effort to complete this sentence I have tried a number of finishes, but none seems to work. For example:

"Than a rabbit." (I don't think even the *Daily News* would claim that. Funnier possibly—but not faster and livelier.)

"Than it used to." (Well, maybe, but I don't remember the old slow and deadly *Daily News* very well.)

"Than it ought to." (This, I think, comes close.)

"Than *The New York Times.*" (Also a promising candidate.)

"Than your grandmother." (Now here they would have an argument with me. My grandmother—both of them, really—were very fast and lively. Well, I don't mean to call them fast, exactly—it isn't right to call your grandmother fast, I realize. But they would both have given the *Daily News* a good run for their money.)

"Than a brothel." (I rest my case.)

WHEN YOUR HONEY'S ON THE TELEPHONE

THE NEW YORKER, *February 22, 1958*

Well, now, that's a nice sentimental title, isn't it? So—are we all ready for a glowing story about this darling girl, and how she calls you up on the telephone, and an hour later, dripping darlingness, you hang up in a blaze of glucose, and your whole day is made, and everything is absolutely wonderful from then on?

All right. Now, do you want the facts? The facts are that I am very fond of honey, and I have it for breakfast now and then, and the telephone often rings while I'm eating it—my number is quite a lot like that of Mt. Sinai Hospital, and a voice generally says, "Give me the maternity ward"—and while I am taking the phone off the cradle, the wire dangles over the honey saucer just close enough to pick up the merest daub of honey, and from then on everything is not exactly wonderful at all. In fact, it's plain hell.

What follows is not wasteful so far as honey is concerned, because a microscopic amount of honey is enough to do it all. Once a speck of honey gets on the telephone wire, it does the work of a whole bevy of bees, if bees and bevies go together.

One morning in my early and innocent days, I made a quick effort to wipe the honey off the wire, but that was a great mistake. An infinitesimal amount of honey—hardly any, mind you—having thus got on my fingers, it quickly transferred itself to the telephone instrument, and from then on there was no way out. Dialling a number a few minutes later, I managed to get just the merest bit of honey—almost none at all, really—into most of those little dial holes, thus rendering the telephone useless for the next eight or ten years, or until they invent something to supersede the dial. Then, taking up a fork to finish my eggs, I transferred the merest molecule of honey to the fork. Picking up my coffee cup, I got a very little bit on the cup handle. At this point, I went into the bathroom and washed my hands, first getting just the smallest speck of honey on the bathroom doorknob. When I came back and took up the fork again, there was the honey, on my fingers. I now had the whole breakfast tray taken away and a new breakfast prepared, with new forks and coffee cups and everything. Then I washed my hands, and started all over. But the telephone rang again—they wanted Rupert's Brewery this time—and I took up the receiver and there was still just the smallest amount of honey on it, and so I got it on the fork again, and when I started to drink my coffee it got on the cup handle again, so I decided there was no use eating breakfast at all that morning. So I began to get dressed, and just the smallest amount of honey got on my trouser belt, so I undressed and took a bath, and when I came out, all clean, I closed the door of the bathroom after me, and there was just this little bit of honey on the doorknob . . .

Well, you get the idea. There was only one thing to do. I had the telephone taken out, and I moved to a new apartment. So nowadays, if I have honey for breakfast, I save time by just moving to a new apartment right away.

A PLAYWRIGHT TELLS ALMOST ALL

THE NEW YORK TIMES, *September 17, 1944*

The wheels of show business are turning again, the Shuberts are grinding, and another theatrical season is on. Locked up in bedrooms in New Haven, Wilmington, and a dozen other tryout centers, any number of playwrights are trying desperately to fix the second act; or the third act; or the first act; or the intermissions. Not only that, but it has to be fixed and copies neatly typed (by the author, of course) in time for 11 o'clock rehearsal. Even then the producer will withhold any word of approval; the director will say that he's afraid he doesn't understand it and will you please explain what's funny about it—"Perhaps my sense of humor is deficient, old fellow, but I do wish you'd tell me"—and there will be at least one actor who can't learn the new lines. ("It's strange, I've never had any trouble before, but these seem to be written so peculiarly.")

Almost every play, of course, is rewritten in some degree during its tryout tour. This is inevitable. In the first place, there is no play in the world that cannot be improved by additional work. And in the second and much bigger place, it is well known that plays have a way of fooling you. No matter how careful your labors, there is an unpredictable factor. Somewhere in the transition from typewriter to stage there is an almost chemical element that intrudes itself between the play and the audience. Sometimes this works to the playwright's advantage, and a simple scene of which little had been expected suddenly throws the audience into stitches, or moves it to tears, as the case may be. This is a good deal like having your bank account gone over and finding that you have two hundred dollars more than you figured. But more frequently, of course, it goes the other way. At a key moment in the play the audience remains sublimely disinterested, or else starts coughing its head off, and that's why all those playwrights are locked up in hotel rooms.

And that, children, is why plays are tried out on the road,

instead of opening cold on Broadway, as the theatrical phrase has it. "But I don't see why you can't tell, just by reading it. Either it's good or it's bad. The thing to do is just produce the good ones and then you won't have all that trouble." Well, of course, the answer is that you can't just tell. Billy Rose recently said to me that he "wouldn't open a can of sardines cold," and that seems to be the consensus of show business. (Mr. Rose intends to violate this rule by opening *Henry VIII* here without benefit of tryout, but, of course, Shakespeare is not sardines.)

But whether the play is good or bad, promising or unpromising, the playwright will retire to his bedroom typewriter with one phrase ringing in his ears. "It needs work." All of the professionals and near-professionals who journeyed out to the opening are united in that opinion. Producer, friends of the playwright, movie scouts, friends of the actors, the local house manager—one and all are agreed. "It needs work," they tell you, and then they are off to have a drink with a good-looking blonde, and the playwright is off to the bedroom, alone.

Sometimes, of course, there is a bedroom conference. For some reason this is always built around six orders of cold cuts, as though the accompanying mustard could be used to hold the play together. But sooner or later—3 o'clock, 4 o'clock—it comes down to that lone figure in the bedroom. If he has a collaborator, of course he is in a much better spot, because there is nothing like a game of gin rummy to get your mind working.

Moss Hart and I, apropos of all this, have planned out a marvelous old age for ourselves. Using a little group of spies who will hang around rehearsals, we will be equipped with advance information as to which shows are in the most trouble. Probably we will confine ourselves to large and expensive musical comedies since these always have a good chance of going wrong. Then, on opening night, there we will be in Hartford, having that bad dinner at the hotel before the opening. At the next table will be the authors and the composer, along with their wives, all being treated to a large dinner by the producer, who will charge it to production. The jokes will be popping back and forth, and the happy authors will have barely a moment in which to toss us an offhand greeting.

But we will have our revenge. There we will be, third row on the aisle, watching every unfortunate moment as it unfolds on the stage. The big comedy scene that runs ten minutes without a laugh in it; the long ballet that you know will come out entirely; the confused plot about the corset manufacturer and the burlesque girl. Finally at ten minutes to one the curtain will fall. Meanwhile a good percentage of the audience has already left, so it is not hard to get up the aisle. We walk up jauntily, Moss and I, and there are those same authors standing in the back of the theatre. They are not quite so jolly as they were during dinner. As we pass them we each wave a gay hand in their direction and together we give voice to an immemorial dictum: "Well, boys, it needs work." . . . Then we go out and get drunk.

If this seems cruel, you must remember that the playwright puts up with a lot. (I suppose the actor does too, and so does the audience from time to time, but I am frankly writing from a specialized viewpoint.) There is no one in the world who cannot tell an author how to fix his play, and the poor guy has to stand there and listen courteously. And at the end he must say, "Thank you very much. You are absolutely right," instead of what he wants to say, which is, "What the hell do you know about it?" Having listened for many years to the dramatic opinions of all kinds of persons, I would like to suggest a basic change in the manner of printing the telephone directory, so that this generally secondary profession may receive recognition. "Baldwin, Walter J.," I would have it say, "furs and dramatic critic." "Stuffnagel, Rufus W., garbage collector and dramatic critic." And so on.

I once knew a playwright who had a sweet moment of revenge, although it was not strictly along the lines I have indicated. He had written a musical comedy and was out on the road with it, prior to coming to New York. It is a rule of the theatre that the producer must pay the author's hotel bill during this period, and the producer, a careful fellow, decided after three or four days that he would save money by sending the author home. The playwright, however, was a conscientious chap who thought he could still improve the show, so he stayed on at his own expense. Two nights later his golden moment arrived. The producer phoned up from the lobby that he had an idea about the second act, and could they have a talk? "Certainly," said the playwright. "Come right up." But when the producer got upstairs the playwright met him out in the hall. "We'll have to talk here," he said. "You're not paying for my room."

Generally speaking, it always seems to the poor author as though a combination of circumstances begins to work against him the moment he gets his first idea for the play. There is the little matter of casting, which can best be summed up by Mr. Shaw's monumental observation: "You start out with certain ideal types in mind," he said, "and you finally settle for their being all white."

Occasionally, in a moment of desperation or of inexperience, the playwright will decide that what his play needs is a Movie Name. Heaven help him from then on! The Movie Name will assure him that he or she is simply cra-zy to return to the theatre. "It's the only thing that counts after all—I can't tell you how I hate Hollywood. The theatre is real—I want to play before audiences! It's the only thing that gives you satisfaction!"

So the Movie Name is engaged and for about four weeks after the New York opening everything is wonderful. Visiting movie stars, friends of the Name, flock back to the dressing room every night after the show, agape with admiration. "Oh, my dear, you were wonderful! Of course, if I could do what you're doing—if I could come back to the theatre and play a wonderful part like this —well, I just can't tell you what I'd give!"

But after about six weeks all of the Name's Hollywood friends have seen the play, no one is coming back to the dressing room any more, and the whole thing begins to pall. Then, too, it seems that a big Hollywood studio wants her for a simply gorgeous part. Of course, there's a contract and the Name has to stay on, but things are not much fun after that and the performance does not exactly improve. And then presently, contract or no contract, the whole thing comes to an end. It turns out that the lady is going to have a baby, or else she sprains her wrist or something and simply must have an operation. "If you don't believe me, my dear, just look at the X-rays."

And a long time afterward it turns out that the real reason the Name wanted to come to Broadway was that she was beginning to slip in Hollywood and a hypodermic was needed. . . . Personally I love Hollywood and I am in favor of leaving it right where it is. A wise manager once said to me: "Always try to have a play instead of a star. Remember, a play can never send for you to come back to its dressing room."

Many the woes of playwriting, and somewhere along the line the critics ought to be listed. The critics are hard to take, but alas, they are generally right. I will not try to deny that I have been aggravated. (Has this suddenly turned into a personal article?) Just a year ago one of the brighter boys wrote a review of the season just ahead, in which he solemnly announced that it could not possibly be any good. That, I submit, is clairvoyance, not criticism.

So, taking one consideration with another, it's a tough business, and I wouldn't be in any other. " 'The play's the thing,' " as Max Gordon once remarked, " 'wherewith I'll catch the conscience of the King,' plus a hundred thousand dollars of somebody else's money."

LIFE'S CALENDAR FOR FEBRUARY 1922

1   W   Screw propeller for steamships invented by John Erics-
son, 1838. Mrs. Hamilton Fish decreed that soup plates
should be tipped *from* the diner, not *toward* him, 1901.

2   Th   Zoos closed in honor of GROUND-HOG DAY, 1922.
United States purchases Florida for $5,000,000, 1819;
New Yorker gets room at Palm Beach hotel for half that
amount, 1922. Joseph T. Davis, taxi driver, Chicago, Ill.,
finds he has change for $5, 1967.

3   F   Horace Greeley born, 1811; Douglas Fairbanks goes
West, 1916. Man living in Hartman's Centre, Neb.,
remembers to buy safety razor blades the day he runs out
of them, 1917.

4   Sa   Hinges invented by Cassius J. Hingus, 374 Appian Way,
Apt. 4C, North Rome, 242 B.C. Confederate States of
America formed, 1861. Self-leaking fountain pen in-
vented, 1896.

5   Su   Roger Williams, founder of Rhode Island, lands in
America, 1631. Roger Williams finds Rhode Island, 1635.
Five hundred thousandth United Cigar Store robbed,
1924.

6   M   Aaron Burr born, 1756. Lowney's Cocoa fails to win
Grand Prix at exposition in Quito, Bolivia, 1971.

7   Tu   Long distance telephone opened between New York and
Chicago; first conversation begins: "I can hear you just
as plainly as though you were in the next room," 1892.
Can of sardines opened with key provided for the purpose, 1911.

8   W   William Tecumseh Sherman born, 1820; Georgia banks
remain open, 1922. Citizen of Valparaiso, Ind., keeps
sponge damp in humidor after first week, 1918.

9 Th William Henry Harrison, ninth President, born, 1773. Samuel Jones Tilden born, 1814. Weather Bureau established by Congress; coins phrase "Probably Colder," 1870. Non-Chinese cigarette girl discovered in New York cabaret, 1922.

10 F France cedes Canada to England, 1763. Royal Mounted Police sell it to W.S. Hart, 1918. Student of economics locates trunk store not having special sale, 1912. Enterprising clothing firm begins making vest pockets large enough for vest pocket kodaks, 1946.

11 Sa Daniel Boone born, 1735. Thomas Alva Edison born; completes first day's sleep in one and a half hours, 1847. Interpretative dance prologues for motion pictures invented, 1917.

12 Su Abraham Lincoln born, 1809.

13 M First magazine in America published in Philadelphia; Gold Medal Flour takes back page, 1741. Whipped cream first put on bouillon by Elizabeth H. Vantyne, afterwards Mad Bess, 1901.

14 Tu ST. VALENTINE'S DAY. Alexander Graham Bell patents the telephone, 1876; playwrights' union gives thanks, 1876-1922 incl. Arizona admitted to Union; annual output of picture postcards showing Grand Canyon increases four million, 1912.

15 W Battleship Maine sunk in Havana Harbor, 1898. Citizens of Xenia, Ohio, celebrate Better Ink week, 1926.

16 Th Fort Donelson surrenders to Grant, 1862. Chorus men first wear straw hats and carry on chairs, 1867.

17 F Ordinary egg laid by Winsted, Conn., hen, 1906. Charlie Chaplin "discovered" by highbrow magazines, 1917, '18, '19, '20, '21, '22.

18 Sa Jefferson Davis becomes Confederate President, 1861. Safety razors reach two for a nickel, 1928.

19 Su Ohio admitted to Union, 1803. Edison patents the phonograph; Watson, the needle, 1878.

20 M Panama Exposition opens in San Francisco; Dolly Dainty

Bead Company takes option on tower of jewels, 1915. American newspaper admits that rival sheet carries more agate lines of advertising, 1922. German scientist discovers that cheaper form of concrete can be obtained by mixing regular concrete with German marks, 1924.

21 Tu Washington Monument dedicated; Spalding's notes increase in baseball business, 1885. United States Steel Corporation incorporated in New Jersey; Charles M. Schwab predicts era of prosperity, 1901.

22 W George Washington born, 1732. *Good Housekeeping* shows how to decorate luncheon table with little hatchets, 1918. James Russell Lowell born, 1819. New York Giants, in training quarters, discover new and phenominal second baseman, 1908-1922, incl.

23 Th First express company started, 1839; first collection at both ends, 1840. Battle of Buena Vista, 1847; Battle of Buena Vista flunks 10,000 high school pupils, 1922.

24 F Man found in Worcester, Mass., who understands a barometer, 1908. Statistics show increase in cost of living, 1938.

25 Sa Maryland founds first representative government in America (and about the last), 1639. Charles Cotesworth Pinckney born, 1746. The revolver invented; "Didn't know it was loaded" used for first time in newspaper, 1836.

26 Su Fifteenth Amendment, giving negro full rights as citizen, adopted, 1869. Negroes still trying to get them, 1922. Stage telephone rings *on* stage, 1976.

27 M Henry Wadsworth Longfellow born, 1807; 76 parodists of "Hiawatha" retire with independent fortunes, 1888. Citizen of Portsmouth, N.H., actually finds himself with as many trouser hangers as he has pairs of trousers, 1917.

28 Tu Maryland gives a charter to the Baltimore & Ohio Railroad, 1827; total of 27,836,927 persons feel pretty sore at Maryland about it, 1922. Revolving door supplants electric chair at Sing Sing, 1929.

NOW IT CAN BE TOLD; AUTHOR OF LATEST "PINAFORE" OBLIGES*

THE NEW YORK HERALD TRIBUNE, *June 17, 1945*

These Sunday pieces, tracing a show from inception to completion, must inevitably have something of a pompous implication about them—"just look what a wonderful thing I did!" Disclaiming any charge that *Hollywood Pinafore* is a masterpiece, I would be coy as blazes if I did not add that, in my opinion, it is a darned good show, enormously enhanced by the performances of Mr. Moore, Mr. Gaxton, Shirley Booth and the rest. In retrospect it seems to me that my admiration for Gilbert and Sullivan caused me to stick a little too closely to the *Pinafore* form. But the box office at the Alvin is a lively place these nights, and don't take my word for it. Ask Max Gordon.

So now we come to the story. Along about the first of February, Bill Gaxton crossed over to my table in the Oak Room at the Plaza to make one of the worst suggestions I have ever heard. He and Victor Moore had come East for a show that had failed to jell, and they had the wonderful idea of reviving *Of Thee I Sing.* I asked him if he had read it recently. He hadn't. I pointed out that for sundry reasons a revival of *Of Thee I Sing* would be unforgivable in war times, and that was that.

At the moment I was already deep in *Hollywood Pinafore,* but it had not occurred to me that the Messrs. Gaxton and Moore would fit into it. Two days later I called them up and said that a strange thing had happened. Miraculously, the show fitted them perfectly. We got together that afternoon and the thing was settled.

It seemed to me, in my innocence, that no show could be simpler than *Hollywood Pinafore.* One set, and anybody could sing the music. Hadn't I sung it myself, ever since I was eight? There would be none of the normal troubles of a musical show—there wouldn't

*This article was first published on the Sunday prior to the New York opening of *Hollywood Pinafore.—ed.*

even be any light cues. First act in the morning, second act at night, and there you are. Why, you'd hardly even need a stage manager, far less than the three I eventually would end up with. And I also reckoned without Jo Mielziner.

Now Jo is an artist, and a great one, but he always thinks you're putting on a small city, not just a show. We were to open in Baltimore, and when Jo finished the set it seemed much easier to move Baltimore to the scenery instead of vice versa. And I was right about the light cues, except for one small detail. It turned out that the show was to be lighted through holes in the ceiling, and putting together the ceiling and its complicated lighting equipment would require just eighteen hours and about twenty men. (It's a beautiful job, and I don't regret it, but it turned out that Jo had just come from lighting the San Francisco Conference, and I think he got the two of us mixed up.)

There were other surprises. It turned out that Mr. Sullivan's music, which anybody could sing, was all cut up into parts quite incomprehensible to the layman—basses, and sopranos, and first and second tenors, and contraltos, and intermezzos, and mezzanines, and heaven knows what. For this little job we were lucky enough to obtain the incomparable Lyn Murray, and from Mr. Murray I learned a great deal. The chief thing I learned was never to do it again.

From Mr. Murray I also learned that it would take four weeks to select a satisfactory chorus. I wandered in and out of the theater during these trying auditions, and from the dark depths of the auditorium, as each applicant sang, would come a phrase that sounded the death knell. "Thank you very much," Mr. Murray would say. "Thank you very much," and that would be the end of it. When a candidate showed promise, Mr. Murray never would bother to thank her. Instead would come a question: "What is your range, please? How high do you go?" Then I knew there was a chance.

Costumes. I'm not sure I can go into costumes—it is too painful. Most of them reached Baltimore at a quarter to seven on the night of the opening, brought down by dog sled when all other means of transportation had failed. Materials had been selected months in advance, dyed, re-dyed, dyed again. Measurements were ready and waiting; seamstresses sat with needles ready, awaiting the gong. And if you ask me why, with all these precautions, the costumes still arrived in Baltimore on the night of the opening, I can only fall back upon a cliche and say: "That's show business." I can further advise you to stay out of it.

Happily the full burden of these distractions was borne by a young man named Arnold Saint Subber, and not for nothing is he known as Saint. I believe Mr. Subber is down on the program as "Production Assistant" or some such thing, but he was far more than that. Except for the fact that it would have looked strange on the program, he might have been billed as Whole Darned Show. Mr. Subber weighed about forty-three pounds when the show went into rehearsal, and thirty-four when it opened. You have to look at least three times to see him at all, but what there is to him is wonderful.

My simple little show started rehearsals in four different theaters or halls, which should have warned me. The magnificent Antony Tudor was instructing his ballerina somewhere in Carnegie Hall, a lightning-thinking young man named Douglas Coudy was taking the other dancers through their paces at the Alvin; Mr. Murray was billeted with the singers on the New Amsterdam Roof, and the principals and myself were hard at work at the Lyceum. Mr. Subber was everywhere, and I mean everywhere. He fitted into places that no other human being could get himself into, and would often step out from behind a thin pipe.

Yes, a simple one-set show. When the various heads of departments met to lay out a schedule for the Baltimore hegira I counted no less than twenty-two people, each with a special and highly necessary function. I should add that the schedule thus laid out was rigidly not adhered to. Show business again.

HOLLYWOOD PINAFORE

or The Lad Who Loved a Salary

Book and Lyrics revised by George S. Kaufman
(WITH THE DEEPEST APOLOGIES TO W. S. GILBERT)
Music by Sir Arthur Sullivan

Hollywood Pinafore was produced by Max Gordon (in association with Meyer Davis) at the Alvin Theatre on Thursday, May 31, 1945, with the following cast:

JOSEPH W. PORTER, head of Pinafore Pictures . . . . . VICTOR MOORE

MIKE CORCORAN, a director . . . . GEORGE RASELY

RALPH RACKSTRAW, a writer . . . . GILBERT RUSSELL

DICK LIVE-EYE, an agent . . . . WILLIAM GAXTON

BRENDA BLOSSOM, a star . . . . ANNAMARY DICKEY

LOUHEDDA HOPSONS, a columnist . . . . SHIRLEY BOOTH

BOB BECKETT, a press agent . . . . RUSS BROWN

MISS HEBE, Mr. Porter's secretary . . . . MARY WICKES

MISS GLORIA MUNDI . . . . DIANA CORDAY

MISS BEVERLY WILSHIRE . . . . PAMELA RANDELL

LITTLE MISS PEGGY . . . . ELLA MAYER

DOORMAN . . . . DAN DE PAOLO

SECRETARIES . . . . { JACKSON JORDAN
ELEANOR PRENTISS
DRUCILLA STRAIN

GUARD . . . . ERNEST TAYLOR

Actors, Actresses, Assistant Directors, Cameramen, Technicians, etc.

Within this adaptation of Gilbert and Sullivan's *H.M.S Pinafore*, Mr. Kaufman, in his own words, "has brazenly borrowed a single number from *The Pirates of Penzance*."—*ed.*

SCENE: *The office of Pinafore Pictures Studio, Hollywood. A gorgeous room —the walls are done in grey satin and red marble. A center stairway leads to two balconies Right and Left. This, of course, is the "Poop Deck" of Pinafore. On each balcony there is a door. Two curved desks are formed by the curving rails of the stairways. On each desk are three telephones of varying colors, and back of each desk is a beautiful blonde. There is a uniformed Doorman at the center door. Actors and actresses in various costumes are arranged on steps. Both secretaries are speaking alternately on the telephones as the curtain rises.*

GIRLS: Pinafore Pictures!
Pinafore Pictures!
Mr. Joseph Porter?
Mr. Porter's in the projection room!
An Egyptian mummy on Stage 12. Must be female!
Pinafore Pictures!
Try Selznick!
Try Metro!
Mr. Porter is in his private bungalow!
Try Warners!
Mr. Porter is in the barbershop!
Pinafore Pictures!
Pinafore Pictures!

CHORUS: We are simple movie folk
Of the wood that's known as Holly;
And we lightly bear the yoke
Of a life of lovely folly.
We go to work at dawn
And we carry on
Till the cool of the evening comes;
We're in ermine and jade,
For we all get paid
Terrifically fancy sums
Oh, Joy! Oh, Joy!

DOORMAN: Miss Gloria Mundi—$1500 a week. (MISS MUNDI *enters dressed in black sequins.*)

GLORIA: . . . On a wage so low
I am plunged in woe
A most unhappy miss
I must go bare
Or else just wear
A miserable rag like this.

DOORMAN: Miss Beverly Wilshire—$5000 per week. (MISS WIL-SHIRE *enters—a tall blonde dressed in slacks dragging a mink coat behind her*)

BEVERLY: . . . Mine's a name you often see
Up in lights on a marquee
For a glittering Star am I
If you care to take a guess
At the cause of my success
There're two little reasons why.

DOORMAN: Miss Peggy—$8000 per week. (MISS PEGGY *enters—dressed like a girl of six.*)

PEGGY: . . . For a little girl of six
I have quite a bag of tricks
I'm sweet in a Fauntleroy suit;
I am very good for biz,
And the reason is:
I'm terribly goddam cute!

DOORMAN: Silver Tassel—$10,000 per week. (PAGE BOY *enters leading collie on jewelled leash.*)

CHORUS: We are simple movie folk
Of the wood that's known as Holly;
And we lightly bear the yoke
Of a life of lovely folly.
But before we go away
We have this to say,
Of an author world-renowned:
Mr. Gilbert if he knew
What we're going to do
Would be whirling round and round.
Oh boy, oh boy, before we go away
Oh joy, oh joy, we have this to say
He'd burrow in the cold, cold ground.

At the conclusion of the number the secretaries' telephones ring incessantly, and the Doorman announces the arrival of Hollywood's greatest columnist, Louhedda Hopsons, a buxom woman, draped in jewels and carrying a pencil, a notebook, and newspapers.

LOUHEDDA: Hail, Pinafore men! To Louhedda hearken!
Brief is my stay—I found no place to park in.
Pray hold naught back! I've come to gather news.
You'd be surprised the drivel I can use!

Actors and actresses flock around her, chattering with excitement. They ask Louhedda for the latest news.

LOUHEDDA: Ah, for that you must buy my papers! *(Hands each group a newspaper. She sings:)*
I've wonderful stories of Hollywood's glories,
To mellow your little insides;
I've news of divorces, and Louis Mayer's horses,
And just who are going to be brides.

I'm Czar and Czarina of this entire scena,
And here is my policy true:
If you'll butter *me* up, not give me the knee up,
Then I'll gladly butter up *you.*

I'm called Little Butter-up, dear Little Butter-up;
Good reason why it should be;
The pages I clutter up, mush that I utter up—
Sweet Little Butter-up, me!

Last night, seeking topics, I went to the tropics
And got a most wonderful break.
I know who was sittin' with Barbara Britton,
And also Veronica Lake.

Poor Rita's divorcin' that awful man Orson
(I'm making that up to please Hearst);
And Alice Faye may be expecting a baby

A year from next October first!
"That's exclusive"

My mere disapproval can mean your removal;
Take care not to merit my scorn;
So you who have known me will do well to phone
me
Before you get married or born.
ALL: She's called Little Butter-up,
Dear Little Butter-up;
Good reason why it should be.
LOUHEDDA: Words she will splutter up
No one can shut her up
Sweet Little Butter-up, me!

All exit except Louhedda. Bob Beckett, Pinafore Pictures' public relations counsel, enters. Louhedda whips out her pad and pencil and asks Bob what news he has for her. Bob, lowering his voice, confides that Mr. Porter, for untold thousands, has purchased the motion picture rights to *The Raven,* by Poe. Louhedda reminds Bob that it doesn't matter who *writes* a picture, the only thing of importance is who will *star* in it. Bob, very secretly, says, "Brenda Blossom." As Louhedda writes, Bob adds that it will be photographed in Technicolor, from a screenplay by Ralph Rackstraw. At the mention of his name, Louhedda recoils.

LOUHEDDA: Ralph Rackstraw . . . Hast ever thought that beneath a gay and frivolous exterior there may lurk a cankerworm which is slowly but surely eating its way into my very heart? What then would you say?
BOB: *(Looking at her ample bosom)* I'd say he had quite a way to go.
DOORMAN: Mr. Richard Live-eye. Ten percent of everybody's salary.

Although "dressed to kill," the newcomer has a patch over one eye. Bob asks what happened. Dick says, "I received it from a client. 'Tis but ten percent of what *he* got." Louhedda leaves to watch some underwater filming at the studio and Bob asks Dick what is new with him.

DICK: I just put through the biggest deal of my life! I sold Warner Brothers the motion picture rights to the Bible!

BOB: Where did *you* get them?

DICK: What's the difference? I *sold* them! And I just sold Clark Gable to Metro!

BOB: But Metro already *has* Clark Gable.

DICK: They forgot all about it. I got him the best deal he ever had—a million dollars a minute! And I get ten percent! . . . But what happens? They don't appreciate me! They bar me from the studios! . . . From every restaurant! From every home! From the A. & P. And know why? Because I am an agent! I am hated by all! But you don't know what I have to go through to sell you. *(He sings:)*

When an Agent's not engaged in his employment
Or preparing his felonious little plans
His capacity for innocent enjoyment
Is just as great as any honest man's.
His sympathetic heart he has to smother
When dirty work is aching to be done.
Taking one consideration with another
An Agent's life is not a happy one.

He must work from twelve to one for all that's in it
If he rings a bell a tall brunette responds
If he only leaves his office for a minute
He is chased by sixty-seven gorgeous blondes.
One will kiss him for some favor that he did her
And another thinks it might be lots of fun.
If you really stop and carefully consider,
An Agent's life is not a happy one.

He must lunch with either Grable or with Hedy
He must dine with Marlene Dietrich or Bacall
He is made to go with Betty Hutton steady
He just never sees a homely girl at all.
He must motor out to all the private beaches
He is forced to lie a-basking in the sun
How would you like that if you were in his breeches?
An Agent's life is not a happy one—happy one.

Louhedda, actors and actresses re-enter. The Doorman announces, "Ralph Rackstraw! Writer! Seventy-five dollars a week!" and he exits disgustedly. Ralph enters, holding script, wearing convict stripes. All on stage turn their backs.

RALPH: Wherever I roam one and all turn away
    They dare not face those who gain such trivial pay
    They sing "How much a day?"
CHORUS: They sing "How much a day?"

RALPH: Alas, where is my share of admiration
    Mine is a life of sitting in the gall'ry.
    O'erlaid with grievous pain my situation;
    I love—and love, alas, above my sal'ry.

    A maiden often seen
    Upon the silver screen,
    Bewitching, fair, and thrilling;
    For whom producers sigh
    And with each other vie
    To give her bigger billing.

    A writer, lowly paid,
    Mayn't hope for such a maid;
    I curse her ev'ry damn beau.
    My life can ne'er be hers;
    I cannot buy rich furs,
    Nor take her to Mocambo.

    Since first I fell in love
    With one so far above,
    I'm twenty-two pounds lighter.
    Oh, pity, pity me!
    A movie star is she!
    And I a lowly writer.

Dick says that if Ralph wants to marry Brenda, he should make *anything* of himself except a writer.

DICK: The maidens of this town marry producers, executives, directors, actors, cameramen, make-up men, clothes designers, scene designers, insurance men, doctors and dog-catchers, but they do *not* marry writers.

RALPH: But *some*body has to marry writers.

DICK: I see no reason.

The Doorman announces the arrival of "Mike Corcoran, director. Five hundred thousand a year, under a capital gains set-up."

MIKE: My boys and girls, Good Morning!

ALL: Sir, Good Morning!

MIKE: Are you ready for a take?

ALL: We are, and retakes!

MIKE: Why do you laugh at all my jokes,
     And listen to my dull stories?

ALL: You're the director!

MIKE: I'm a big director at Pinafore

ALL: And a good director, too.

MIKE: And I put it as a fact
     That most of you can act
     As well as a kangaroo.
     When it says "directed by"
     Then my all-observing eye
     Has watched ev'ry light and prop;
     Ev'ry picture from my hand
     Breaks the record at the Strand
     And I never, never make a flop.

ALL: What, never?

MIKE: No, never!

ALL: What, never?

MIKE: Well, hardly ever!

ALL: He hardly ever makes a flop

(Three cheerleaders enter with sweaters and megaphones initialed "P P")

Then give three cheers and one cheer more
For the best director here at Pinafore!
Then give three cheers for a *wonderful* director

MIKE: My pictures always tell a simple tale—
ALL: We are hanging on your ev'ry phrase.
MIKE: Every episode is planned
> For a child to understand,
> And I worship Mr. Will H. Hayes.
> If two people are in bed
> They must both be wed or dead.
> It's a proper Will H. Hays decree;
> I defer to his ukase
> On the length of an embrace,
> And I never use a big, big D.
ALL: What, never?
MIKE: No, never!
ALL: What, *never?*
MIKE: Only in Gone With The Wind.
ALL: Hardly ever use a big, big D.
> Then give three cheers and one cheer more
> For a *clean* director here at Pinafore!
> Then give three cheers for a *nice clean* director!

All go out except for Mike and Louhedda. She is, as ever, ready for news. She remarks that he looks depressed and wonders whether it is because he has not yet had his morning coffee. Mike responds that he is despondent because his daughter, Josephine, who changed her name to Brenda Blossom, is sought in marriage by Joe Porter, but "she won't even go with him to Chasen's, or Lucey's, or Romanoff's, or the Brown Derby." Louhedda says, "Ah, poor Joe Porter! Ah, but sadder still, the fact that I can't put it in my column!" So Louhedda exits in one direction, Mike in another.

Brenda enters to a now empty stage and sings a lament that although she is a star and has many things others long for, she is in love with Ralph and can't have him. Her father, Mike, re-enters and reminds her of the heights to which she can ascend if she marries Joe Porter. She tells her father that she is in love with a writer. Mike asks what he has written.

BRENDA: But little, father. Only a celluloid in which Roy Rogers did appear.

MIKE: Roy? Not Ginger? . . . but tell me, how did you meet with this writer? Writers are held within a structure of their own—they are not permitted to stray from it.

BRENDA: I know, father. But my steps took me near to the building in which the writers labor, and suddenly a voice came to me, and I looked up. There was his face, pressed against the bars. He was crying "Let me out of here! I'm just as sane as you are!" You know, father, I think he *is* just as sane as we are.

MIKE: But stop and think, my child. Why then did they put him *in* there? Surely there was reason.

Brenda's protestations of love are interrupted by Joe Porter's arrival, accompanied by the admiring crowd of sisters, cousins, and aunts to whom he has given jobs in the studio.

DOORMAN: Mr. Joseph W. Porter, head of the studio! *Two million dollars a year!* Plus bonuses.

As Joe Porter enters, the actors and actresses on stage all get down on their knees. Porter is followed by his secretary, Miss Hebe.

PORTER: I'd like to get the afternoon light in this room. Will you see if you can arrange to have the sun set in the East after this?

HEBE: I'll speak to someone.

PORTER: I am the monarch of the joint;
        All that I have to do is point.
        I pay the piper and I call the dance—
HEBE: And we are his sisters and his cousins and his aunts.
ALL: And we are his sisters and his cousins and his aunts,
        His sisters and his cousins and his aunts.

PORTER: For when a picture's fine,
        The credit's always mine,
        I give myself a big advance—

HEBE: And so do his sisters and his cousins and his aunts.
ALL: Yes, so do his sisters and his cousins and his aunts,
    His sisters and his cousins and his aunts.

PORTER: But when the preview's drear,
    I generally disappear,
    And seek the seclusion that the bathroom grants—
HEBE: And so do his sisters and his cousins and his aunts.
ALL: Yes, so do his sisters and his cousins and his aunts,
    And so do his sisters and his cousins and his aunts,
    His sisters and his cousins
    Whom he reckons up by dozens,
    And his aunts.

PORTER: How many stars did I discover yesterday?
HEBE: Six, Mr. Porter.
PORTER: All girls.
HEBE: Yes, sir.
PORTER: That's funny, isn't it?
HEBE: Yes, Mr. Porter.
PORTER: *(To Secretary at Left desk)* What is your name?
LEFT SECRETARY: Bernice Greaseheimer.
PORTER: Bernice Greaseheimer . . . that wouldn't look right on the marquee. Henceforth it will be . . . *(He thinks)* . . . Sylvia Sin. You're going to be a star. Put on a bathing suit and have some stills taken.
SECRETARY: Yes, Mr. Porter.
PORTER: Then take off the bathing suit.
SECRETARY: Yes, Mr. Porter.
PORTER: *(To Hebe)* Get another girl to take her place.
HEBE: Yes, Mr. Porter. *(Snaps her fingers. A second beautiful blonde comes in as* MISS GREASEHEIMER *leaves.)*
PORTER: Wait a minute. I'll make a star of her too. Get another girl. *(A third girl comes in)*
HEBE: This is going to run into money.
PORTER: I'll wait a couple of weeks. Miss Hebe, invite everyone to a party this evening, on stage one. . . . We're going to barbecue an agent. All of you men get back to work. *(All leave, including*

DOORMAN.) That's better. Wouldst you know how I got this way?
(He sings:)

> When I was a lad I tried my hand
> At ev'ry business in the land.
> My list was most diversified—
> I sold umbrellas and insecticide.
> But I could not make *any* thing go.
> So now I am the ruler of the studio.

CHORUS: But he could not make *any* thing go
so now he is the ruler of the studio.

PORTER: I drove a truck and I worked in a bank,
And at both those jobs I *really* stank;
I also made asbestos pies,
And I manufactured artificial butterflies,
But in all that time I never said "No,"
So now I am the ruler of the studio.

CHORUS: But in all that time he never said "No,"
So now he is the ruler of the studio.

PORTER: At getting to jobs I was often late,
Because of watching other people excavate
But I promptly answered ev'ry dinner bell,
And I played a nifty hand of auction pino*chell.*
Which makes it highly apropos
That now I am the ruler of the studio.

CHORUS: Which makes it highly apropos
That now he is the ruler of the studio.

PORTER: I cleaned the windows and I scrubbed the floor
Of a place that I don't mention any more.
I went upon the stage and I dropped the spear,
And I sat upon a bench in Central Park one year.
But you oughta see my bungalow
Since I became the ruler of the studio.

CHORUS: But you ought to see his bungalow
Since he became the ruler of the studio.

PORTER: I got a job as a sandwich man
But I found the work entirely too pedestrian;
I read the picture magazines
And I made a lot of money playing slot machines.
I flunked as a brakeman on the B. and O.
So now I am the ruler of the studio.
CHORUS: He flunked as a brakeman on the B. and O.
So now he is the ruler of the studio.

PORTER: So all shlemiels, whoever you may be,
If you want to rise to the top of the tree,
If you wouldn't be regarded as a darned old fool,
Be careful to be guided by this golden rule:
Just turn your back 'neath the mistletoe,
And you all may be rulers of the studio.
CHORUS: Just turn your back 'neath the mistletoe,
And you all may be rulers of the studio.

The chorus exits and Mike enters. Porter asks him that if there is a certain group connected with the studio known as "writers," he would like to see one. Mike bids the eight writers enter—they are all in convict clothes and chained together at the feet. Porter asks if they have sharp pencils for writing; they answer yes. He then asks if they are comfortable in their building. Ralph steps forward and asks if the writers could have a little more straw.

PORTER: Straw? To sleep on?
RALPH: No, sir. To stuff the characters with, sir. One cannot make scripts without straw.

Porter takes Mike into his office for a conference, followed by his sisters, cousins, and aunts. Ralph suggests to the other writers that they dig a tunnel and escape, for "If once we get out of Hollywood we would be free men. It is the law." Bob reminds Ralph of the options the studio has on the men. All on stage sing the "Studio Writers Song."

ALL: A writer fills the lowest niche
Of the entire human span;
He is just above the rat and should always tip his hat
When he meets the garbage man.

His lips should tremble and his face should pale
His steps should falter and his eyes should quail
He should live somewhere in a 'dobe hut,
And he always should be ready for a sal'ry cut.

A writer does not own the chains
That bind him head and toe;
If before he falls asleep he should count a lot of sheep,
They belong to the studio.

He should work ev'ry morning, ev'ry noon and night,
And all he should do is write and write
Till he falls right over and his eyes protrude,
And this should be his customary attitude.

The writers exit. Joe Porter re-enters because he is lonesome; "My office is so big I can't see anybody." Dick Live-eye enters and offers to make amends to Porter for taking advantage of him at a recent card game.

DICK: I want to be your agent . . . I'll give you ninety percent of everything you make.

Porter agrees, but says that the patch over Dick's eye scares him. Dick says that the *reason* he wears it is to scare people. There's nothing wrong with him at all.

PORTER: Say! Can I try it?
DICK: Sure! *(Gives him patch)*
PORTER: *(Puts on patch)* Now do I scare you?
DICK: Sure you do! . . .
PORTER: You know, if I had one on each eye I could scare people twice as much. *(And he exits)*

A girl asks Dick why Porter and he entered into their business agreement.

DICK: Why? Because it's Hollywood! Things aren't *supposed* to make sense in Hollywood! We're all crazy. Don't you know that? *(And he sings:)*

Never mind the why and wherefore!
This is Hollywood and therefore
We're expected to be utter-
Ly devoid of thought or care;
We put Kreml in our butter
And rub syrup in our hair!
We are crazy, we are crazy!
Not a single thing we know!
And we pick many a daisy
Out a-strolling in the snow!
Yet in spite of all these strictures
We turn out the damndest pictures! . . .

Ring, pianos, we are dippy!
We put pepper in our drinks!
Won't you jump the Mississippi?
Won't you manicure the Sphinx?

Never mind the why and wherefore
This is Hollywood and therefore
It's a gold-encrusted steeple
In a di'mond-covered tent;
Anyone resembling people
Is a nasty accident.

Dick exits as Brenda and Ralph enter. He tells her that he has not yet finished with his writing chores on *The Raven*, but confides that Brenda will play the title part. He says, "You will play *The Raven*, a private detective." Instead of continuing discussion of the film, he suddenly pours out his love for her. Brenda is quick to remind him of the gulf between them. She says, "Your proffered love I haughtily reject. Go, sir, and learn to cast your eyes upon some extra girl—they should be lowered before a star who has won the Academy Award!"

They sing a duet in which Brenda says she would be happier if either he were more highly born, or she more lowly. Ralph threatens to commit suicide if he can't have her, but Brenda, overcome, admits she loves him and they make plans to marry, in song.

BRENDA AND RALPH: This very night
　　　　　　　　Most quietly
　　　　　　　　With just the right
　　　　　　　　Publicity
　　　　　　　　A wedding bell
　　　　　　　　Will sound its chimes
　　　　　　　　We'll only tell
　　　　　　　　The New York Times
　　　　　　　　We shall be one
　　　　　　　　At half past ten
　　　　　　　　And that means none
　　　　　　　　Can part us then!

Joe Porter, in a generous spirit, raises Ralph's meager seventy-five-dollar-a-week salary to *eighty* dollars a week. Everyone rejoices including Dick, who gets ten percent of the new salary. However, as the first act draws to a close, Dick ominously predicts that the wedding will not take place.

DICK: He thinks he's won his Brenda dear,
　　　But me, I personally fear
　　　A bit of thunder from above
　　　Will end their ill-assorted love
　　　And thwart their dearest wish.

　　　Joe Porter ere the day is done,
　　　Will also have his little fun.
　　　Unless absurdly wrong I am
　　　They'll all end up at Monogram
　　　A pretty dish of fish.

The entire cast sings a reprise of the "Screen Writers Song," as the curtain falls.

ACT TWO

Moonlight. Mike Corcoran leans on the column and sings.

MIKE: Fair Moon, I'll ask until
    Upon my grave they pile stones:
    Why wasn't I named DeMille,
    Or Mamoulian or Lewis Milestones?
    Born 'neath a smiling star,
    Gayest of sybaritics,
    Their pictures always are
    Welcomed with joy by the critics.
    For me the stars exert no spell,
    I am a soul for all to pity:
    My latest film, 'tis sad to tell,
    Has closed at Radio City.

Louhedda has already been told of Mike's daughter's love for a writer, but Mike further confides that if he can't get Brenda to marry Joe Porter, Porter will assign someone else to direct *The Raven*. Louhedda suggests a plan: if Mike were to marry her, daily in her column, syndicated in 530 papers, she would mention his name as the greatest of directors. "Even the heart of Joe Porter would melt against that avalanche of mail," she says. As Mike looks at her appraisingly, trying to decide if she is worth it, Louhedda adds, "Just think! I would have the exclusive story of the marriage. And if there is to be a baby, I would be the *first* to know it!" Without giving her an answer, they both exit.

Joe Porter, Miss Hebe, and chorus enter. Porter says "Let there be more light" and the lights come up at once. But Porter is very unhappy and none of the girls can cheer him up. It seems they can't juggle, do card tricks, or swim. Porter asks, "What the hell are they doing in Hollywood?"

GIRLS: We want to marry Clark Gable.
PORTER: Oh.
HEBE: That's funny—so do I.

PORTER: What has Clark Gable got that I haven't and where can I get it?

HEBE: It's a long story.

By now, Porter understands that Brenda isn't interested in him, and threatens that he can take *any* girl and make her into a star.

Bob crosses the stage with Sylvia Sin, Porter's first-act "discovery."

BOB: You see, it's this way. First you get your picture in the movie magazines! . . . Then it gets printed in *Look!* . . . And then finally you get on the cover of *Life!*

SYLVIA: *Life!* That'll be wonderful!

BOB: Sure! You'll do fine as long as you don't make a movie.

Louhedda re-enters and tells Joe Porter that she has a secret she won't divulge until Porter promises to hire Mike as director of *The Raven*. Porter wants the secret first. Louhedda, in song, tries to give Porter hints as to what it might be—but only succeeds in confusing him more. As they exit, Dick and Brenda enter.

DICK: Pssst!

BRENDA: Mr. Live-eye.

DICK: I would have speech with you.

BRENDA: Speech with me?

DICK: Speech with you. I shall have most of the speeches, but it will be with *you*. Tell me—have you an agent?

BRENDA: *(Nods)* The firm of Drawingbord and Smorgasbord.

DICK: Smorgasbord is a good man. But I am a better.

BRENDA: Alas, I have a long contract.

DICK: How long?

BRENDA: Eighty-five years—with options.

DICK: Smorgasbord is a *very* good man. *(Aside)* I must persuade her to break the contract. I must frighten her. *(Aloud)* Know you the plan that Mr. Porter has prepared for you, providing you yield not to his entreaties?

BRENDA: Plan? What, pray?

DICK: You will never be heard of again! He will doom you to a life of obscurity!

BRENDA: You affright me! He will exile me to some distant rock?

DICK: Worse! No human eye will ever behold you! He will put you upon the *stage!*

BRENDA: *(Recoiling a step)* The stage!

DICK: Know you that upon the stage some actresses receive as little as a thousand dollars a week?

BRENDA: It cannot be!

DICK: 'Tis true! Know you that a stage actress, upon arrival in New York City, is met by no press agent, no American Beauty roses, and sometimes by no more than a crowd of two hundred people! It's a living death.

BRENDA: Oh, pity me!

DICK: No photographs in the night clubs, no pictures in stage magazines—there *are* no stage magazines!

BRENDA: He could not inflict such torture!

DICK: But he will! And one thing more—one last indignity! On the stage you have to *act!*

BRENDA: No, no! *(Goes on her knees, clasps hands)*

DICK: *(Down to her)* And should you give a bad performance upon the stage, the critics actually *say so*—in print!

BRENDA: Alack-a-day! No!

DICK: Yes! All this if you do not wed with Joe Porter! . . . Methinks I've scared the hell out of her! *(He exits)*

Brenda, confused, contrasts in song the luxurious life that awaits her if she doesn't marry Ralph against the drab life that awaits her if she does. At the song's conclusion she is still in a quandry. Dick re-enters.

DICK: I just want to be the agent for John D. Rockefeller—that's all I ask.

Bob enters.

BOB: So I said to Selznick, "You can't talk like that to me!" and he said, "I can't, can't I?" and I said, "No, you can't." So he did.

Bob and Dick are joined on stage by Joe Porter, Miss Hebe, and Ralph to have a story conference to plan the pictures for the coming year. Dick thinks the studio ought to produce a "prestige picture." As he explains it, "A prestige picture is a picture that loses money, but it gives you prestige." Everyone agrees, including Ralph. Porter feels that, even though Ralph is going to write the picture, he shouldn't have any say-so at the conference. So Ralph is promptly gagged. Porter gets an idea to buy a play off the New York stage. "You can generally lose money on those," he says.

PORTER: What happens if a prestige picture *makes* money?
DICK: Oh, you can't do that.
PORTER: I just wondered.

Since there was a recent trend of doing biographical films, they try to think of someone to do a film about.

DICK: Let's see . . . Lincoln, Pasteur, Disraeli, Nora Bayes . . .
MIKE: All of the well-known ones have been done. They're *too* well-known.
PORTER: We need a well-known man that nobody has ever heard of. . . .
MIKE: How about a man like Thoreau? A famous naturalist?
PORTER: What's a naturalist?
MIKE: A naturalist is a man that behaves naturally.
PORTER: The Hays office wouldn't stand for that.

They decide to do *The Life of Joe Porter, or From Rags to Rushes.*

DICK: I'll cast it!
MIKE: I'll direct it!
BOB: I'll advertise it!
HEBE: I'll skip it!
DICK: It'll be the greatest picture ever produced! You know why? *(Sings)* He is a movie man
PORTER: I am a movieman
DICK: From the housetops let us cry it:

That he is a movieman!
    He's the last man to deny it!
ALL: That he is a movieman!
DICK: Might have been a bare back rider.
PORTER: On a horse or something wider,
DICK: Or chef with frying pan.
ALL: Or chef with frying pan.
DICK: But in spite of all temptations
    Toward other occupations,
    He remains a movieman!
ALL: He re-mai-ai-ai-ai-ai-ai-ai-ns a movieman!

And the conference is ended. Dick relates some bad news to Porter—it seems that Porter hasn't got the rights to *The Raven* after all.

DICK: You don't have to worry, though—I've just had a great idea. Why don't you buy Poe's *The Stork*?
PORTER: Poe's *Stork.* What's that about?
DICK: What do you think it's about? A stork. *The Raven* is about a raven, isn't it?

But it turns out that *The Stork* isn't available either.

DICK: *(Slyly)* Well, now that you haven't got a picture for her, there's no use keeping Brenda Blossom on salary, is there?
PORTER: I was sort of thinking of marrying her. She wouldn't get any salary then.
DICK: That's so. The only trouble is . . . I don't know whether I ought to say this . . .
PORTER: Is what? Everybody's mysterious around here. Are *you* going to be mysterious too?
DICK: Me? No-o-o-o! *(Sings)*
    Joe Porter, I've important information,
    Sing hey, the kindly boss of all who work,
    About a certain intimate relation,
    Sing hey, the merry maiden and the jerk.
PORTER: Dick Live-eye, you can take your information,

Sing hey, the ten-per-center that you are,
And put it with your fondest aspiration,
Sing hey, funiculi, funicular!

DICK: If *you* hide on the balcony and glance down,
Sing hey, sing nonnie and alack-a-day,
You'll find they're going to catch you with your pants
down,
Sing hey, you won't look very good that way.

PORTER: I don't know what it is that you want fixed up,
Sing hey, it all keeps ringing in my head,
It's all so abracadabra and mixed up,
Sing hey, I think I'd like to go to bed.

DICK: Joe Porter, your young lady is a-sighing,
Sing hey, and you can paste this in your hat,
This very night with Rackstraw to be flying,
Sing hey, what have you got to say to *that?*

PORTER: Dick Live-eye, I will hide up in the gall'ry,
Sing hey, if what you're telling me is sound,
I'll take away the louse's raise in sal'ry,
Sing hey, for I'm the toughest guy around.

(As the music stops)

Let there be no light!

(Blackout)

*(*BRENDA *enters and a small spot is thrown on her)*

BRENDA: I will hesitate no longer. 'Tis Ralph I love, and naught
else matters. We shall away this night to Yuma, and be wed.

(The light goes out. Now a similar spot is thrown on MIKE. *He is dressed
in a great cloak behind which he can conceal himself)*

MIKE: In this costume out of wardrobe they will know me not.
I must stop her flight, if I am to direct Poe's *The Raven.*

(Spot on DICK *on balcony)*

PORTER: But wait! Everybody's getting married! Where does that leave me?

HEBE: *(Linking her arm with his)* Even a writer needs a secretary.

PORTER: That's right. So he does! To do his writing! We'll have a triple wedding, but separate honeymoons.

BOB: Three loving pairs.

DICK: And I get ten percent!

The entire cast sings the finale.

ALL: We are simple movie folk
Of the wood that's known as Holly;
And we lightly bear the yoke
Of a life of lovely folly.
So, we end as we began
We submit this trifling filbert
With apologies to Gilbert
And also Sullivan
With apologies to Gilbert and Sullivan
With apologies to Gilbert and Sullivan.

THE END

NOTES FOR A FILM BIOGRAPHY

THE NEW YORKER, *August 11, 1945*

I went to see *Rhapsody in Blue* the other night, and as an intimate friend of George Gershwin's I was struck by the fidelity with which it followed his life. Ah, the memories it brought back! That night when the Rhapsody had its first hearing, when George rushed from the concert platform straight to the bedside of his dying music teacher, dear Professor Frank! It was I who buttoned his greatcoat about him on that historic occasion, I who whispered into his ear, "Mind the snow, George." (I was a little hurt that this was left out of the picture.) Too, I recalled so well the sweet Julie Adams—Julie, who sang the leads in all of George's shows and who fell in love with him so helplessly, so self-sacrificingly. I saw Julie just the other day, and we chatted over old times. She is in the WACS now, still sacrificing. And what a pang went through me when I heard the screen figures of George and Ira once more playfully referring to each other by those pet names that I knew so well, "Mr. Words" and "Mr. Music." It was a bit of life, I tell you.

As I pondered upon this and other screen biographies, thinking, too, of the coming life stories of Cole Porter and Jerome Kern, it occurred to me that the picture companies, desperate for subjects, might someday be offering up their millions for the story of my own life. Fearing that the bidding may be something less than spirited, and always with an eye to a couple of million dollars, I am taking the liberty of pointing out a few of the more dramatic episodes in my life, and suggesting how they may be enhanced for the greater enjoyment of the picture-going public. For the guidance of the producers I shall first describe each episode as it actually took place, then sketch in a few small adornments. These are purely suggestions, and I am sure that the screen writers will find ways to enlarge upon them.

The facts: As a little boy of seven, in Pittsburgh, I wheedled a penny out of my father and went across Walnut Street to Shornhorst's grocery store, where I bought some candy. I then returned home.

Suggested treatment: When I am in the middle of the street a runaway horse comes along, dragging behind it a buggy in which are a man and a little girl. The little girl, a beautiful child with golden hair, is crying out with terror and clinging desperately to the side of the buggy. Without a second's hesitation I throw myself at the foaming beast and drag it to a stop about a block farther down, just in front of a house on which there is a placard reading, "Stephen Collins Foster, American composer, was born in this house on July 4th, 1826." The camera moves slowly along the walk and up to the placard, which dissolves to reveal a Mississippi levee scene in which a group of darkies are singing "Old Black Joe." There follows a medley of Stephen Foster melodies, with Lena Horne and Bill Robinson. When this is over, the camera comes back to the street, and the man, who has now had time to get out of the buggy, says, "My boy, you don't know what you have done. I am James B. MacFarlane, the richest man in Pittsburgh, and this is my daughter, Beatrice." I am lifted up into the buggy and taken to the big house on the hill, where an enormous party is in progress, with Sousa's Band to play the dance music. Mr. Sousa plays "Stars and Stripes Forever," followed by a medley of all the other famous Sousa marches, during which the camera shows highlights of the American Revolution, the War of 1812, Perry on Lake Erie, the fight between the Monitor and the Merrimac, and finally Teddy Roosevelt and his Rough Riders going up San Juan Hill. At this point Mr. MacFarlane says, "It so happens that President Roosevelt is in Pittsburgh this very day, campaigning for reelection, and I have asked him to drop in." We then hear a great cheer in the street, and Teddy Roosevelt enters. Sousa's Band strikes up "Hail to the Chief," but Roosevelt raises his hand and says, "No! My favorite song is 'Shine On, Harvest Moon,' just the way Nora Bayes and Jack Norworth used to sing it down at Tony Pastor's." So Mr. Sousa's Band plays "Harvest Moon," and the camera cuts to Nora Bayes and Jack Norworth at Tony Pastor's. After that everybody is introduced to Teddy

Roosevelt, and Mr. MacFarlane says, "This is my daughter Beatrice. She is only six years old, but we think she has a very good voice and we would like her to sing for you." Little Beatrice sings "My Dolly's Face is All B'oken," and at the finish there is a closeup of Mr. Sousa, who is heard to remark, "That little girl will be a great figure upon the concert platform." Then it is my turn to be introduced to the President, and Mr. MacFarlane tells how I stopped the runaway horse, and Mr. Roosevelt says, "My boy, that is in the finest American tradition. I would like to help a boy like you. What would you like to be when you grow up?" There is a long pause, and then I say, "Nothing." Everyone agrees that I have a good chance to make it. Then Mr. MacFarlane says to Mr. Roosevelt, "Mr. President, what do you think of the future of the world?," and Mr. Roosevelt says, "We have just finished a great war with Spain and I hope that it will be the last of all wars. But America must be prepared, for I fear that we will have a great war with Germany in 1917. I wonder," he says, "what the war songs will be like in those days." As he is speaking, the music strikes up and we hear a medley of war songs from 1917—"Over There," "Tipperary," "How Ya Gonna Keep 'Em Down on the Farm," etc.—and at the same time the camera shows great guns booming and shots of the battlefield. When I get home my father says, "Where the hell have you been all this time?," and I say, "I stopped a runaway horse and was at Mr. MacFarlane's house on the hill and President Roosevelt was there." Of course Father thinks I am lying and he turns me over his knee and spanks me with a hairbrush as we fade out.

Episode No. 2

The facts: I took a short trip to London. One day I went to the offices of the American Express Company, where I was expecting a money order from home for fifty dollars, which I badly needed. The clerk said he didn't know anything about it, and would I please not block the line?

Suggested Treatment: Before I can think of an answer to this crack, a distinguished, white-haired old gentleman enters, accompanied by a beautiful girl. He goes right up to the cashier's window and says, "Bleakley, I will take a hundred thousand pounds, please." The clerk says, "Yes, Mr. Ambassador." This gives me a hint. It is

James B. MacFarlane, now our Ambassador to England. I say to him, "Mr. Ambassador, you don't remember me, do you?" He says, "No." Immediately, however, the beautiful young lady says, "Oh, but I do! You are George S. Kaufman, who stopped that runaway horse and saved our lives so many years ago." "How wonderful!" says the Ambassador. "You must live at the American Embassy while you are here!" Naturally, I agree, but before we leave the Express office the Ambassador turns to Bleakley and says, "I think I will take along those three shares of stock that you are holding for me." "Three shares for the Ambassador!" cries Bleakley, and everybody gives them, resoundingly. (A certain amount of comedy is necessary in a picture of this sort.) Anyhow, on the way to the Embassy, we drive along the Strand, and presently the Ambassador says, "There is the famous Savoy Theatre, where Gilbert and Sullivan presented all their celebrated operettas, beginning in 1881." As he speaks, the front of the Savoy Theatre slowly changes to the way it was in 1881, and the fashionable English ladies and gentlemen of the day are shown arriving at the playhouse. Presently the strains of the English anthem are heard, and everyone comes to attention. It is Queen Victoria, accompanied by Disraeli. As they enter the theatre, Disraeli is heard to remark, "Your Majesty, it is essential that England should control the Suez Canal, or we face war with Germany in 1914 and again in 1939." After a medley of all the Gilbert-and-Sullivan operettas has been played, we continue our drive toward the Embassy, and the Ambassador, looking out of his car, says, "Oh, there is Albert Hall!" "Let's stop and talk to him," I say, "because I know his brother, Frank Hall." (As I have said, a certain amount of comedy is necessary.) The Ambassador explains that he means the famous concert hall, adding, "My daughter Beatrice, who is now a well-known concert singer, is giving a recital there this very evening." At this we dissolve to the interior of Albert Hall that evening. There is, of course, a fashionable audience, and the camera pans slowly along the lobby, revealing the Prince of Wales, Lady Astor, Winston Churchill, Ramsay MacDonald, Stanley Baldwin, Rudyard Kipling, and Gilbert Miller. Then the Ambassador and I are shown in a box, all ready for the concert to begin. The strain that we are under shows in our faces—will Beatrice make good before this distinguished gathering? Beatrice sings "Ave

Maria," which brings an ovation from the crowded house, so she sings "Ave Another Maria." After the applause has died down, the Ambassador turns to me and says, "By the way, Mr. Kaufman, what about your career? What became of your wonderful plan to do nothing?" "I think I have succeeded in it pretty well," I reply a bit stiffly. "Indeed you have," says the Ambassador graciously. "Your teachers must be very proud of you." The camera then cuts to two of my teachers, back in Pittsburgh. One of them, Miss Hornaday, is running a two-balls-for-a-nickel concession in Kennywood Amusement Park, and the other, Miss Funk, is in jail. It is Christmas Eve and Miss Funk is singing "Silent Night." The camera then comes back to Albert Hall and after the concert we all go to a famous night club, where Gertrude Lawrence, Beatrice Lillie, and Noel Coward are performing. Noel Coward does a medley of all his song hits. In the middle of the last number there is a terrific disturbance out in the street and everybody rushes to the door. The Ambassador, looking at the building across the street, says, "The lights are going out in the Polish Embassy!" Germany has marched; it is war!

Episode No. 3

The facts: Two weeks ago I carried a couple of shirts around the corner to the Chinaman. He said he would have them ready on Thursday.

Suggested Treatment: I sail for China, where James B. MacFarlane is now our Ambassador and his daughter Beatrice is giving recitals in the Chinese music halls. The Ambassador gives a party for me at the American Embassy, where the famous Chinese composer, Tinkle-Foo, is one of the guests. After a medley of Tinkle-Foo's compositions has been played . . .

But that's enough to give the general idea. The picture companies will please line up on the left.

LIFE'S CALENDAR FOR MARCH 1922

1   W   First bank in the United States chartered; manufacturers of loose bricks for fireplaces become despondent, 1780. William Dean Howells born; New England becomes self-conscious, 1837.

2   Th   U.S. Department of Education established, 1867. Thousands still unable to read Congressional Record, 1922. Folding card table, belonging to Dravosburg, Pa., family, found to have nothing wrong with any of its legs, 1918.

3   F   War declared against Algiers, 1815. Grocer in St. James, N.Y., when asked if eggs are fresh, answers "No," 1903.

4   Sa   Vermont admitted to Union, 1791. Inauguration Day instituted; excursion rates invented, 1793.

5   Su   Don Stewart, of Columbus, O., invents new explosive, six times stronger than dynamite, for removal of lids from boxes of shoe paste, 1919. Riveting machine gets out of order; effort made to have day declared State holiday, New York, 1922.

6   M   Philip Henry Sheridan, famous advocate of horseback riding, born, 1831. Massacre of the Alamo, 1836. Little Wonder Pyrography Company instigates massacre of thousands of Indians on leather cushion covers, 1895.

7   Tu   Diner in Pocatello, Idaho, breaks world's record by eating 7826 oyster crackers before the meat course arrives, 1905.

8   W   England passes Stamp Act, 1765. Los Angeles, Cal., celebrates completion of entire month without a sensational scandal, 1905. Pancho Villa raids Columbus, N.M., 1916.

9   Th   Villa captured and promptly hanged by Gen. Pershing,

1916. Battle of Monitor and Merrimac, 1862. Guest at a friend's club fails to read everything on bulletin board, New York, 1891.

10 F   Valve for steam engines patented; work begun on valve handle wheeze, 1849. Pancho Villa captured and hanged by Gen. Pershing, 1916.

11 Sa   Gareth Frippy, first victim of a tooth-paste-squeezed-on-shaving-brush accident, dies at Franklin, Tenn., 1908. Pullman Car Company celebrates installation of its 1000th variety of spring faucet, 1922.

12 Su   General Post Office established by Congress, 1789. First complaint about it, 1789. Great blizzard, 1888. Pancho Villa captured in Mexico by pursuing troops and promptly hanged, 1916.

13 M   Standard time system established in U.S.; slogan "Now It Can Be Told" invented, 1884. Man walking across continent fails to deliver letter to Mayor Hylan, 1920.

14 Tu   Andrew Jackson born, 1767. H. J. Heinz completes life work by mixing No. 43 and No. 51 and getting No. 57, 1900.

15 W   Conference to end all wars begins at London, 2319. Pancho Villa shot and killed by own men in Mexico, 1916. Non-Congressman's daughter used to christen battleship, 1908.

16 Th   James Madison born, 1751. West Point Military Academy established, 1802. Plans completed for first Army-Navy Game, 1802.

17 F   ST. PATRICK'S DAY. First submarine goes under water, 1898. Soda fountain clerk places chocolate sundae in front of person who ordered it, 1912.

18 Sa   Grover Cleveland born, 1837. First Pension Act passed, 1918. American Legion wonders if series is completed, 1922. Harold L. Milchheim, Duluth, Minn., writes name and address on space provided for purpose on triangular coupon in magazine advertisement, 1926.

19 Su Call issued for First Colonial Congress, 1690. William Jennings Bryan, afterwards known as Beau Brummell, born, 1860.

20 M Pancho Villa narrowly escapes being captured in mountains of Mexico, 1916. First art photograph taken by light of match held cupped in sitter's hands while he lights cigarette, 1872.

21 Tu Bank of New York incorporated, 1791. Pin-wheel effect with parasols first used by chorus girls, 1843. Raphael Tuck and Sons begin designing next year's holiday cards, 1922.

22 W Scott bombards Vera Cruz, 1847. Emil J. Waldmann, Des Moines, Iowa, enters the Cabinet as first Secretary of Bootlegging, 1931.

23 Th Patrick Henry makes the Liberty-or-Death speech, thereby giving school children something to do on Friday afternoons, 1775. Aguinaldo captured by Funston, 1901. Last papier-maché scimitar removed from cozy corner, 1917.

24 F Rhode Island purchased from the Indians, 1636. Magazine publishers plan special asbestos editions for use in Turkish Baths, 1922.

25 Sa Movie producers begin printing Los Angeles city directory as prologue to films, 1914. Twelve hundred lodge brothers attend a theatrical performance not "in a body," 1923.

26 Su Husband in Macon, Georgia, helping wife to hang a picture, gets it right the first time, 1897. Driver of coal wagon gets off car tracks as soon as a car comes up behind him, 1920.

27 M Ponce de Leon, seeking Fountain of Youth, discovers Florida, 1513. Ten thousand middle-aged business men, also seeking Fountain of Youth, decide it was Paunch de Leon, 1922.

28 Tu Mexican War begins; Hearst gets out an extra, 1846. New variety of extra seat in taxicab, requiring to be

turned around three times before it opens, invented, 1924.

29 W John Tyler, tenth President, born, 1790. Six families living in Parsons, Kan., join forces to work out a particularly difficult jigsaw puzzle, 1921.

30 Th Ether first used as anesthetic; first patient tells about operation, 1842. U.S. buys Alaska from Russia, 1867. James Oliver Curwood obtains Alaska for exclusive scenario use, 1918.

31 F Pancho Villa killed by jealous woman in Mexican mountains, 1916. Exit MARCH, with mint sauce.

GOD GETS AN IDEA

THE NATION, *February 19, 1938*

The Lord got up one morning, brushed His teeth, and took a look at the world below.

"Things aren't very good," He said.

"No, Sir," said His secretary.

"It seems to Me," said the Lord, "that a lot of it's My fault. Maybe I haven't been trying hard enough. There must be a lot of people down there that don't even know I exist."

"But surely, Sir—"

"No, I mean it. I've been listening to the radio recently. And I'll bet you Lucky Strikes are much better known than I am."

"But, Sir—"

"But nothing. This is a new age, my boy, and we've got to use new methods. I'm going on the air. Get Me the biggest advertising man in the business."

So they got him—the biggest advertising man in the business. He heard the whole idea through, and shook his head uncertainly.

"You mean the whole talk would be religious?" he asked.

"Of course," said the Lord.

"It's pretty risky," said the advertising man. "We got in a lot of trouble with Mae West lately, on a thing something like that."

"But this would be serious," said the Lord. "In a world torn by strife and hatred, ruled by cruel and ruthless dictators—"

"Hold on," said the advertising man. "You can't say anything about the dictators, you know. Germany's sure to protest, and then we'll get in wrong with the government."

"But they're at the root of most of the world's trouble."

"Well, maybe. But we get our license from the government, don't forget. And we've got all kinds of clients, too. A lot of them don't like to hear that kind of stuff."

"Then suppose I just talk about peace? Just peace."

"That would be better. Of course it doesn't sound very exciting —it won't be easy to find a sponsor. But I'll see what I can do."

So he went after a sponsor. Jello thought it was a good idea, but finally decided that Jack Benny was a better bet. Packard turned it down cold. The Bayer people were impressed, but said that peace wouldn't sell aspirin. Now, if He would talk on another subject . . . Chase and Sandborn already had Edgar Bergen, but thought something pretty good could be worked out between God and Charlie McCarthy. And so it went. Most of them said they were sorry they couldn't use Him right then, but they would bear Him in mind, and if anything came up . . .

The best he could offer, said the advertising man, would be a sustaining program. That meant He not only wouldn't get paid for it, but would have to pay for the band Himself.

"What band?" asked the Lord.

"Why, the band that would go on with you," said the advertising man. "You didn't expect just to talk, did You?"

"Yes, I did, kind of," said the Lord. "You see, I've got a good deal to say."

"They won't listen for more than five or six minutes," said the advertising man. "They're not used to it. Now the way I see it is this: we open with a bit of your theme music, something like 'Have You Met Miss Jones?' Then comes a snappy announcement—'JQX takes pleasure in introducing an old Favorite'—something like that. Then You do six minutes, maybe six and a quarter. And after that the band again, with something hot."

"Maybe," said the Lord, "we had better let the whole matter drop."

"No," said the advertising man, "it sounds to me like a good idea. All You've got to do is catch on a little bit and we'll get a sponsor and make a lot of money. Now when would You like to go on?"

"The sooner the better," said the Lord, "considering how things are. What about this Sunday night?"

"This Sunday?" said the advertising man. "Good heavens, no! Roosevelt is on!"

BILLING, SCHMILLING . . .

A Parable for Showfolk

SATURDAY REVIEW, *April 18, 1959*

(The scene is a vaudeville street drop. Enter HAM *and* EGGS, *in old vaudeville tramp costumes.)*

HAM: I don't want to hear any more about it! We've been Ham and Eggs for years, and that's the way it's going to stay.

EGGS: But it's not fair! Ham and Eggs. Ham and Eggs! All the time we've been together! Why shouldn't it be Eggs and Ham? I'm just as important as you are. Why should I take second billing all the time!

HAM: Look! We've had a great run as Ham and Eggs—we've played every restaurant in the country with that billing and we've always been a hit. People wouldn't dream of asking for Eggs and Ham. It just doesn't sound right.

EGGS: It doesn't sound right because you don't want to change —that's why.

HAM: I want to do what's best for the act—you know that. We've been a hit for three hundred years—ever since the Pilgrims landed at Plymouth. And that Mrs. Williams put us together because she was short of frying pans.

EGGS: But it's the Eggs that people really want. Ham is just sort of something that comes along with them.

HAM: Then why have I been up there first all this time? It's the public that decides. I've been first because they think of me first. Ham is the backbone of the act.

EGGS: I know where Ham comes from, thank you. And I tell you it's *Eggs* that draws 'em in, every time.

HAM: But once they're in it's Ham that holds 'em there—gives them something to chew on.

EGGS: Just try advertising Ham alone some time—see how far

you get. But put Eggs up there alone and they'd still come in. Besides, there are always two of me and only one of you. I don't see why I always have to come second.

HAM: But you don't always come second! What about Eggs Benedict? You come first there.

EGGS: Who the hell is Benedict? Nobody ever heard of him.

HAM: Of course they have. What about Benedict Arnold? He's famous!

EGGS: Oh, that's just great! Benedict Arnold—that's who I come ahead of. Thank you very much. . . . Well, let me tell you this. I'm not just going to sit on that pan and take it any more. I've got something in mind and we'll see whether—

(A MESSENGER BOY *enters. "Telegram for Mr. Eggs! Telegram for Mr. Eggs!")*

EGGS: Here you are, boy! *(He rips open the message, eagerly)* Listen to this—you think you're so smart. *(Reads)*

"HEREBY OFFER YOU SENIOR BILLING ON MY ACT. YOUR NAME TO COME FIRST ON ALL RESTAURANT FRONTS AND MENUS."

(Signed)
BACON.

BALLADE OF THE UNFORTUNATE FISHERMAN

LIFE, *September 7, 1922*

With native guide, and hook and line,
    I've angled in the lakes of Maine;
I've fished in the historic Rhine,
    I've tried it in the River Seine.
    And when my efforts all were vain,
And meekly I've inquired the reason,
    The Man Who Lives There would explain:
"Somehow it ain't so good this season."

"Now, last year, say—" one's very spine
    Thrills as they tell of that campaign;
But this year fish no longer dine—
    Too dry, perhaps, or too much rain.
    I've sat for days—I've knelt and lain—
In perfect silence watched my P's an'
    Q's, but caught this same refrain:
"Somehow it ain't so good this season."

On trails of very lonesome pine,
    In lands of waving sugar cane,
The selfsame fortune has been mine—
    Experience is all I gain.
    Wherever travels boat or train,
At every lake whose banks have trees on,
    They always say, when I complain:
"Somehow it ain't so good this season."

L'Envoi

Prince—if a Prince thou art—and deign
    To notice verse that's halt and wheezin',
Forgive the bard his wearied brain—
    Somehow it ain't so good this season.

LIFE'S CALENDAR FOR APRIL 1922

1 Sa Little boy who tied a string to a purse on April 1, 1882, celebrates fortieth anniversary of event by paying $24 for a pair of tickets to a Broadway musical show, 1922.

2 Su Bootleg whiskey invented; Socrates first victim, 399 B.C. United States mint established; W. I. Burns begins series of magazine articles on how he runs down counterfeiters, 1792. Charles L. Frantic elected first mayor of Manhattan Transfer, 1924.

3 M Washington Irving born, 1783. B.V.D. joke first used in musical comedy, 1802. Edward Everett Hale born, 1822. David C. Gripple, Worcester, Mass., walks a mile and a quarter for a Camel, 1922.

4 Tu Hendrik Hudson discovers Hudson River, East Side settlers up to then having been afraid to cross Fifth Avenue, 1609. Speaker at banquet stays within five minutes of time allotted, 1917.

5 W New York Chamber of Commerce established; regular business men's lunches invented, 1768. Mrs. Mary Lascelles pays clipping bureau bid of $827,526, 1922.

6 Th First Constitutional Congress meets in New York City; members attend Hippodrome as guests of Charles B. Dillingham, 1789. Candle stays erect in candlestick, 1902. Peary reaches North Pole; Dr. Cook's name not in guest book, 1909. U.S. declares war against Germany, 1917.

7 F New York man walks under ladder and receives letter telling him that his aunt has died and left him two apartment houses, 1912.

8 Sa Duel between Henry Clay and John Randolph, Georgetown, Va.; Mayor of Georgetown starts probe, 1826.

Man hears own name distinctly pronounced by page in hotel, 1938.

9 Su La Salle takes possession of Louisiana; Herman J. Fingle appointed State superintendent of praline factories, 1682. Lee surrenders to Grant at Appomattox; Augustus Thomas begins first Civil War play, 1865.

10 M S.P.C.A. organized, 1866. Entire family goes through family entrance of saloon, 1908.

11 Tu Mayor of Carthage throws out first ball at opening of season of Afro-Indo Baseball League, 152 B.C. Italian Cabinet resigns, 1914-'22 incl.

12 W Henry Clay, famous breeder of pigeons, born, 1777. First pony express; movie cameraman wounded by poisoned arrow, 1860. Fort Sumter bombarded, 1861.

13 Th Thomas Jefferson born, 1743. James Harper born, 1795. *Harper's Monthly* prints first anecdote about what little W_____ said when Bishop F_____ came to tea, 1842.

14 F Abraham Lincoln assassinated, 1865.

15 Sa Westinghouse patents the air brake, 1869; New York subway passengers celebrate fiftieth anniversary by falling off their seats when trains stop, 1919.

16 Su Slavery abolished in District of Columbia, 1862; copy-readers on Congressional Record laugh hysterically at the idea, 1922. Lillian E. Dosp, telephone operator, wins world's trilling record by taking one and three-quarter minutes to pronounce the word "three," 1922.

17 M Virginia secedes from the Union, 1861. Man buys hat in Fifth Avenue shop without being introduced to salesman by floorwalker, 1921.

18 Tu General Scott wins battle of Cerro Gordo, 1847. San Francisco earthquake, 1906. Woman refolds newspaper in original creases, 1965.

19 W Battle of Lexington, 1775. Clayton-Bulwer treaty, providing for joint occupancy of Nicaragua Canal, signed; fireworks and dancing in streets of New York and London, 1850. Publishers' blurbs invented, 1852.

20 Th S. Loo Chung, of Canton Falls, China, pays election bet lost on Ming dynasty by rolling lichi nut the length of the Great Wall, 1352-1412. Bell tinkles when actor pulls stage bell rope, 1918.

21 F Lady fingers invented by wife of Lord Gareth Finger, 1871. Proprietor of drug store stabs soda clerk for serving customer prior to purchase of check, 1919. Annual call of Great North Woods heard again in magazines, 1922.

22 Sa Indian Territory thrown open to settlers, 1889. Toastmasters begin introducing Irvin S. Cobb as Irving S. Cobb, 1913. U.S. forces capture Vera Cruz, 1914. James Buchanan, fifteenth president, born, 1791.

23 Su Shakespeare dies; blow almost kills James K. Hackett, 1616. Stephen Douglas born, 1813.

24 M *Boston News Letter*, first permanent American newspaper, published for first time; Katzenjammer Kids born, 1704. Munsey buys *Boston News Letter*, 1714.

25 Tu U.S. declares war on Spain, 1898. War loan of $200,-000,000 to Great Britain; W.R. Hearst feels it keenly, 1917. Donald M. McSmith, retired painter of bock beer signs, dies, leaving fortune of more than a million, 1921.

26 W Last Confederate army surrenders to Gen. Sherman, 1865. Jamestown Exposition opens; Coney Island yawns slightly, 1907. Unknown vagrant giving name of William Hohenzollern arrested for annoying photographers at Doorn, Holland, with pleas for their services, 1926.

27 Th Samuel F. Morse, inventor, born, 1791. U.S. Grant born, 1822. First bombardment of Spanish War; "Goodbye, Dolly Gray" gets ready to be written, 1898.

28 F James Monroe, fifth President, born, 1758. Stores named in his honor move upstairs, 1900. Early vegetable which owner thought would be a beet turns out to be a beet, 1915.

29 Sa Mrs. James Swipney, New York, on phoning for a moving van for use May 1, is told that she may expect one, 1921. Spring crime wave begins in New York, 1922. Wal-

lace Reid goes through entire picture without a dinner coat, 1929.

30 Su George Washington inaugurated, 1789. Louisiana Purchase, 1803. Summer heat turned on in telephone booths, 1900. Pathé News photographer goes crazy trying to decide which public school Maypole dance he'll photograph tomorrow in Central Park, 1922.

IN ADMIRATION

Introduction to BETTER BRIDGE FOR BETTER PLAYERS, *by Charles H. Goren,* 1942

In my peregrinations among bridge experts, it so happens, I have met the author of this book only once and have never yet sat down at a bridge table with him. After reading *Better Bridge* I feel that I have saved a good deal of money by avoiding him, because with my penchant for cutting I am sure that I would have been stacked up against Mr. Goren every rubber. I trust that the reader will not think that this considerable saving has influenced my judgement of his book, although I must admit that I am gratefully inclined toward him.

Speaking strictly as an amateur, it seems to me that *Better Bridge* is a monumental job and probably the definitive book on the subject. An enormous number of words continue to be written about bridge—daily articles pop up in every newspaper; whole magazines are devoted to it. Certainly I haven't read them all, but this book, I think, is as clear and thorough a statement of the game as anyone could ask. I would say, off-hand, that anyone who cannot play bridge after digesting this book had better quietly give up the game. (And I'll furnish a list of names on request.)

There is one little thing that has always struck me about bridge books and articles, and this is as good a time as any to take it up. I always follow the printed hands with great care, sometimes going so far as to get an actual deck and lay out the cards. And this is my point—that no matter who writes the books or articles, South holds the most terrific cards that I ever saw. There is a lucky fellow if I ever saw one.

Picking out one of South's hands at random from Mr. Goren's book, I find that he held the following cards:

♠ A K Q J 8 6 4
♥ A

♦ Q J 3
♣ K Q

As a matter of fact, that is one of the smallest hands South ever holds. So it occurred to me that if I could manage to sit South a few times I might get some of those hands. I tried it over a period of months, generally making some excuse about my back to the window or something, and my average hand was about this:

♠ 9 8 7 3
♥ K 3 2
♦ 8 7 3
♣ J 3 2

And yet this pretense that South is a terrific holder is stoutly maintained by all the bridge writers. The only reason I can think of is that there is something slyly political in it—they are banding together to give South those hands because cotton is not selling very well or they had to give up their slaves or something.

And now here is where I am going to turn bridge writer myself, because those hands with a queen and a jack in them have finally brought me to the point of inventing a bridge convention of my own. Most players, of course, are familiar with systems like the Blackwood, designed for the showing of aces and kings. My system is somewhat the same, except that it is designed to show deuces and treys instead. Since I never get aces and kings, I see no reason why I should be deprived of the fun of using the system.

Take, for example, the hand that I have just indicated:

♠ 9 8 7 3
♥ K 3 2
♦ 8 7 3
♣ J 3 2

Let us see how it works. North opens with a club, and South responds with one no-trump. North now bids two no-trump, which in my system calls for the showing of deuces and treys. So South bids three diamonds, showing two deuces. North now bids three no-trump, which is an invitation bid asking for treys. South, having all four treys, bids four no-trump, and the contract is doubled and set eleven hundred. This is the only system under which this result can be obtained.

Now that I am getting my wind, there are a number of other points that I would like to touch upon. Mr. Goren, exhaustive though his volume is, has said not a word about kibitzers, nothing about such important subjects as choice of seats, or how to avoid cutting the worst player in the game. Not a word do I find, either, about the ingenious coup known as the Coffee House, which I have brought to a fine point of perfection and which has saved me many a rubber.

Take, for example, a hand in which the trump distribution is as follows:

```
            Q 6 5 4
        ┌──────────────┐
        │       N      │
    K   │ W          E │  3
        │       S      │
        └──────────────┘
          A J 10 9 8 7 2
```

You are West, with the singleton king, and South is playing the hand. When the dummy goes down you groan and say, "Probably you've got a hundred honors too." Obviously this leads South to believe that the king of trumps is in East's hand; he finesses and you make your king. Simple when you understand it.

As for the choice of seats—how to select the winning chairs—that is a matter on which science is now working, and I may have some very interesting news for you in a future article. For the present I can only say that some highly promising results have been obtained with rabbits, but as yet I can only hint at the possibilities. Eventually, I am sure, it will be possible to predict with complete accuracy which way the cards will be running on a given afternoon or evening, and when this happens no one will ever lose a rubber. Meanwhile Sam Fry, who is no slouch of an expert, has suggested that the various bridge clubs post a simple statement on the bulletin board each day, saying whether the cards are running North-South or East-West at that particular time. I suppose that will have to suffice for the present, until science points the way.

For some time I have had another interesting idea in mind, which it seems to me would do away with a great deal of the bidding difficulty that the average player now encounters. Excellent as are the present systems and conventions, we all know that sometimes a wrong result is arrived at. The trouble, it seems to me, lies far deeper than the bridge writers think, and I am surprised that some farseeing person has not brought it up before.

As I see it, the basic error lies in the fact that the two partners are seated in the wrong positions. What is the purpose of the bidding? Obviously, as any of the bridge writers will tell you, the idea is to arrive at the best contract. Then why seat the two partners in such a way as to put them at an obvious disadvantage? Instead of sitting across from each other, in chairs, they should sit side by side on a small bench. In this way each could see clearly into the other's hand, and a great deal of folderol about bidding systems could be scrapped immediately. At one time I experimented with an alternative suggestion calling for transparent cards, so that the partner across the table could look right through the backs. But this penalized the nearsighted, and I feel that the new seating arrangement is simpler and surer.

Of course these are just ideas. Some of them need work, and meanwhile I would suggest that temporarily you put your faith in Mr. Goren—at least until you hear from me further. As I said before, he's written quite a book.

IF MEN PLAYED CARDS AS WOMEN DO

First produced in Irving Berlin's *Third Music Box Revue,* at the Music Box Theatre, on September 22, 1923, with the following cast:

JOHN	JOSEPH SANTLEY
BOB	PHIL BAKER
GEORGE	HUGH CAMERON
MARC	SOLLY WARD

The playlet was also used in the Paramount film, *Star-Spangled Rhythm,* performed by RAY MILLAND, FRED MACMURRAY, FRANCHOT TONE, and LYNNE OVERMAN.

SCENE: *The scene is* JOHN'S *home. A card table has been set up in the middle of the room, with four chairs around it, and above it is another table on which are piled the necessary adjuncts for a poker game—a fancy cover for the table, cards, chips, a humidor. For the rest, you have only to imagine an average and good-looking room.*

RISE: *As the curtain rises,* JOHN *enters from another room, then turns and calls back through the open door, as though he had forgotten something.*

IMPERTINENCE FROM THE AUTHOR: *It is perhaps unnecessary to remark that the sketch derives its entire value from the fact that it is played in forthright and manly fashion. In other words, the actors must not imitate the voices of women.*

JOHN: And don't forget, I want things served very nicely. Use the best china and the filigree doilies. *(He starts to close the door —remembers another instruction.)* And at eleven o'clock just put the cigars and drinks right on the table and we'll stop playing. *(He closes the door and advances into the room. He looks the place over; rubs a suspecting finger along the table top in a quest for dust. He moves one chair a fraction of an inch and seems to think that that makes a difference in the appearance of the room. Then there comes a knock on the outer door.* JOHN *darts*

to the mirror and takes a quick look at himself; adjusts his tie.) Come in!
(BOB enters.) Hello, Bob!

BOB: Hello, John! I thought I'd run over early to see if I could help you with the lunch.

JOHN: Thanks—everything is ready. I baked a cake. Oh, say! That's a new hat, isn't it?

BOB: Why, no—don't you remember? It's the one I got at Knox's in the Spring. Then when they began wearing the bands higher, I said to myself, why should I buy a new hat when I can have a man in and get him to put on another band for me, just as easily as not? Do you like it?

JOHN: Very attractive. I wonder how it would look on me? *(Takes it; starts to try it on, then smooths his hair before he finally puts it on. He looks at himself in the mirror; turns.)* What do you think?

BOB: Lovely! Makes your face look thinner. *(Looks at the card table.)* Who's playing tonight?

JOHN: George and Marc.

BOB: Really? *(He takes his seat.)* Tell me—don't you think George is looking older these days? How are he and Ethel getting along? Any better?

JOHN: Not as good.

BOB: Funny what she saw in him. *(There is a knock on the door.)*

JOHN: Come in! *(GEORGE enters.)*

GEORGE: *(Greatly surprised, as though they were the last people he had expected to see)* Hello, boys!

JOHN: Hello, George! Well, well, well!

BOB: *(Rises)* Hello, George! Never saw you look so young!

GEORGE: *(In great excitement)* Say, I just met Ed Jennings down the street and what do you think? He says Jim Perkins told him that Will Harper's wife may leave him!

BOB: You don't say so! *(Sits again.)*

GEORGE: What do you think of that? *(His excitement dies a little; he looks around.)* The room looks lovely, John. You've changed things around, haven't you? Awfully nice. But if you don't mind just a little suggestion—I'm not sure that I like that table up there where you've got it. *(Another critical look.)* And if you had these chairs re-upholstered in blue—

JOHN: Well, what do you think of a plain chintz?

GEORGE: That would be nice. Oh, say! I've got a T.L. for you, Bob.

BOB: Oh, good! What is it?

GEORGE: Well, you owe me one first.

BOB: Oh, tell me mine! Don't be mean!

GEORGE: Well, all right. Frank Williams said you looked lovely in your dinner coat.

BOB: That *is* nice.

JOHN: How's the baby, George?

GEORGE: Awfully cranky lately. He's teething. I left him with the nurse tonight—first chance I've had to get out. *(Takes a seat at the table.)* Who else is coming?

JOHN: Just Marc.

GEORGE: *(With meaning)* Oh, is he? I want to speak to you boys about Marc. Don't you think he's been seeing a lot of that Fleming woman lately?

BOB: He certainly has. He was at the Biltmore, having tea with her yesterday—I know because a cousin of Tom Hennessey's saw him.

JOHN: Which cousin is that?

BOB: I don't know whether you know him—Ralph Wilson. He married that Akron girl—they have two children.

GEORGE: *You* remember—one of them is backward.

JOHN: Oh, yes! I heard that. *(Another knock on the door.)* Come in! *(*MARC *enters.)*

MARC: Hello, everybody!

GEORGE, JOHN *and* BOB. Hello, Marc!

MARC: I'm sorry to be the last, but we have a new maid, and you know what that means.

JOHN: That's all right. Say, I like the cut of that vest, Marc. Look, boys! Don't you like that vest?

MARC: It is nice, isn't it?

GEORGE: Oh, lovely! Turn around and let's see the back. *(*GEORGE *and* JOHN *both get up and examine his clothes, pull down his trousers, etc.)*

MARC. I had it made right in the house—I have a little tailor that comes in. Four dollars a day.

GEORGE: Excuse me—there's a little spot—*(He moistens a finger and rubs* MARC'S *lapel.)*

JOHN: Well, shall we play a little poker?

MARC: *(Sitting)* Yes, sure. Oh, John, may I trouble you for a glass of water?

JOHN: Why, of course, Marc. *(GEORGE and BOB sit again.)*

MARC. I'll get it myself if you'll tell me where—

JOHN: Oh, no—that's all right. *(He goes out. A pause. The men look at each other, meaningly. Their heads come together.)*

MARC: John doesn't look well, does he?

BOB: No. Did you notice those lines? He can't hide them much longer.

MARC: He was very good-looking as a boy.

GEORGE: Isn't this room the most terrible thing you ever saw?

(MARC goes to the table up stage; picks up a cigar and shows it to the others. They are scornful.)

MARC: Huh! Ten cents. *(Pause.)* I really wanted to get that water myself. I'd like to see his kitchen. *(JOHN re-enters with the water.)* Oh, thanks, John. *(MARC drinks.)*

JOHN: Is it cold enough, Marc?

MARC: *(Indicating that it isn't)* Oh, yes. Of course, I generally put ice in, myself. *(Sits.)*

GEORGE: Say, we had the loveliest new dessert tonight!

BOB: Oh! What was it? It's awfully hard to find a new dessert.

MARC: *(With emphasis)* Is it?

GEORGE: Well, it was a sort of prune whip. You make it out of just nothing at all. And then, if company comes when you don't expect them—

BOB: I want the recipe.

MARC: How many eggs?

(JOHN up at the rear table. Turns on this speech.)

JOHN. Does it take much butter?

GEORGE: Oh, no—very little. I'll bring you the recipe Tuesday afternoon.

(MARC feels a rough place on his chin. Rubs it, then takes a good-sized mirror out of his pocket and stands it on the table. Examines his chin. Then takes

out a safety razor and starts to shave. After that he takes out two military brushes and combs his hair. The others pay no attention to this. JOHN *is at the rear table, with his back to the audience;* BOB *is seated, fooling with the cards;* GEORGE *is seated, calmly smoking. After* MARC *has put everything away,* BOB *breaks the silence.)*

BOB: Are we ready?

JOHN: No! Wait just a minute. *(He brings down the fancy table cover, which he spreads on the table.)* There we are!

MARC: *(Feeling it)* That's nice, John. Where'd you get it?

JOHN: Why, I bought a yard of this plain sateen down at Macy's—

GEORGE: Really? How much was it?

JOHN: A dollar sixty-three. It was reduced. Then I had this edging in the house.

BOB: Awfully nice!

MARC: Oh, say! Walter Sharp just got back from Paris—

GEORGE: He did?

MARC: Yes. And *he* says they're wearing trousers longer over there.

GEORGE: Really? *(There is quite a fuss about it.)*

JOHN: *(Brings chips and takes his seat)* What'll we play for?

BOB. Oh, what's the difference? One cent limit?

GEORGE: Does it matter who deals? *(Takes the cards from* BOB.*)*

MARC: Say, did you hear about Eddie Parker?

JOHN: No.

MARC: Well, it seems he saw these advertisements about how to get thin, and he thought he'd try them. You know Eddie's taken on a lot of weight since his marriage.

GEORGE: Twenty pounds—absolutely.

MARC: Well, they sent him some powders and he began taking them, and what do you think?

GEORGE: Well? *(*MARC *whispers to him.)* You don't say so?

JOHN *and* BOB: *(Excited)* What was it? What was it? *(*GEORGE *whispers to* JOHN, *who whispers to* BOB; *great excitement.)*

MARC: Who has the cards?

GEORGE: Here they are. *(Starts to deal—poker hands.)*

MARC: I don't want to play late. I've been shopping all day.

GEORGE: And I have an appointment at the barber's tomorrow.

I'm going to try a new way of getting my hair cut. *(The deal is completed.)*

BOB: *(Picking up a few cards)* Which is higher—aces or kings?

GEORGE: Now, who bets first?

JOHN: Are these funny little things clubs?

MARC: What are the chips worth?

JOHN: Let's have them all worth the same thing.

BOB: A penny apiece. . . .

GEORGE: Say, Lord & Taylor are having a wonderful sale of nightgowns!

MARC: What do you pay your maid?

BOB: Sixty-five, but she isn't worth it. *(The three start talking at once about maids, and* JOHN *has a hard time being heard.)*

JOHN: *(Excited)* Boys! Boys! Listen to this! Boys!

ALL: Well?

JOHN: *(Excited)* I *knew* there was something I wanted to tell you!

ALL: *(They must not speak together)* What is it?

JOHN: Well, now in the first place you must promise not to breathe a word of it to anybody, because I got it in absolute confidence and I promised I wouldn't tell.

GEORGE: What is it?

MARC: Well?

BOB: Well?

JOHN: It's about Sid Heflin! Now, you won't tell anybody? At least, don't let on you got it from me!

ALL: No!

JOHN: Well, I'm told—and I got this pretty straight, mind you —I'm told that he's going to—ah— *(He puts the message across with his eyes.)*

MARC: I don't believe it!

BOB: What do you mean?

GEORGE: When?

JOHN: In April!

MARC: April! *(They count on their fingers, up to four.)*

GEORGE: What do you mean?

JOHN: Exactly! They were married late in January! *(They all throw down their hands and begin talking at once.)*

CURTAIN

THE GREAT KIBITZERS' STRIKE OF 1926

THE NEW YORKER, *November 12, 1949*

Since I was a close observer of events leading up to the national strike of bridge kibitzers some years ago, and subsequently a member of the committee that helped to bring about a settlement, I think it is fitting for me to set down the true story of those turbulent days. There has long been a belief that the trouble started when a kibitzer named Lefkowitz—not Sam Lefkowitz, who later demanded that kibitzers be allowed to double any slam contract, but a cousin of his, named Marty—applied a hotfoot to a player during a six-no-trump contract. The Lefkowitz hotfoot case was not without its points of interest, and the depositions taken in the hospital are now preserved in the Library of Congress, but it was not the cause of the kibitzers' strike.

On the night of May 12, 1926, in the old Cavendish Club, on East Sixty-fifth Street, a player named Jymes, or Hymes, or something—the records are unfortunately vague—concealed a queen of spades from a kibitzer, known simply as Commander Smith, during the play of a hand. By holding the spade queen behind the four of diamonds, Jymes completely confused the kibitzer in his calculations, leading him to believe that he would make only three spades instead of four. Since this was during the old game of auction, before contract became popular, not a great deal was thought about it at the moment and nothing was said. Smith himself stayed in his place for the rest of the evening, but it was noticed when the game broke up that he failed to ask, "What time are you boys playing tomorrow?"

On the following night, Smith didn't show up. It was the first night he had missed in eleven years, but still no one was worried; it was simply assumed that he was dead. This had happened before to kibitzers, and the procedure in such cases was well established. One of the players would deal and say, "Did you notice that Bill

Clunk died last night? One spade," and his partner, when it came to his turn, would say, "Yes, I did. Two spades." Or diamonds, or hearts, or whatever it might be. So the players would kitty out three dollars for flowers, and that would be that. (How times have changed! Under today's rules, the death of a kibitzer calls for the cessation of play for a full ten seconds, and the next four hands are automatically doubled.)

But to get back to Smith, when the next day's papers carried no obituary notice, the players began to be worried. That evening, Smith was absent again, and this time one of the players put in a phone call to Smith's house. Smith was home, reading a book! Not a bridge book, either—some sort of novel. The fat was in the fire for fair!

The following night, two more kibitzers were missing, and from then on the thing grew by leaps and bounds. Smith held an indignation meeting at his home on the fourth night, with nearly fifty kibitzers in attendance. Subcommittees were formed and chairmen were appointed in Queens and the Bronx; inside of three weeks there was not a kibitzer on duty in Greater New York. Picketing was started in front of the Knickerbocker Whist Club, and a rock was shied at Oswald Jacoby's head as he was entering the club. Happily, it hit an old lady who was not even a bridge player.

There was, of course, consternation within the clubs. With no kibitzer to say, "You should have played it the other way around" or "Only a fathead would have led the king of diamonds," post-mortem discussions were routine and without color. Without kibitzers, the players became careless and listless; games simply dragged along, sometimes without comment of any sort. The players began to lose weight, had no appetites. In many cases, games were actually cancelled.

Jymes, or Hymes, or whatever his name was, eventually offered public apology to Smith for concealing the spade queen, but by then it was too late. Sympathy strikes were springing up all over the country, a national kibitzers' union was formed, and cardplayers were presented with an ultimatum in the form of a set of rules. Among the stipulations were these:

Recognition of the union as the only bargaining force for kibitzers, and an agreement that no game should be started without at least two kibitzers in attendance.

Cessation of play if a kibitzer was called to the telephone.

The right of the kibitzer to call a revoke if it was confirmed by another kibitzer.

If a kibitzer had to go home before the end of the game, the results were to be telephoned to him as soon as the game was over.

The right of the kibitzer to put his glass of water on the bridge table.

And many others.

Negotiations were deadlocked for four months, and in that time there were many outbreaks of violence and sabotage. In a Minneapolis bridge club, the six of clubs exploded in a player's hand, and was found afterward to have been dusted with TNT. In Dallas, a deck of cards was found to have three aces of spades in it, and this crime was traced to a kibitzer who had managed to get a job in a card factory. In New York City, fifteen thousand kibitzers held an indignation meeting in Union Square, and many were beaten by the police when they tried to parade without a permit. In the ensuing riot, three people were trampled to death. In Seattle, a player who went down one on a cold slam claimed that he had been quietly given a needle by a kibitzer who had jostled him on the sidewalk. Ely Culbertson was burned in effigy.

On September 28th, President Coolidge appealed to both sides to settle the controversy before there was further property damage or loss of life. Leaders of the two factions assembled in the White House on October 9th, and on the night of October 22nd, at a little after ten o'clock, the formal announcement of peace was made. I do not want to claim too much credit for the settlement, but when the conference had been deadlocked three days over the question of penalties for a kibitzer's foot on a player's chair, it was I who suggested a happy compromise. The foot, I said, should be amputated, not burned off.

LIFE'S CALENDAR FOR MAY 1922

1 M First one-cent post card issued; country postmaster jokes inaugurated, 1873. Battle of Manila Bay, 1898. Four Presidents press buttons in White House, opening the Chicago, Tennessee, Pan American, and Louisiana Purchase Expositions, 1893, 1897, 1901, 1904.

2 Tu Stonewall Jackson shot, 1863. First elevated train in New York; Mrs. Amos L. Blunt, 219 East 14th Street, first woman to adjust complexion in mirror of chewing gum machine, 1878.

3 W First medical school established in America, 1765. Mrs. M.L. Image, Chiswick, England, strangled at breakfast table by white mouse, thus accounting for woman's fear of rodents, 1782. Eighteen English lady diarists refused permission to land at Ellis Island, month's quota having been completed, 1922.

4 Th Haymarket riot, Chicago, 1886. Ordinary vegetable observed in window of delicatessen store, 1924.

5 F Death of Napoleon, 1821. West Indian apartment house slave traffic begins, 1897. Some slaves establish permanent soviets, 1898.

6 Sa First flight of heavier-than-air flying machine (Langley's), 1896. Herbert L. Moist, inventor of silencer for street car and elevator whistlers, born, 1900.

7 Su Columbia River discovered by Captain Gray, 1792. Rex Beach begins counting the salmon in it, 1899. Lusitania torpedoed, 1915. Lid of roll top desk slides down without sticking, 1921.

8 M Battle of Palo Alto, 1846. Battle of Spottsylvania Court House, 1864. Hostess in Dodge City, Iowa, remains perfectly calm when guest tips back on Chippendale chair,

1919. Mayor Hylan begins annual spring attack on at-tackers, 1922.

9   Tu   John Brown (of Ossawatomie) born, 1800. Harlem, New York, family passes entire evening at home without put-ting on the "Mother Machree" record, 1918.

10   W   Ticonderoga captured, 1775. Record for number of side dishes in country hotel broken by McKinley House, St. Clair, Ohio, by introduction of individual containers for piccalilli, gherkens, and chow chow, 1899.

11   Th   Peter Stuyvesant arrives in New Amsterdam, 1647. Min-neapolis has weekless week, 1921. *American Magazine* runs article about man who didn't turn out to be success-ful, 1928.

12   F   First marriage in Plymouth Colony; possible children proposed for membership in Boston Sewing Circle, 1621. Marshall T. Lapelle, of North Bedlam, Me., found to be using Christmas gift pipe rack, 1904.

13   Sa   Jamestown, first English settlement in America, founded, 1607. Several members of colony complete "My American Impressions," 1608. U. S. declares war on Mexico, 1846. Photographs of Prince of Wales without an elephant again appear in rotogravure sec-tions, 1922.

14   Su   MOTHERS' DAY. Convention to draft Constitution meets; Anti-Saloon League representative arriving five minutes too late, 1787. Citizen of Perth Hornet, N.J., discovered to be without radio outfit, 1923.

15   M   Cape Cod discovered; Cod Liver Oil business incorpo-rated for $100,000,000, 1602. First regular aero mail ser-vice inaugurated in United States, 1918; everybody still waiting to receive a letter by it, 1922.

16   Tu   Mrs. Emil J. Newhaus, Akron, Ohio, first woman to play a game of solitaire without overlooking any moves, born, 1879. Ten million men who had put away last year's straw hats take them out of the closets and decide to buy new ones, 1922.

17   W   Money Order System established by Congress; all post offices ordered to put money order windows as far as possible from stamp windows, 1864. Expert accountant

estimates that railroads annually waste $892,365 by printing "Not Good If Detached" on round trip tickets, 1919.

18 Th International Peace Conference opens at The Hague; permanent Court of Arbitration established and nobody even smiles, 1899. President Wilson signs the Conscription Act, 1918. Entire day passes without new dentifrice being put on the market, 1921.

19 F   Albert C. Walker, salesman in Duluth, Minn., receives five-dollar bill from customer and fails to ask: "Haven't you anything smaller?," 1918. Drama League endorses the Drama League, 1922.

20 Sa Death of Christopher Columbus, 1506. Idea of putting string into rock candy first conceived, 1833. Paper cup full of water successfully carried to woman during intermission at theatre, 1920.

21 Su American Association of the Red Cross founded at Washington, 1881. Boy selling magazines on train admits that one of them is not "Just Out Today," 1897. Piece of dairy lunch pie analyzed by chemist and found to contain nearly 17% pie, 1921.

22 M   Woman waiting for elevator, on ground floor of big office building, takes a long chance and does not ring for the elevator to stop; elevator starter faints, 1920.

23 Tu First National Convention of Workingmen in New York; Judge Gary Takes Steps, 1872. William Randolph Hearst demands the sales tax, 1947.

24 W   The Savannah, first steamship to cross the Atlantic, sails for Liverpool, 1819. Samuel F. H. Morse sends first telegraph message from Baltimore to Washington, 1844. Brooklyn Bridge opened despite everything that New York can do about it, 1883.

25 Th Ralph Waldo Emerson born, 1803. Man who gets wrong number on telephone does not insist on knowing which wrong number it is, 1912.

26 F   Last Confederate Army surrenders; scenario writers

begin work on movies in which Northern Lieutenant falls in love with proud Southern beauty, 1865.

27 Sa Cornelius Vanderbilt, founder of the Vanderbilt fortunes, born, 1794. Chambermaid in hotel in Templeton, Pa., shot by guest who discovers that top of sheet is three inches from the edge of the mattress, 1901. John Golden admits he produces clean plays, 1918, 1919, 1920, 1921, 1922.

28 Su Harvey Schneide, of Wheeling, W. Va., believes a "Wet Paint" sign and does not touch the surface to see if it is really wet, 1914.

29 M Wisconsin admitted to the Union, 1848. Man who purchased used car on May 14 observed in drug store buying carbolic acid, 1922.

30 Tu MEMORIAL DAY. Hall of Fame opened, 1901. Floorwalker in New York department store describes location of glove counter in such a way that the customer is able to find it, 1907.

31 W Walt Whitman born, 1819. First photograph of man looking into fireplace, 1878. Johnstown flood, 1889. Seventeenth Amendment, famous for being the one before the Eighteenth, adopted, 1913.

THE GREAT CAVIAR RIOTS

THE NATION, *February 10, 1940*

> Owing to the Russian situation, the shortage of unsalted caviar in this country threatens to become acute—*News item*

It was in the spring of 1940 that a shocked public was first brought to face with the facts regarding the unsalted caviar shortage. True, there had been mutterings on Long Island for some time, but few were prepared for the sensational figures disclosed by the Gallup caviar poll, which showed that 81.6 percent of the population of Southampton had been without unsalted caviar for almost a month. A private survey disclosed a serious lack of unsalted corpuscles in children between eight and sixteen, and an outbreak of rickets was feared.

Naturally a wave of indignation swept the country. *The New York Herald Tribune* laid the blame squarely at the feet of Mr. Roosevelt. "While the National Labor Relations Board is giving its biased decisions," said the *Tribune* editorially, "people are riding the streets without a spoonful of caviar to their names. Laws are passed to prevent the grinding down of the lower classes, but the grinding up of the upper classes continues unabated. Communism has reached us at last."

Matters thereupon went from bad to worse. In Tuxedo Park an elderly woman, unable to obtain unsalted caviar, actually ate salted caviar, and of course became violently ill. When the government still failed to act, a huge parade and protest meeting were planned for New York City. Five hundred limousines manned by chauffeur and footman, and each containing a genuine First Family, drove up Park Avenue, followed by a thousand butlers and personal maids on foot. A delegation from the Racquet and Tennis Club rode as a unit, bearing aloft a huge placard: BELUGA OR BUST. The parade was followed by a mass-meeting at Madison Square Garden, held in conjunction with the Horse Show.

As the situation became more desperate, *Town and Country* opened caviar lines in Cartier's. Butlers and footmen who stood in line received a single tablespoonful of unsalted caviar, which was then rushed to Long Island in iced containers. In this way much suffering was alleviated, but it soon became evident that no real relief could be granted unless the government took steps. Even at this point, however, few could have predicted the outcome: that the Republicans would sweep into power as the result of the stubborn refusal of the Roosevelt Administration to act.

The climax came with lightning rapidity. As always, decisive action was brought about by the rise of a real leader—in this case Mrs. Bellington Belcher, of New York and Newport. From her villa at Newport, that summer, Mrs. Belcher quietly mailed engraved invitations to about a hundred of her friends. They read as follows:

Mrs. Bellington Belcher

Requests the Pleasure of

Mr. and Mrs. _____ 's Company

on Thursday Night, August 22d, 1940

at Ten o'Clock

to Consider Rioting

White Tie

A date was secretly set for the uprising—Tuesday, October 29, shrewdly chosen because of its proximity to Election Day. It was a day that was to go down in history as Unsalted Tuesday.

On that fated evening an unusual number of Rolls-Royces and

Isotta-Fraschinis could have been seen quietly converging at Madison Avenue and Sixty-first Street. Well-groomed men and women in evening clothes walked quietly into the Colony Restaurant. The casual observer would have noted nothing unusual, but a careful eye would have detected suspicious bulges in the rear pockets of the gentlemen, an unusual fatness in the ladies' evening bags. Later these bulges were to turn out to be tightly rolled copies of *Spur* and *Tatler*, deadly weapons when wielded by desperate men. In the ladies' bags accounting for the fatness, were old copies of the "Social Register," which they were later to hurl with disastrous effect.

From her seat at the head of the table Mrs. Bellington Belcher gave the signal. Spreading a bit of caviar on her toast, Mrs. Belcher lifted it to her mouth, tasted it, and then uttered just one word:

"Salted!"

It was the agreed signal. In five minutes the room was a wreck. Not a glass, not a plate, remained unbroken. Handfuls of salted caviar were hurled against the walls; the noses of the headwaiters were rubbed in it. When the police arrived ten minutes later, the place was a shambles.

Arrests were made, of course, but the weight of public sympathy was such that the prisoners were immediately released. The following morning Mrs. Belcher executed her master-stroke. The country was flooded by campaign brooches on which the words "Vote Republican" were spelled out in black pearls, in imitation of caviar. Tiffany's had made a special rate for ten million of them.

With the election going Republican, of course, there was an abundance of unsalted caviar from that time on. This was accomplished through a new government bureau, the UCC (Unsalted Caviar Commission), of which Mrs. Belcher herself was made the head.

EXPECTANT PLAYWRIGHTS SAVED
TWO FACES EAST; OR,
WHY EILEEN WASN'T BORN IN CAPTIVITY*

NEW YORK WORLD-TELEGRAM, *February 15, 1941*

Out in Hollywood last year, visiting one of the movie studios, I happened to walk past the building in which the scenario writers had their offices. As I went by I heard screams and shrill cries and looked up to see dozens of anguished faces pressed against the window panes. Their voices floated out to me, piteously pleading: "Let us out of here! Let us out! We're as sane as anybody! For God's sake, let us out! We're perfectly sane!"

Dimly I made out a few of the faces—Joe Fields, Jerry Chodorov, Aldous Huxley.

That was my introduction, if you call it an introduction, to the authors of *My Sister Eileen*. Months later, after the play had opened, they told me the whole story one day—told it lightly and almost gaily, now that it was all over. Several times I had hinted that I was eager to hear it, but in the beginning the memory of it all had been so painful that they could not bring themselves to speak.

Then, finally, one day it came out. I have no space to go into it here—the months of privation, the brutality of the guards, the unspeakable food, finally the smuggling into the writers' quarters of two files, concealed in an old scenario. Their escape and recapture, the weeks of solitary confinement with a B picture, escape again—the full story is one of the great human documents of its time, and someday, when they can smile again, I hope that the boys themselves will write it.

They had shaved off their beards and were fairly happy again

*This piece was written as the introduction to the Random House edition of the play *My Sister Eileen*, which Kaufman directed on Broadway in 1940.—*ed.*

when I encountered them months later in New York, safe in a hotel. Locking the door, they brought forth the script of *My Sister Eileen* and some of the worst candy it has ever been my misfortune to eat. In the ensuing weeks they did valiant work with the script; the candy, however, got no better.

Out of the depths of their misery—it seems to me that they have fashioned a gay and heart-warming comedy, preserving all of the humor and the tenderness of Ruth McKenney's stories, and converting the whole into a workmanlike play. I am not exactly alone in this belief, incidentally. Eight or nine play reviewers and most of the theatergoing public are of the same opinion. And Max Gordon.

They are quite remarkable lads, the Messrs. Fields and Chodorov. To my certain knowledge they wrote about six plays, not one. (All of them *My Sister Eileen,* of course.) Their industry was equaled only by their fantastic speed. It was a rare day, in the weeks preceding rehearsals, that they did not come along with eight or 10 new scenes. I would leave them happily at 4 o'clock in the afternoon, feeling sure that they had so much work ahead that I would not hear from them for weeks. Along about five-thirty, just as I was playing four spades doubled—my partner's fault, incidentally—the telephone would ring. It would be Joe and Jerry. "We finished those scenes," they'd say. "And, oh, yes—we've got a new second act."

The results are now on view in New York and Chicago, and presently, if I know Max Gordon, they will spread over the rest of the land. It has all been one of those happy events in the theater that come along but rarely—happy both because of the results and the extraordinary dispositions of the Messrs. Fields and Chodorov. Not all the charm went into the script, by a darned sight.

So, in sending them on their way into the book world, I would like to voice both a prediction and a hope. I predict that they are in the theater to stay—that they will write many a gay and happy comedy. And I sincerely hope, as they write them, that they will have better candy around the house.

MY BOOK AND I

THE NEW YORKER, *May 26, 1951*

To tell the truth, I am just a little bit behind in my reading. My friends tell me there is a new one out in the Graustark series, called *Beverly of Graustark,* but, what with one thing and another, I haven't got around to it yet. I began the first Lanny Budd book bravely enough, intending to shoot right through the series, but for some reason I let Upton Sinclair get nine volumes ahead of me, and now it's a little hard to catch up. I notice, by the way, that Mr. Sinclair has given up on that series. I knew I'd get him sooner or later.

But in many years I do not recall having quite the fight with any book that I have had—and am still having—with *Samuel Johnson*, by Joseph Wood Krutch.* My usual procedure with a book is, roughly, as follows: I hear about a book or read a notice of it. I say to myself, "Now, there is a book that is just my dish. I have always been interested in books of that sort. I must read it." So I buy it. It stays in the wrapper for two or three days after it arrives, because a lot of things have a habit of coming up. I open it, finally, with great pleasure. "Ah!" I say to myself. "Just the kind of book I like!" I put it prominently on my desk, right on top of a pile of books that I am just crazy to read.

The next few months pass quietly, what with playing bridge, and going out to dinner, and talking to people, and things like that. Then comes an important moment. Flushed with energy, I move the book from my desk to my bed table. Now I am really ready to start.

Several weeks pass and I don't start. I can explain this. I have a habit of reading all the newspapers every day, and there is nothing quite so luxurious as reading newspapers in bed. Then, there are the magazines—*Time,* and *Life* and even *The New Yorker.* These come out

*Joseph Wood Krutch, a professor at Columbia University and dramatic critic of *The Nation*, repeatedly wrote disparagingly of Kaufman's skills as a dramatist. This piece, then, was Kaufman's way of getting even with Mr. Krutch.—*ed.*

every week, and once you settle down to them, you will be surprised how quickly Thursday and Friday come around.

Along about this time, the book begins to get in the way of the newspapers and things, so I move it back to the desk for a couple of months. Then the publishers bring out another book, and it's just my dish, so I buy it. In this way, one thing leads to another, and pretty soon it's later than you think.

If there is one subject I am completely fascinated by it's Samuel Johnson, and when I heard that Mr. Krutch was taking a sabbatical year in which to write a book about him, I didn't even wait for the publication date. I ordered the book at once. Little did I think at that time that whereas Mr. Krutch would be on the book for one year, I would be on it for seven, and only up to page 9 at that.

In these seven years, *Samuel Johnson* has piled up the following history with me: It has made three round trips to Hollywood, staying twice at the Garden of Allah, and once at the Beverly Hills Hotel, where the dust jacket was slightly spotted by a highball glass; it has gone twice to Florida and got quite a little sand in it, some of which I am still shaking out; and last summer it visited England and the French Riviera.

On each occasion, I took it with me in the firm conviction that I was finally going to get somewhere with it, and I still feel that it is exactly my dish. I was fascinated by the very opening sentence, and remember it as though it were only six years ago: "Samuel Johnson was a pessimist with an enormous zest for living." You must admit that that is an intriguing sentence, one that will catch the reader up and hold him. It has held me for seven years.

Also, I have enormous respect for Mr. Joseph Wood Krutch, a scholar and a gentleman. The fact that I have carried his book halfway around the world with me is certainly proof of that. I'll bet he hasn't got another reader who has shown such loyalty. I don't deserve any particular credit for this; *Samuel Johnson* just happens to be my kind of book.

In Hollywood, someone wanted to borrow it once, but I felt that I would get at it any minute, so I refused to lend it. In Florida, as I have already implied, I used to carry it with me to the beach. I remember that it got buried in the sand one day, and I was frantic until I found it again. I lost the dust jacket four or five years ago, but the book itself is in splendid condition. Why shouldn't it be?

The place where I left off, on page 9, was absolutely enthralling: "The father was proud of his son—foolishly so, in that son's opinion—but he showed his pride in clumsy ways which humiliated an intelligent child." Think of the heartbreaking stories that will illustrate the child's humiliation, the sufferings of his sensitive soul! I can hardly wait for page 10.

And I mean to read it, I promise you. I am taking it with me to California soon, and, if necessary, to Europe again in the summer. It is exactly my dish.

NOTES OF A CO-AUTHOR*

THE NEW YORK TIMES, *November 2, 1941*

Walk around the reservoir any morning—any reservoir, for that matter—and it's an even bet that you will run into Edna Ferber. Miss Ferber is a walker. That daily walk, she says, is essential to her physical and mental well-being. Me, I'm different. In the words of Ring Lardner, the only exercise I get is when I take the studs out of one shirt and put them in another.

Miss Ferber also has a preference for height. Her home in Connecticut—and a very handsome one it is—stands on top of a great hill, and she is never happier than when briskly ascending a mountain. Height clears and stimulates her mind, she will tell you. Here again I have to enter a demurrer. I have tried out the theory in miniature by getting up on a chair when I had a knotty problem to solve, and I can testify that it isn't worth a nickel.

But I am not adamant on either subject—I should say that a certain sweet reasonableness is one of my outstanding characteristics. So, looking around for a place to work last March, and wanting both hills and open spaces, we ran a finger over the map and hit upon White Sulphur Springs. Neither of us had ever been there, but somebody's cousin had gone down the year before and she reported that it was wonderful. Just far enough South to be warm without being uncomfortable, marvelous food, everything.

We had a great idea for a play. Refugees. Not just ordinary refugees, mind you, but the great figures of the artistic and scientific world. Molnar, Fritzi Massary, Einstein, Fritz Thyssen. It was to be a play that was both serious and gay, a play with compassion and gallantry in it. Looking back, I don't know what made us think that that would be a good idea. Bits and pieces of it had already been

*This article was first published on the Sunday after the New York opening of *The Land Is Bright*, a play by Kaufman and Edna Ferber, which premiered at the Music Box Theatre on October 28, 1941.—*ed.*

used in several plays, and Dorothy Thompson and Fritz Kortner had written exactly such a play, and got nowhere with it. I suppose it was our eagerness to write a play, any play, that misled us. We had written just three plays together in fourteen years.

So we went to White Sulphur. I would like to digress for a paragraph and say a word about the laying out of train schedules. I don't know who does this little job, but all over the country trains are run for the benefit of people who start their day brightly at 6:30 A.M. True to type, the White Sulphur train left about 5 in the afternoon and pulled in at 7 the next morning. In these cases, however, the railroads make a magnificent and meaningless concession. You may stay in the car, they inform you, until 7:30. This is always told you with a great air of fixing the whole thing—not even an international banker, they imply, would want to sleep later than 7:30. Imagine! Why, that's the middle of the day! As one who went into show business because it was the one profession in which I could sleep late, I find this extremely aggravating. I don't ask that every train in the world be run for the benefit of the theatrical profession, but it would be pleasant just once in a while.

At all events, we arrived—on time, of course. A splendid cold rain greeted us as we came down the steps; the car had been pulled off onto a siding, and there wasn't a porter in sight. It was at that precise moment that the refugee idea began to slip. As days passed it was destined to get worse and worse, but I should say that the instant of our descent of those car steps was when it first started to go.

We stayed in White Sulphur for ten days, and it rained and was cold for nine of them. Whenever the downpour slowed to a drizzle Edna was into her stout boots and off into the hills.

We started out with a strict working schedule. We would meet for lunch at 1 o'clock—that was my breakfast, of course—and we would discuss the play until 5, when we were off for our sulphur baths. (A very trying goings-on, those sulphur baths, by the way, and I strongly suspect the ensuing massage of being nothing but disguised exercise.) Then at 8 again for dinner—we agree to talk play all through dinner, and as far into the night as we could stay awake. In this way we would not only come back to town with a complete scenario but probably two or three other plays as well.

The first day's session started in businesslike fashion. . . . Now! I should say the scene should be Molnar's apartment—he's more or less the leader of the group—the others would all flock around him, come to visit. . . . Fine! How about an old house down in Gramercy Park? There could be a woman who's let them have the house—old New York family. . . . Now, these people are all trying to adapt themselves to life in America—of course, over there they were tremendously important and here they just have to take any jobs they can get. . . . One of them goes out and discovers ice cream sodas —that'd be good! . . . Oh, yes! And chewing gum! How about a scene where one of them chews gum for the first time! . . . Fine! And I know! Texas! Somebody tells them they ought to leave New York —go to Texas! So they look up Texas in the encyclopedia—there could be a wonderful scene. . . .

For the first hour we interrupted each other in our excitement —the ideas came thick and fast. Then they began to slow up. What did they do in the second act? What did they do in the first act, for that matter? Just sit and talk about America, or the way it used to be in Vienna? . . . Well, now, one of them could be an actress and she could have a lot of trouble getting a part, and then be a big success. . . . Ye-es. But that's rather hard to show, isn't it? I mean, you wouldn't want to put a whole scene in the theatre. . . . Well, she could come back from the opening night with a big bunch of flowers in her arms. . . . Yes, but if she does I don't want to be there. . . . I suppose you're right. . . . I know! She isn't a success—she's a failure! . . . Well, maybe. . . . But then, what are we trying to say in the play? Besides, that's awfully depressing. . . .

I'll tell you what! Maybe if we knocked off and didn't work tonight—first day and everything. We'd be much fresher in the morning—afternoon, I mean. I notice they show a movie here at 9 o'clock every night—we could drop in on that. . . . All right. It wouldn't hurt—one evening. Might be good for us, as a matter of fact.

The next day we started off very brightly. . . . House in Gramercy Square. . . . Yes. . . . Fritzi Massary at the piano—there's an idea! You know, she was a big musical comedy star in Vienna—*Sari* and *The Merry Widow*, all those things—and she could sing bits of her old songs! . . . Oh, wonderful! . . . Now, let's see—what happens in the play? . . . Well, the business man—he's just a peddler in the beginning—of course he was a big shot over in Europe, and then he becomes successful here. . . . Ye-es. But that's sort of like the actress, isn't it! . . . Well, of course she's a woman and he's a man. . . . Ye-es. How about their falling in love! . . . Yes, that's good. . . . But still. . . .

Say! Have you been around the place—looked the hotel over? Quite interesting. They've got a lot of photographs back there—celebrities that have stopped here. . . . Well, let's look at them! That's wonderful—why didn't you say so! . . . Oh, look! Douglas Fairbanks. . . . Mrs. Harrison Williams. . . . C. Bascom Slemp. . . .

It was when we started looking at photographs of C. Bascom Slemp that we realized the refugee idea was in a bad way. We had touched bottom. But this was only the second day, and neither of us was willing to face the other and utter the dread words. We had no play, that was the simple truth of it. But for nine days out of the ten we kept pretending we had. Along about the third day Edna discovered a climbable mountain somewhere in the vicinage, and then she was happier. She started climbing it every day, and staying up there longer and longer, until I felt sure she was coming down with another Ten Commandments. We got to seeing the movie every night, no matter what it was. *The Three Mesquiteers*, *Hopalong Cassidy*, anything. Another look at Mrs. Harrison Williams, and C. Bascom Slemp.

Occasionally we would get a break. Leland Hayward got to calling up from California—he was in the middle of selling Edna's "Saratoga Trunk" to the movies for twelve million dollars or something—and when Leland gets on long-distance, time is but water. An hour would pass, two hours. . . . Jack Warner says. . . . Cary Grant, Irene Dunne. . . . I would sit happily waiting, doing nothing. But eventually even Leland would hang up, and there we would be again. . . . Einstein, Fritz Thyssen. . . .

In desperation we began joining the old ladies in the lounge at 4 o'clock every day. Tea and organ music. "Drink to Me Only With Thine Eyes." . . . I even kibitzed a bridge game one evening, with the players averaging seventy-six years. There were three revokes in one hand, but nobody noticed. I kept right on kibitzing, too—it was the only game in town, as the old joke goes. . . . Losing my mind completely, I even took a walk one day. It was a terrible experience, but better than Einstein and Fritz Thyssen.

On the tenth day we faced each other and had it out. Each started to convince the other, but it was evident in two seconds that neither needed any convincing. . . . I'm so glad! I feel as though a weight had fallen off me! We don't know those people—how can we write them! The only person we know in the whole play is that American woman who comes in—you know, old New York family. . . . Yes, we could write her. . . . Hold on, there! Old New York family! Why not? Those are people we can write! We know them, or know about them? . . .

Atlantic City—Edna was through with height—she wanted sea level. The train reached North Philadelphia at 7:14 in the morning, as usual, and 7:20 found us breakfasting in the railroad station, wondering what we were doing there. After all, there was a handsome empty house in Connecticut, to say nothing of my own in Bucks County. In heaven's name, then, what were we doing in a railway station in North Philadelphia at 7:20 in the morning, trying to write a play? But dismal though the setting, we were happy. The first act had fallen into place almost overnight, and already there were bits and pieces of the second.

The boardwalk, of course, was made to order for Edna. She walked and walked and walked. I sat. We had our palms read, played bingo, dropped in at auction rooms. . . . "Worn by Marie Dressler in the celebrated movie, *Dinner at Eight!*" boomed the voice of the auctioneer. . . . Strange that we should happen to enter just at that moment.

Peculiarly enough, I have no recollection of the actual writing. That seems to be true with most plays, so far as I am concerned. The whole business of getting ready to write, finding the actors, rehearsals, out of town—bits and pieces of all that linger in the mind. But all I can tell you about the weeks of writing is that the meals at Ferber's house were elegant. I can remember the food in detail, but none of the work.

Casting. A horrendous business, brutal for the actors, equally trying for the authors. . . . Would you mind removing your hat? . . . Thank you. . . . Would you sit over there where the light will strike you? . . . Now, we don't like to ask this, but would you mind reading just a few lines for us? We know you're a good actress, of course—it's just a question of whether the personality is right for this particular part.

Rehearsals. Clothes, make-up. Endless hours of clothes and make-up. . . . Well, of course, I think it gives her a bad figure. The skirt is way too long—it makes her look unattractive, and she's a very attractive girl. . . . Well, I don't know what we can do. That's the way the skirts were in those days—we've already taken quite some liberties. . . . Well, all I can say is, if that's the way the girls looked in the Twenties I don't know how they ever got a man. . . . Yes, but after all, they did. . . . Now, he's not going to wear that! . . . But he has to wear it—that's what the suits were like. . . . Well, then, can't he do something with his hair! Anything! . . . I know if I were a girl and a man looked like that . . . But a minute ago you said the men wouldn't look at the girls. . . . I still think so—I don't know how they ever got together.

Washington. The tempo of the town made the play seem trivial, unimportant. The dynamic Max Gordon, a thwarted statesman, was all over the place. Interviews with Knudsen at 8:30 in the morning, seeing Morgenthau at 11. Sundry dignitaries came to the theatre—the Vice President, Mrs. Roosevelt, Senator Barkley, Mr. Hughes. . . . Gordon was down the aisle after them with the fall of the curtain, primed with a double-barreled question. "Did you like the play and is Russia going to hold?" Slightly confused by the form of the query, and probably hearing only the last half, they would blurt out a great "Yes!" In a flash Gordon would be up the aisle again, grabbing Edna and me by the arms. "Wallace is simply crazy about it! Greatest play he's ever seen!"

New York again. The opening.

LIFE'S CALENDAR FOR JUNE 1922

1 Th Battle of Chesapeake and Shannon; Lawrence coins "Don't give up the ship!" 1813. Chattanooga, Tenn., man removes top from milk bottle without stabbing himself with fork, 1922.

2 F Maine goes dry, 1851; as Maine goes so goes the country, 1919. Lawrence M. Moth, piano tuner, Minneapolis, Minn., arrives for work *after* 9:30 A.M., 1919.

3 Sa Jefferson Davis born, 1808. Hobson sinks the Merrimac in Santiago Harbor, 1898. New Yorker, realizing that he has been wearing winter hat since May 15, drowns himself in Hudson, 1921.

4 Su Non-Washburn-Crosby Flour advertisement appears on back of *Saturday Evening Post,* 1912. Ford Motor Co. increases capitalization from $2,000,000 to $100,000,000, or 1 1/2 cents for every Ford joke, 1915.

5 M First chapter of *Uncle Tom's Cabin* published in magazine, Harriet Beecher Stowe receiving $300 for serial rights, 1851. First registration day for Great War, 1917. Three hundred and twelve toddle top companies file petition in bankruptcy, 1922.

6 Tu New York taxicab driver slows up to allow another car to get ahead of him, 1914. American newspaper revolutionizes journalism by printing photograph of girl in wedding dress without using caption "A June Bride," 1938.

7 W Caius Publicus Lock and Fabius Cornelius Key decide to collaborate on inventions, South Rome, 212 B.C.

8 Th Andrew Jackson dies, 1845. Guest arriving at home of friend restrains himself from facetiously placing his hat on bust of Shakespeare standing in entrance hall, 1901. Albuquerque, N.M. resident fills in one of those "The

movement of my watch is No. ____" blanks in a pocket diary, 1919.

9 F First given point passed by a parade, 1437. John Howard Payne, author of "Home Sweet Home," once popular song now used as signal to end dances, born, 1791.

10 Sa Wyoming Territory gives votes to women, 1869. Jeff hits Mutt instead, 1894.

11 Su Percy Mackaye starts first civic masque factory, 1832. Corn Exchange Bank and Schulte Cigar Stores bid for last remaining corner site in New York City, 1940.

12 M First naval engagement of American Revolution, 1775. Charles Goodyear gets patent for manufacturing rubber fabrics, 1844; Mrs. Goodyear starts telling him not to forget his overshoes, 1845.

13 Tu France declares war on England in aid of American colonies, 1778. Fire in express office in Atlantic City destroys 1200 tons of prizes consigned to Japanese rolling ball shops on Boardwalk; damage, $2.35, 1909.

14 W FLAG DAY. Three million persons in New York City alone ask why flags are being shown, 1922. Harriet Beecher Stowe born, 1811. First diving suit patented; short story writers begin looking up life and habits of octopus, 1834.

15 Th King John signs Magna Carta, 1215. Franklin performs kite and key experiment, 1752. First Liberty Loan closes successfully in spite of the posters, 1917. Pure silk shoe-lace, advertised as 30 inches in length, actually measures 30 inches, 1921.

16 F International commission appointed to find out why restaurants bring on the butter fifteen minutes ahead of the bread asks permission to handle disarmament question instead, 1922. Soda clerk serves glass of water with sundae without being asked for it, 1940.

17 Sa Battle of Bunker Hill, 1775; double-header in Boston, 1922. Joke from German weekly remains comic after translation into English, 1923.

18 Su United States declares war on England, 1812. Battle of Waterloo, 1815. Guest at banquet breaks world's record by balancing a water glass on three spoons and then two forks and a knife on top of the glass, 1922.

19 M West Virginia admitted to Union, 1863. Old-fashioned insurance agent, seeking audience with business man, admits he is an insurance agent, 1901.

20 Tu De Soto dies, 1542. Queen Victoria succeeds to throne, 1837. Second families found in Virginia, 1922.

21 W McCormick patents the reaper, 1834. Republican convention renominates Taft after bitter struggle, thereby achieving world's greatest technical victory, 1912. Famous juggler loses $10,000 on wager that he could eat Saratoga chips with a fork, 1922.

22 Th Restaurant opens in Atlanta, Ga., with so many sugar bowls that waiters are not required to steal them from other tables, 1913. Record-breaking attendance at funeral of pool player who always put the chalk in his pocket, 1922.

23 F William Penn acquires Pennsylvania from the Indians, thereby making himself responsible for the Philadelphia Athletics, 1683. First successful typewriter patented; installment terms invented, 1868.

24 Sa John Cabot lands on Labrador, 1497; Henry Cabot Lodge lands on Wilson, 1918. Taxi driver polite on a rainy night, 1960.

25 Su Custer's last fight, 1876. Tailor makes suit exactly as ordered, 1891. Motor truck not containing liquor or stolen silk passes through New Jersey at dead of night, 1922.

26 M First American troops arrive in France; 319 different accounts of their first words on French soil cabled to American newspapers, 1917. Henry J. Dolmann, Cascade Park, Pa., successfully tightens small screw in eyeglasses with his thumbnail, 1922.

27 Tu Little Nuisance Laundry expelled from Union for deliv-

ering shirt to customer with one button unfastened, 1906. Mayor Hylan admits he knows nothing about art, 1943.

28 W Battle of Monmouth; George Washington says something more than "Pass the hatchet," 1778. Viscount Lascelles mentioned in newspaper for first time since the wedding, 1922.

29 Th Great Britain levies the Stamp Tax, 1767. W. J. Perkins, of Louisville, Ky., becomes raving maniac at dinner table when he discovers that he has been given fork with bent prong for ninth consecutive night, 1922.

30 F Congress sets aside Indian Territory; Indians satisfied to break even, 1834. New York girl seen without bead necklace, 1922.

THE MEEK INHERIT THE EARTH

THE NATION, *October 1, 1938*

The Meek were going quietly about their work one day, emptying garbage pails and cleaning spitoons, when a telegram arrived, collect:

> BEG TO ADVISE ACCORDANCE WITH TERMS
> LAST TESTAMENT CREATOR JUST ADMITTED
> PROBATE YOU HAVE INHERITED THE EARTH
> HEARTY CONGRATULATIONS OUR LONG
> EXPERIENCE INHERITANCE CASES PUTS US
> UNIQUE POSITION SERVE YOU STRONGLY
> ADVISE COMMUNICATE IMMEDIATELY.
>
> *Chetbourne Van Cortlandt Chetbourne*
> *Attys Law 120 Broadway New York*

A few days later the Meek duly assembled in the outer office of Chetbourne, Van Cortlandt, and Chetbourne, having walked up sixteen flights of stairs because the elevators were crowded. The young lady at the switchboard regarded them rather haughtily.

"Yes?" she inquired.

"We—we'd like to see a member of the firm," was the reply, "but—but we can come some other time if it isn't convenient."

"What do you want to see 'em about?" asked the young lady.

"Well, it's—it's nothing important, but—we got a telegram from them."

The young lady took the telegram into the inner office, and was back again in no time with quite a different manner. "Mr. Chetbourne, Senior, will see you in about an hour," she said. "Wait out in the hall."

Promptly in an hour and a half Mr. Chetbourne swung wide the door of his office and invited them all in. Mr. Van Cortlandt was also present, and so was the other Mr. Chetbourne. Mr. Chetbourne, Senior, took charge, bade everybody welcome, and even asked them if they'd have a drink. Nobody took one—except Mr. Van Cortlandt and the two Mr. Chetbournes.

"Now," said Mr. Chetbourne, "to begin." He picked up a pile of important-looking papers. "Under the terms of the Lord's will, you and your assigns are named as sole heirs and beneficiaries. Under these terms, and with certain exceptions to be noted hereafter, you—ah"—Mr. Chetbourne consulted the documents—"you have inherited the earth. It's quite a tidy inheritance."

One of the Meek coughed diffidently. "Would you—would you mind telling us just what the exceptions are?"

"Of course if you'd rather not—" said another.

"No trouble at all," said Mr. Chetbourne. "The exceptions are Germany, Italy, and Japan. Although the will is of divine origin, we are informed that it will not be recognized in those countries. The same applies to all territory that they hope to control in the future."

"That—that takes in a good deal of ground," said the Meek.

"It includes Europe, Asia, South America, and part of Africa," replied Mr. Chetbourne, "but there is still a lot left. Legally, of course, the whole thing is yours, and you can fight if you want to."

"It's all so unexpected," said the Meek, "We've got more than we know what to do with, anyhow."

"Then that's settled," said Mr. Chetbourne. "Now, we have had no official word yet from England, but our London representatives inform us that Great Britain will almost certainly attempt to break the will. In that event Canada, the high seas, and the remainder of Africa will be thrown into litigation."

"Maybe we'd better just let them have it," said the Meek.

"On the contrary," replied Mr. Chetbourne, "I think you would have a very good chance of winning the case. After all, it is the Lord's will."

"Well, whatever you think best," said the Meek.

"Then, as your lawyers, we strongly advise fighting. That brings us to the question of counsel fees."

"How much will they be?" asked the Meek.

"It is customary to agree upon a small percentage of the inheritance," said Mr. Chetbourne. "Let us say the Eastern seaboard, running as far west as the Mississippi."

"Yes, sir," replied the Meek.

"Now," said Mr. Chetbourne, shifting his papers, "there is the matter of inheritance taxes. I think that the Middle West and Northwest would about cover those—let us say from the Canadian border to somewhere in the state of Arizona."

"Yes, sir," said the Meek again.

"And I have here a bill for back income taxes which seem to have been overlooked by the previous owner. However, those will be amply taken care of by the territory in the Southwest, extending northward to somewhere in the state of Arizona."

The Meek shifted a little in their chairs. "Could we trouble you for a glass of water?" they asked.

"We are nearly through," said Mr. Chetbourne. "You can get it at the public fountain downstairs. Now, where were we? Oh, yes. That leaves you—ah"—Mr. Chetbourne looked at a map spread out before him—"that leaves you Yuma, Arizona, completely free and unentailed. I understand it's very pleasant there."

"Yes, sir," said the Meek, getting to their feet.

"One thing more," said Mr. Chetbourne. "We shall of course have certain cash disbursements, not covered by the agreed counsel fee. If you happen to have any cash on you—"

The Meek had only about $12, but Mr. Chetbourne was quite nice about it. He took it without complaint.

MOTHER GOOSE AND THE GOLDEN EGG

A Play for Very Little Children

———

Saturday Review, *February 21, 1959*

(A cute little girl of about eight, named SALLY, *comes out onto the stage and starts to recite.)*

SALLY: Sing a song of sixpence,
                            A pocketful of rye,
                      Four and twenty blackbirds
                            Baked in a pie.
                      When the pie was opened,
                            The birds began to sing—

(But a MAN *in his shirtsleeves, weighing about two hundred pounds, makes an entrance at this point and interrupts.)*

THE MAN: What's the idea this?

STAGE MANAGER: Idea what?

THE MAN: Don't give me that—I'm from the Musicians' Union. You know the rules well as I do. Them four and twenty blackbirds! You going to have four and twenty blackbirds come out and sing you got to hire four and twenty standby blackbirds from the Union. *You* know that!

STAGE MANAGER: But I don't see—

THE MAN: Another thing! This King Cole or somebody you had yelling for three fiddlers. From now on he yells for six fiddlers, two horns, drums, and an oboe.

STAGE MANAGER: But it seems to me—

*(*ANOTHER MAN *has entered. Two hundred and fifty pounds.)*

2ND MAN: Talk to you a minute?

STAGE MANAGER: Sure!

2ND MAN: Pastry Makers' Union! Where you going to get this pie?

STAGE MANAGER: But it isn't a real pie. She just—

2ND MAN: Talk about a pie gotta have a real pie off-stage. How big this pie?

STAGE MANAGER: It's not big. It just—

2ND MAN: Holds a lot of birds, some kind.

STAGE MANAGER: Blackbirds. Little bits of things. They—

2ND MAN: How many of 'em?

STAGE MANAGER: Uh—four and twenty. But they're very—

2ND MAN: Four and twenty of 'em. Need a pie six foot-three diameter.

(But a THIRD MAN *has entered. Two hundred and seventy-five pounds.)*

3RD MAN: Pie Carrier's Union! How many men going to carry that pie?

STAGE MANAGER: Nobody carries it. It's just off-stage.

3RD MAN: Somebody got to *put* it off-stage, don't they?

STAGE MANAGER: Uh—yes—but we—

3RD MAN: My advice put on four men before the matinee tomorrow.

(But a FOURTH MAN *has entered. Three hundred pounds.)*

4TH MAN: Society Prevention Cruelty Blackbirds! How long them birds going to be in that pie?

(But the curtain is down.)

AMAZING ANECDOTES

Playwright Lists "Events" That Led to Production of **The Small Hours***

THE NEW YORK TIMES, *February 11, 1951*

In recent seasons I have noticed an increasing tendency among playwrights to write interesting little Sunday articles explaining what their plays are all about, and why. Presumably they do this because the circumstances of their writing are so unusual as to warrant detailed description, or maybe they are just trying to get their names into print.

But whatever the reason, Miss Leueen MacGrath and I are not going to be left at the post, to use a nautical term. Lest somebody begin to think, at this point, that we are plugging *King Lear*, let me hasten to add that we are the authors of a play called *The Small Hours*, which will open at the National Theatre on Thursday. And it is of that that I would write.

First, I would like to tell an enormously amusing story about how we came to write this play. Every time I think of it I have to laugh. We were sitting at breakfast one morning, about two o'clock in the afternoon, and suddenly the telephone rang. I answered, and it was a wrong number. Well, this got me thinking. "Wouldn't it be funny," I said, "if we wrote a play together?" (Originally there was some connection between the phone call and my getting the idea to write a play, but I don't remember the details.) There was a glass of orange juice in my hand at the time, and as I emptied it into my coffee I looked at Miss MacGrath rather quizzically and repeated my question. "Wouldn't it be funny," I repeated, "if we wrote a play together?" I will never forget Miss MacGrath's answer if I live to be thirty-five. "Yes," she said.

---

*This article was first published on the Sunday prior to the New York opening of *The Small Hours*, a play by Kaufman and Leueen MacGrath, which premiered at the National Theatre on February 15, 1951.—*ed.*

Well, the more I thought about this the more I thought about it. Did she mean, "Yes, it would be funny," or "Yes, we ought to write a play together"? When the play went into rehearsal, six months later, I still had not asked Miss MacGrath what she meant. Miss MacGrath and I, as it happens, are married to each other, but there still are some things you do not ask a woman.

The naming of the play brings me to another amusing anecdote, almost as dull—I mean, almost as funny—as the one I have just related. From the beginning I had the idea that we would name the play *Mrs. Roberts*, on the theory that some obliging typesetter might accidentally drop a letter and thus bring a nice rush of business to the box-office. Miss MacGrath, on the other hand, voted for *The Ingrown Toenail.* As a result we combined the two names and called it *The Small Hours.* The full title, as a matter of fact, is *The Small Hours, or, Over Max Gordon's Dead Body.*

This brings me to Max Gordon. Mr. Gordon is the producer of the play. When we first decided to write it we told Mr. Gordon immediately and he asked a most sentient question. "Is it in one set?" he said. We said, "no," but that it was in twenty-six sets, which was the next best thing. Mr. Gordon said, "The next best thing to what? The bankruptcy court?" Well, of course, this was absurd, because we were not going to use our own money.

This brings me to the money. The full story of how the money was raised is a really hilarious tale, and will be published separately as a book some day. During that time we had barely a piece of furniture in the house, because everything resembling a blunt instrument was being used. But it all ended happily and the backers will be standing out in Forty-first Street on Thursday night, cheering the audience on.

And now a word about the nature of the play itself and what we are trying to say in it. Both Miss MacGrath and I believe that in the theatre of today characters should not be used merely as characters, but that they should tell a story. If the characters do not fit into the story, then an attempt should be made to fit the story into the characters. Of course, if the characters do not fit into the characters, that is something else again. Then it is better just to let the whole thing drop, put the backers' money in your pocket, and leave town.

I am aware that all playwrights do not follow this theory, but I feel that there has been a great change in the theatre in recent years, what with the films, and television, and crokinole. There was a time when plays could be presented merely as plays and the audience would sit there and that was that. Now it is all different. I forget just how, but I do know that forces are at work and we should think about that, and maybe even write Sunday pieces about it. Or else there will be no more theatre.

That is what we are trying to bring about in *The Small Hours.* No, I don't mean that—I mean, we are not trying to bring about no more theatre, but in a different way . . . Maybe it would be best if you just went to see *The Small Hours.* I'm sure you'll understand what we mean.

LINES WRITTEN AFTER FOUR WEEKS IN A HOSPITAL

THE NEW YORKER, *May 1, 1954*

Nurses all—and I mean the breed—
Share one clamorous, blinding need:
Not to assist you in getting well,
Or hurry in when you ring the bell;
Not to banish the sense of gloom
That somehow penetrates your room;
Not, as a fellow might believe,
To soothe your brow or to cool your feve;
Not to lessen, with gentle hand,
The tightening pull of a stomach band;
Not to carry you in, complete,
A single meal that is fit to eat;
Not to silence the bloody bore
Who's talking out in the corridor;
Not to massage the aching bone,
Or even to leave you *just alone.*
Their one ambition is quickly said:
All they want is to make your bed.

Wriggle your toes or shake your head,
What do they do? They make your bed.
Request an orange juice instead,
First they want to make your bed.
Ask for a needle, a bit of thread,
Still they have to make your bed.
Tell 'em you'd like some whole-wheat bread,
What'll they do? They'll make your bed.
Years ago you were leeched and bled;
Nowadays they make your bed—
Fold the sheets and adjust the spread—
Make and make and make your bed.

LIFE'S CALENDAR FOR JULY 1922

1 Sa STRAW HATS ONE-THIRD OFF. Battle of Gettysburg, 1863. Battle of San Juan, 1898. Boiling water is poured over piece of French pastry without cracking varnish, 1922.

2 Su James A. Garfield assassinated, 1881. Diner in restaurant successfully summons waiter by tapping on water glass with knife, 1897.

3 M Battle of Santiago, 1898. American character in English novel does not say "I calculate," 1906. Modern boy asks what fire crackers were, 1922.

4 Tu INDEPENDENCE DAY (sic). Nathaniel Hawthorne born, 1804. Stephen Collins Foster born, 1826. Patent Bureau established; patents begin to pend, 1836. Vicksburg surrenders, 1863. King of Norway gets annual mention in newspapers, 1920.

5 W David G. Farragut born, 1801. P.T. Barnum born, starting one-a-minute series, 1810. Manufacturers decide to toast Lucky Strike tobacco instead of soft-boiling it, 1916.

6 Th John Paul Jones born, 1747. Republican Party founded, 1854; no dancing in streets, 1922. Iowa inventor attains huge income by designing portable bath tubs for consumers of Eskimo Pies, 1925.

7 F Sitting down invented by Adam, 12,973 B.C. Rupert Hughes discovers the movies, 1915. Last remaining American household substitutes doilies for table-cloths, 1937.

8 Sa Emmett J. Carwell, first man to return a pair of guaranteed hose to the dealer, born, 1871. *Vanity Fair* reader breaks all records by finding the Table of Contents in 4 minutes and 13 seconds, 1919.

9 Su German submarine Deutschland crosses the Atlantic, 1916. Germany wishes it hadn't, 1922. New York newspaper agrees to print picture of Babe Ruth, 1922.

10 M Wyoming admitted to Union, 1890. Bryan makes crown of thorns speech, 1896. Walter C. Gripple, Boise City, Idaho, remembers to close top of talcum powder box when packing suitcase, 1918.

11 Tu John Quincy Adams born, 1767. Hamilton-Burr duel, 1804. Salt water taffy invented at Atlantic City, 1875. Advertising manager for Campbell's Soups buys a rhyming dictionary, 1887.

12 W First editorial on "New Amsterdam as a Summer Resort," 1665. Mr. Emerson decides on shade of blue bottles for Bromo-Seltzer, 1872.

13 Th Civil War Draft Riots in New York, 1863. Cyrus W. Field lays the Atlantic cable; American papers begin to reprint London editorials, 1866. First international conference called to decide what to do with meerschaum pipes after they are colored, 1930.

14 F First world's fair opened in New York; Grand Prix for suspender buttons goes to Little Magnet Suspender Button Co., 1853.

15 Sa Georgia readmitted into Union, 1870; Georgia still acts as though she hadn't been, 1922. Battle of Chateau Thierry, 1918. Built-in flasks invented for hip pockets, 1925.

16 Su Printing invented, 1451; book reviewing starts, 1452. Velvet Joe turns philosopher, 1906.

17 M Resident of Montpelier, Vt., instructed by physician to take daily exercise lays out strict schedule of gymnasium work and sticks to it, 1901. World's largest American flag unfurled, 1789-1922, inclusive.

18 Tu Census of cooks reveals seven people on Western Hemisphere who know how to make cranberry jelly properly, 1922. Actor, playing scene over telephone, pauses between lines long enough to create illusion of someone speaking at the other end, 1926.

19 W First Woman's Rights Convention, 1848.

20 Th Joke about pretty girls and dry bathing suits invented, 1731. Last railroad man buys a Hamilton Watch, 1927.

21 F Battle of Bull Run, 1861. Hottest July 21 on record; thirteen real oranges used to provide Orange Drink for 17,-500,000 persons throughout United States, 1922.

22 Sa Color photography invented, 1890; 64 companies announce that they have finally solved problem of adapting it to motion pictures, 1922. A. H. Woods, announcing plans for season, declares he is through with bedroom farces, 1922.

23 Su U. S. Grant dies, 1885. Woman smoking cigarette actually knocks all the ashes into receptacle, instead of around it, 1923.

24 M Brigham Young founds Mormon colony in Utah; Brighamy begins, 1847. Lumpless mashed potatoes discovered in hotel, 1915.

25 Tu Smokeless powder first used, 1891. Man found in Red Bank, New Jersey, who does not believe his wife would make a wonderful interior decorator, 1917.

26 W Yorick J. Billingsgate, Nashville, Tenn., purchases a stamp from a friend and finds that he actually has the two cents in change, 1917.

27 Th First wireless communication between United States and Japan; W. R. Hearst sees menace, 1915. Man waiting to cash a check for $5 at paying teller's window does not find customer ahead of him with 20-minute payroll to be made out, 1924.

28 F First railway mail car; "lone bandit" invented, 1862. Artificial fruit looks real, 1960.

29 Sa Fourteenth Amendment adopted; Eighteenth gets closer and closer, 1868. Expressman carried trunk out of house without being told to look out for the chandelier, 1894.

30 Su Sliced peaches invented, 1179. William Hodge gets a regular play, 1980.

31 M Each of seven New York newspapers simultaneously proves by sworn statement that its circulation is larger than those of other six, 1922. Toupee fools somebody, 1973.

INTERPRETATION

The Nation, *May 13, 1939*

President Roosevelt entered the Executive Office the other day, smiled at his assembled secretaries, and said, "Good morning!" That was all that he said—"Good morning!"

Now there was a time, in my simple-hearted innocence, when I would have taken that remark for just what it seemed to be—"Good morning!" and nothing more. But my days of innocence are over. I have been reading Walter Lippmann and Dorothy Thompson, to say nothing of a few others, and I am a considerably smarter fellow than I used to be. And although the President's "Good morning!" may carry not even the slightest connotation to the uninitiated, I should like to point out as a trained observer, that this was perhaps the most significant statement Mr. Roosevelt has made since he entered the White House.

In the first place, exactly what did the President say? He said, "Good morning!" Not "Good afternoon!" or "Good evening!" mind you, but "Good morning!" And why did he specifically select morning, out of all the available periods of the day? Surely the reason is obvious. Because it is in the morning that the sun rises. And *where* does the sun rise? In the east, of course. East is the Orient, east is Japan. And so the President's statement begins to take form and pattern.

Here for the first time we have definite proof that the Presidential mind is at last concerned definitely with the Japanese-Chinese situation. Plainly Mr. Roosevelt is taking this opportunity of stating his views on the Japanese aggression, but we must not hastily assume from this that he contemplates invoking the Neutrality Act. On the contrary, the President gives us definite indication that no such plan is in his mind. Witness his use of the word "good." Why this particular word? Because in his judgement the war in the Orient is progressing satisfactorily at the present time, from the standpoint

147

of the democratic powers, and consequently he is disinclined to take any overt step. At the same time, however, he gives sharp warning to Japan that the situation is being closely watched.

Now let us go a step farther. With the European situation so acute, Mr. Roosevelt's statement obviously must be read with an eye to its effect on the totalitarian powers. In fact, it is to the totalitarian powers that the message is plainly addressed. Why? Let us consider a moment. We know that it is Mr. Roosevelt's custom to enter the Executive Office at nine o'clock in the morning, and it was at precisely that hour that the statement was made. But when it is nine o'clock in the morning in Washington it is two o'clock in the afternoon in France and England. In other words, lunch time. Again bearing in mind his use of the word "good," what is the President saying to France and England? Obviously he is telling them that they may continue to eat their lunch in peace, and that in the event of war this country may be counted upon for limitless food supplies.

But lunch has already been eaten in Germany and Italy. In Berlin it is three o'clock, in Italy four. The Germans, who are traditionally heavy eaters in the middle of the day, are going through a period of drowsiness. But in Italy it is an hour later, and the Italians are alert and keen-eyed.

Now the President's real plan begins to emerge. For is it not clear that his statement constitutes an invitation to the Italians to catch Germany napping, as it were, and to desert the axis while there is yet time? Obviously he does not set forth the full details of his plan in this message; it is put forth largely in the nature of a "feeler." But the ground has been broken for separating Germany from its ally, and in that forthcoming separation the President tells us that America will play a leading role.

On the domestic side the President's statement is no less pregnant with meaning. Again the question must be asked: Why does he select morning? Clearly it is not the big business man who is active in the morning: directors' meetings are customarily held at three or four o'clock in the afternoon. No, the morning belongs to the farmer—it is the farmer who rises at dawn and starts upon his endless round of chores. So now we have renewed assurance from the President of his interest in agricultural legislation, and at the same time a definite intimation that big business must shift for itself. The period of appeasement is over.

Later: An additional statement made by the President late last evening gives evidence of a sharp change in foreign and domestic policy. Upon leaving his office for the day the President said, "Good night!" Obviously all of the foregoing must be read in the light of this new and sensational development.

DEAR EDITOR

Being a compilation of about eleven of those letters to the newspapers

SATURDAY REVIEW, *December 19, 1959*

I want to thank you for your magnificent editorial on the man-eating oyster, and have ordered extra copies to send to my friends. It is high time that someone summed up the courage to speak out. All thinking men will agree with you.

When our magistrates coddle juvenile delinquents, and American citizens, who should be grateful to this great country, do not even hang out the American flag on holidays, we inevitably get the inflation spiral and more strikes. What does Russia really want?

I am a working man who must support a wife and three children, and it is high time that fat, lazy men, returning from a holiday at the beaches, should rise and give their comfortable subway seats to women, who have probably worked all day. Some of them may even be pregnant—I mean the women, of course.

But it is certainly clear that policemen should be given back their nightsticks and encouraged to use them on those punks—I don't mean the women, of course.

As long as the City and the State are allowed to levy new taxes indefinitely, then we will always have the quiz-show scandals. As it is, all we can do is sit around indefinitely waiting for the H-bomb to drop. Meanwhile, decent men fear to walk in the parks after nightfall.

I dare you to print this.

PRO BONO PUBLICO

DOES NEWARK HAVE TO BE WHERE IT IS?

THE NEW YORKER, *September 19, 1953*

I am not, I hope, being unreasonable. As a matter of fact, I have always prided myself on my sense of justice, and if people think I am asking too much, I will let the whole matter drop, and try not to harbor any resentment.

But it will be difficult. Let me state the case as clearly as I can:

I have a farm in Bucks County, and to visit it I travel frequently between New York and Trenton, on the Pennsylvania Railroad. I like Bucks County, and when I depart for the farm, I am in a gay and emancipated mood, eager for a holiday and the wide country-side. On leaving Pennsylvania Station, I am first plunged into a tunnel under the river. This takes about five minutes to pass through, and in a tunnel, as you know, there is nothing to look at except the other passengers, most of whom are, at best, mild entertainment. But I am not asking that anything be done about the tunnel.

Presently, daylight shines through the windows again, and for a moment all is well. But immediately there is another setback, in the form of an enormous burial ground for decayed automobiles. This, like the passengers, is not much fun to look at, but at least it passes with reasonable speed.

I have now, it seems to me, earned a little fun. And, sure enough, away we go into New Jersey. Sing ho! for the open road and that sort of thing. America's heritage—what? So there I am, happy, carefree, emotionally adjusted, all set to be wafted through the bright, wonderful countryside—and what happens?

Newark, that's what happens. Psychologically, to say nothing of industrially, it is all wrong. I have just left New York and a big, massive station; surely I am entitled to go spinning along in the open air for a while. But almost immediately I get another big station, sunshine shut out again, and another city. Not quite so big a station and not nearly so big a city, I'll admit, but in a way that only makes it worse. Newark is not only frustrating, it is anticlimactic.

I am not exactly blaming Newark for being there; I know that years ago the city's founders didn't say, "Now let's put Newark where it will annoy the hell out of Kaufman." I just say it's all wrong for it to be there, and I would like to have it moved.

Now is that so terrible? I am not asking to have a big, sprawly city like Los Angeles moved—though, come to think of it, it would solve a lot of problems if it could be pushed about twenty miles farther west. But I am not asking that. Neither am I asking that Denver or Milwaukee or Omaha be put anywhere else. Only Newark.

And only because I make the trip so frequently. Oddly enough, often as I make it, I never can remember Newark in advance. Out of the tunnel I shoot, gay as hell, zoom past those dead automobiles, nothing on my mind—and there it is again: Newark. Every time, mind you, and I've been making the trip for years. Coming back, it's even worse. We're bowling along, I'm all set for New York (I'll get out quickly, grab a taxi ahead of the crowd; mentally I'm halfway up Park Avenue already), then: Newark. It puts me in a bad humor for hours, and it just isn't worth it.

There must be states out West that would be glad to have a city like Newark. New Mexico, for example. I've travelled across that state all day and would have been pleased and happy to run into Newark at such a time. And wouldn't it be better for Newark, too —to be out where it would be liked, instead of being unpopular where it is? Newark, New Mexico. Sounds right, somehow.

Am I being unfair about this? Selfish? If so, let me know, because that is the last thing in the world I want.

ON GETTING "MR. APLEY" STRAIGHT*

THE NEW YORK TIMES, *November 26, 1944*

Never write a play that depicts the habits and modes of a certain group of people for they will arise to confront you with a thousand accusations of inaccuracy.

Never write a play laid in any particular period, for the same reason.

Never write a play with a room in it, still for the same reason.

And oh, yes—never write a play.

Follow these simple rules and you will live on into a peaceful old age and be a nuisance to your family.

The Late George Apley, as a play, started last February with a lunch at the Hotel Dorset. The lunchers were John Marquand, Max Gordon, Harold Freedman (play agent extraordinary), and myself. Mr. Marquand had a martini, grilled kidneys, salad, coffee and cherries jubilee. I have not forgotten a single detail, because, being a late riser, I have not had lunch since. In fact, nothing less than Mr. Marquand and *Apley* could have got me there at all.

At all events that is when *Apley* started, and it isn't finished yet and never will be. There will always be one more little point to correct. *Apley,* as you may know, is a play about Boston, and in the course of our pre-Broadway tour we played for two weeks in its native town. In every audience of a thousand there were nine hundred critics, and the worst of it was that their criticisms were sound. A few examples:

Felix Frankfurter did not join the Harvard faculty until 1914. (We have him there in 1912.)

*This article was first published on the Sunday after the New York opening of *The Late George Apley,* a play by Kaufman and John P. Marquand, which premiered at the Lyceum Theatre on November 21, 1944.—*ed.*

The Copley-Plaza Hotel was not built until 1915. (We refer to it in 1912.)

Sigmund Freud's fame had not yet penetrated to America at the time of our play. (I am not sure about this and am waiting to hear from the analysts.)

Penetrated or not, Freud never would have been discussed in a Boston drawing room.

A young lady in a ball gown, living in the house next door, could not possibly come in the back way, because the Beacon Street backyards were too muddy in 1912.

A gentleman would not come into the drawing room in his overcoat, and even if he did the butler would follow and retrieve it.

The butler, in passing sherry, would offer it last to the host. (Guilty as charged, but for purposes of stage convenience it was necessary to move him up a notch.)

Mr. Apley's chair, he being the head of the house, would be a much more imposing affair. (Right again, but there just wasn't room.)

And everybody would be much, much more polite. (Yes, they would, but nothing is quite so dull on a stage as lots and lots of politeness.)

However, these quibbles were nothing compared to one quiet little observation in Washington, where Bob Sherwood simply said that any character who did not show some social progress in the course of an evening was just not worth writing a play about. His is a voice that I listened to with respect, and what he said was therefore disturbing. But when I talked it over with John Marquand we both felt that in presenting a figure of reaction we were by no means approving of reaction, but pointing quite a contrary moral.

Wilmington, Washington, Baltimore, Boston—that was our road itinerary. And since I am trying to discourage playwrights I would like to say a few words about trouping these days. Gone are the good old days when a theatrical troupe could have a parlor car entirely to itself, and the trip was one gay round of conviviality. These days the star is up in the baggage rack, and the understudy rides the brakes. Ingenues lug their own suitcases, and the character woman squeezes into a taxi with six OPA men.

And the hotels! Reservations of a month's standing are blandly unproductive, and if one gets a room at all it is still heavily marked with the beer bottles of the night before. Not only that, but you must move out tomorrow. Baltimore was the worst, I think, because Tom Dewey was due on Thursday and the Notre Dame game on Saturday. I beat them both out of town, but of course the poor actors had to stay. I understand that two of them even saw Dewey —Equity, it seems, was powerless.

And what do you think is the hardest thing in the world to obtain these days? A piano. There was none at all to be had in Baltimore; despite a month's foraging. So one had to be brought from Washington, but the whole thing only cost $800 so it was all right.

Just for the record—and for the further discouragement of playwrights—the plagiarism suit has already started. This is earlier than usual, because the aggrieved one usually waits until the play is a success. But this time, it seems, there was a man out West some place who had the brilliant idea of making a play out of *Apley* several years ago. To be sure, he never had the permission of the author, but do you think this made any difference? If so, you don't know the plagiarism boys. There was a heavy correspondence about the gentleman's rights—just as though he had any—and of course he wound up by demanding the inevitable "accounting" if the author himself was so presumptious as to dramatize his own work. Then, for good measure, he delivered himself of a final flourish.

"So Mr. Marquand and Mr. Kaufman," he wrote, "are going to dramatize *Apley*. Well, well! What with the boring longwindedness of Mr. Marquand and the complete dramatic stupidity of Mr. Kaufman, I tremble at the result!"

He may be right.

LIFE'S CALENDAR FOR AUGUST 1922

1   Tu   First national census; Smith family leaps into fame, 1790. First cable car run in San Francisco; Mrs. Emily J. Newhaus, 2346 Golden Gate Ave., gets off backward, 1873.

2   W   Restaurant serves order of buttered toast with butter spread on corners as well as in the middle, 1896.

3   Th   Columbus sails to prove world is round, everybody but Isabella leaving him flat, 1492. Palm Beach suit fits, 1967.

4   F   British capture Crown Point, 1759. James Moose, of Kansas City proves before body of scientists that he knows difference between women's summer and winter furs, 1920.

5   Sa   Battle of Mobile Bay, 1864. Pencil manufacturers begin making attached erasers of concrete, 1917.

6   Su   Detroit surrendered to British, 1812. Succeeding customer fails to pick up United Cigar coupons left on counter, 1907. Nicky Arnstein's name mentioned in conversation, 1924.

7   M   Navy Department organized; busses start going up Riverside Drive so that people can see the battleships, 1789. Ingenue, greeting relative in play, doesn't back kick, 1921.

8   Tu   Smith and Wesson patent modern breech-loading metallic cartridge, 1854. Siasconsett, Mass., girl invents nonbreakable straw for cherry-fishing in lemonades, 1922.

9   W   First commencement at Harvard; H. L. Mencken begins talking about the professors, 1642. Woman in Quincy, Ill., plucks piece of candy with tongs that came with box, 1902.

10   Th   Missouri shown into Union, 1821. Sewing machine patents granted simultaneously to Singer and Wilson, 1851;

no vaudeville show complete without joke about them, 1852-1910, incl.

11 F Robert Ingersoll born, 1833; denies existence of Santa Claus, 1838. Wireless telephone patented, 1892.

12 Sa Hawaii annexed by U. S., 7,625,398 dancers and musicians thereby becoming citizens, 1898.

13 Su First story attributed to a Congressman appears in New York newspaper, 1875. Surrender of Manila, 1898.

14 M Dr. Hugo Tanner, first man to fill an inside straight, born, 1836. Flypaper blown onto floor in Braddock, Pa., lands with sticky side up, 1896.

15 Tu Panama Canal opened, 1914. Carriage starters under rank of Major-General appear in front of New York hotels, 1920.

16 W Battle of Bennington, 1777. New cook in Childs' restaurant dies of stage fright, 1905.

17 Th Clermont, first successful steamboat, starts for Albany, 1807. W. R. Hearst tries the same thing, 1922. Pair of cotton stockings seen on New York street, 1930.

18 F Virginia Dare born, 1587. User of coin-box telephone, on completing conversation, doesn't put finger in return slot, 1919.

19 Sa Five women hanged at Salem for witchcraft, 1692. Baldwin M. Willow, advertising expert, writes health food ad without using "vitamin," 1923.

20 Su Benjamin Harrison born, 1833. Post-office truck goes so slowly that pedestrian can almost read "U. S. Mail" on its side, 1920.

21 M Charles T. Whistle, only photographer who never took a picture of Mayor Hylan on City Hall steps, dies, 1922.

22 Tu "America" wins first cup race, 1851. Stranger in New York searches two hours before finding bootlegger, 1922.

23 W Oliver Perry, hero of Battle of Lake Erie, born, 1785. Movie star "returns to spoken stage" after having actually been away from it, 1925.

24 Th Foundation of Capitol at Washington completed, 1818.

Mark Smith, the one on the right, gets shaved for last time, 1847.

25 F First bank president begins posing for Fatima ads, 1920. Commission appointed to find out what has become of country's mission furniture abandons research, 1922.

26 Sa Claudius Martina, first man to wear pointed mustache, born, 456 B.C. Nineteenth Amendment effective *(sic)*, 1921.

27 Su Battle of Long Island, 1776. J. Charles Button, composer of "Oh, How I Love That Little Mammy of Mine," hanged for matricide, 1921.

28 M Menendez de Avilés discovers and names St. Augustine, 1565. Mae Murray appears in motion picture wearing a dress, 1919.

29 Tu Oliver Wendell Holmes born, 1809. First Atlantic liner placed on end beside Woolworth Building to prove something, 1915.

30 W Walter Montgomery, Evansville, Ind., instructed by wife to be sure to water plant daily while she is on vacation, remembers to do so, 1990.

31 Th Earthquake at Charleston, S.C., 1886. Atlantic and Pacific Tea Co. becomes great, 1890.

ON THE AMERICAN PLAN

by George S. Kaufman and Howard Dietz

First produced in the revue *Flying Colors,* at the Imperial Theatre, on September 15, 1932, with the following cast:

MR. TILLEY . . . . CLIFTON WEBB
MISS MCGONIGLE . . . . PATSY KELLY

SCENE: *The lobby of the Remington Arms Hotel.* MR. TILLEY, *a clerk, and* MISS MCGONIGLE, *a stenographer, are behind the desk.* PAGE BOY *crosses.*

PAGE: Paging Mr. Grimes; Mr. Gormley; Mr. Johnson. Paging Mr. Grimes—*(Exits.* TWO GUESTS *cross, preceded by a* BELLHOP*)*
FIRST GUEST: I had two million dollars in caster stock. If, instead of the stock, I had two million dollars worth of casters, think of all the casters I'd have had. *(Both exit.* PAGE *re-enters)*
PAGE: Paging Mr. Grimes; Mr. Gormley; Mr. Johnson . . . *(Exits)*
TILLEY: *(With a newspaper)* Yes, Miss McGonigle, it looks like another big day for the hotel.
MISS MCGONIGLE: That's good.
TILLEY: *(Indicating paper)* Stock market down another ten points. That means things will be booming here.
MISS MCGONIGLE: *(Looking at her board)* We're about three-quarters full already. They've been coming in steadily since the market closed.
TILLEY: *(Also looks at board)* What are most of them doing—jumping or shooting themselves?
MISS MCGONIGLE: They're mostly jumpers.
TILLEY: I like that. Clean cut. *(Phone rings)* Room clerk! . . . Yes, sir—right away. Front! *(The bell. Calls off stage)* Prussic acid in twelve-eighteen. *(FIRST MAN enters)* Yes, sir—single room? *(Offers register and pen. The MAN nods, signs the register)*
MISS MCGONIGLE: Five-sixteen.

TILLEY: Oh, very nice. That's high enough for a jump and has a nice long mirror in case you prefer shooting. Or were you thinking of poison?

MAN: I think I'll shoot!

TILLEY: Right! Front! *(Hands man gun.* MAN *exits.* MISS MCGONIGLE's *phone rings)*

MISS MCGONIGLE: Hello . . . Just a minute . . . It's that guy in nine-twenty. He says he doesn't like the way that cyanide tastes.

TILLEY: Tell him to mix it with orange juice.

MISS MCGONIGLE: *(Into phone)* Mix it with orange juice. *(Other phone rings)*

TILLEY: Room clerk! . . . I'm sorry, sir, but that's really the best suite in the hotel. Southern exposure. Wide windows and perfect landing space . . . Oh, yes, we keep the street clear. Cars not allowed to park. Very well, sir. *(Hangs up.* SECOND MAN *enters)* Yes, sir?

SECOND MAN: *(As he signs)* Something high up.

TILLEY: *(Extending a key)* Thirty-first floor—you couldn't ask anything better.

SECOND MAN: Thanks.

TILLEY: Stationery?

SECOND MAN: Let me see . . .

TILLEY: *(Counting out note paper)* Two notes are customary—wife and sweetheart.

SECOND MAN: Thanks.

TILLEY: Happy landing! *(SECOND MAN exits. Phone rings)* Yes? . . . Report from the 19th floor. *(Signals* MISS MCGONIGLE *to stand ready)* Yes, floor clerk? . . . 1902 clear. Gentleman just checked out . . . 1907 . . . On his way down . . . You don't say? *(To* MISS MCGONIGLE) He says it was a beautiful take-off. Very well! *(Hangs up)*

MISS MCGONIGLE: I go mad trying to keep these records straight.

TILLEY: Yes, the turnover in this hotel is enormous. *(THIRD MAN enters. Foreigner, with whiskers)*

THIRD MAN: *(Fiercely)* I do not understand your America!

TILLEY: How's that?

THIRD MAN: America! What *is* it?

TILLEY: Miss McGonigle, will you take care of little Russia?

MISS MCGONIGLE: Vacancy on the twenty-eighth floor.

TILLEY: Twenty-eighth floor. Twelve dollars a day.

THIRD MAN: But I have only five dollar. America!

TILLEY: Five dollars! I can give you a room on the second

floor. Of course, it's not high enough for jumping, but that's the best I can do for five dollars. Second floor!

THIRD MAN: America!

TILLEY: I wish you'd stop saying "America." There must be some other country.

THIRD MAN: Give me the key! I try it! I jump hard! America! *(Exits)*

MISS MCGONIGLE: He's the spittin' image of a friend of mine. *(*MISS MCGONIGLE's *phone rings)* Hello . . . Yes? . . . Just a minute . . . *(To* TILLEY*)* It's the housekeeper on the sixth floor. That man in 608 has been in the tub for two hours and isn't drowned yet.

TILLEY: Make a note that drowning is a dollar extra after this. It takes too long.

MISS MCGONIGLE: Yes, sir. *(Into phone)* All right—we'll look after it. *(*FOURTH MAN *enters)*

TILLEY: Yes, sir?

FOURTH MAN: I want a room. *(Registers)*

TILLEY: Front! *(Hands out key)* One-eleven!

MISS MCGONIGLE: *(At her board)* One-eleven occupied! *(A shot off stage)* One-eleven free. *(*FOURTH MAN *exits.* THIRD MAN *returns)*

THIRD MAN: You were right! It was not high enough! America! *(Exits. Phone rings)*

MISS MCGONIGLE: Hello! . . . Got caught in an awning? We'll send right up. *(Hangs up.* FIFTH MAN *enters)*

FIFTH MAN: Good afternoon.

TILLEY: Yes, sir?

FIFTH MAN: I'm a theatrical producer—

TILLEY: *(As* TILLEY *and* MISS MCGONIGLE *hand him a gun)* Say no more! *(*FIFTH MAN *exits. Phone rings)*

BLACKOUT

ALL WE NEED IS HORSE SENSE

THE NEW YORKER, *May 25, 1935*

In the year 1948 the depression was still with us, and it was decided that something really should be done about it. By that time several million persons had written letters to the *Herald Tribune,* complaining about the administration. Most of the writers said that the new ideas of government were proving to be of no avail, and that all we needed in a President was plain horse sense. So great was the insistence upon horse sense that the next step was almost inevitable. It was decided to get a horse.

The idea was first suggested by a farmer in Iowa who had a horse that he was trying to find a job for. The horse was pretty old, and couldn't work anyhow, and the farmer felt that he was not really good for anything else. Of course the farmer's horse was ruled out, but the idea had taken root, and quickly spread. One of its advantages, as the proponents of the idea pointed out, was that it would eliminate the First Lady problem. (It had been decided early that there should be no First Mare.)

Naturally, there were a good many objections before the plan could be put through. The S.P.C.A. fought the idea in the beginning, and Mr. Brisbane wrote an editorial demanding a gorilla instead. The Hearst papers throughout the country printed coupons for several weeks—"Tell Your Congressman You Want a Gorilla"—but the country was pretty well worked up by this time, and demanded a horse or nothing.

Accordingly, the legislatures in thirty-six states met hurriedly to adopt a Constitutional amendment. The matter turned out to be absurdly simple. Since the Constitution restricted the Presidency to "a natural born citizen," it was only necessary to extend the right of citizenship to all horses. A further change was made in the matter of the Presidential age requirement, the Constitution stipulating that a President must be at least thirty-five years old. This was changed to include two-year-olds, since it was felt that a highly satisfactory candidate might be found in that category.

It was decided to pick the winner by means of simultaneous horse races throughout the country. On Election Day, accordingly, everybody went to the races instead of the polling booths, which was a big improvement right away. The fastest horse turned out to be a quite good-looking animal named Hot Baby, and, although this was not exactly what people had expected to call their President, the choice was considered generally satisfactory. It had been decided early that it was not right to ask any horse to be Vice-President, and this office was accordingly given to a man.

On Inauguration Day the horse rode down Pennsylvania Avenue on the left of the outgoing President, and the positions were reversed on the return trip. Meanwhile one whole wing of the White House had been made over to accommodate the new occupant, who found comfortable stalls when he entered his new home. In addition, patriotic citizens from all over the country had sent bags of the finest oats, which, of course, were carefully examined by Secret Service men before they were served to the President.

From the very beginning the plan was a huge success. From his stall in the White House, President Hot Baby passed final judgement on every governmental measure. The proposition would be stated to him, and he would then give a decision by pawing the air with the right front foot—once for "No" and twice for "Yes." One of the great advantages of this system was that he had to say one or the other, so that the country felt a firm grip at the helm and the confidence of business restored. On one occasion a Congressional bloc tried to prevent the passage of a bill for which the President had pawed twice, and the horse was led personally before the combined Houses, after which the bill was passed. Only once did Congress pass a measure over the horse's neigh.

In the second year of the administration the plan was succeeding so well that a move was started to put five horses on the Supreme Court bench, but the Supreme Court itself had to pass on the legality of this, so of course it never came to pass. In fact, it was the Court's first unanimous opinion in years.

Long before the four years were up all the country's troubles had been cured, and the nation was rejoicing. Unfortunately, the politicians thought they had learned the trick by that time, and at the next election a man was again put into the Presidency. Inside of a year, of course, things were worse than ever.

LIFE'S CALENDAR FOR SEPTEMBER 1922

1   F   James Wilkes, first boy to go through college on funds obtained by selling subscriptions to Curtis publications, born, 1889.

2   Sa   Treasury Department organized; meeting called to decide whose picture to put on dollar bills, 1789. Sherman takes Atlanta, 1864. Cream of Wheat served by white waiter, 1922.

3   Su   Treaty of Versailles signed, ending American Revolution, 1783. Theory that one brand of gasoline is better than another first exploited on billboards, 1914.

4   M   LABOR DAY—18,726 newspapers print editorials saying that the real American workingman is all right, but that something must be done about the agitators, 1922. First electric light plant started, 1882; company perfects system for unfailing delivery of bills on first of every month, 1883. Geronimo surrenders, 1886.

5   Tu   First Continental Congress, 1774. Treaty of Portsmouth signed, ending Russo-Japanese War, 1905. Rebuilt typewriter works satisfactorily, 1906.

6   W   Lafayette born, 1757. First Municipal Ordinance passed setting aside Sunday mornings for work on crossword puzzles, 1914.

7   Th   Boston settled by John Winthrop, 1630; Boston settled by New York Giants and other National League teams, 1890-1922, practically inclusive. Table d'hote dinner turns out to be good, 1927.

8   F   St. Augustine founded, 1565. Emmett C. Walker, inventor of hydraulic pump for getting ice cream to the bottom of cones, born, 1879.

9   Sa   New Amsterdam becomes New York, 1664; New York

becomes Mayor Hylan's, 1917. California joins the Union; climate invented, 1850.

10 Su Battle of Lake Erie, 1813. Montgomery, Ala., man rolls 18,000 in six months at Japanese pool, winning translucent tea set, 1918.

11 M Henry Hudson discovers Hudson River, 1609; Jersey's commuters wonder how he ever could have missed it, 1922. Battle of Brandywine, 1777. Battle of Lake Champlain, 1814.

12 Tu First woman murdered in America for helping herself to her husband's butter at dinner table, 1648. Stationers reduce prices of 1922 diaries, 1922.

13 W Battle of Quebec, death of Wolfe and Montcalm, 1759. Matthew J. Basin invents motorcycle that goes less than 50 miles an hour, 1926.

14 Th Francis Scott Key writes "The Star Spangled Banner," 1814. City of Mexico captured by Scott, 1847. Window cleaner arrives at office on *next* to busiest day, 1912.

15 F James Fenimore Cooper born, 1789. William Howard Taft born, 1857. First patent for gasoline automobiles issued to George B. Selden, 1895. New York Stock Exchange members break into front pages by smashing three straw hats, 1922.

16 Sa Battle of Harlem, just as though anyone would fight for it, 1776. Francis Parkman born, 1823. Line about preferring the upper berth anyhow first used, 1886.

17 Su Washington publishes his farewell address, 1796. Battle of Antietam, 1862. Woman buys new hat and does not wear it until three days later, 1908.

18 M Cornerstone of National Capitol laid by President Washington, 1793. Hannah Minor, first woman to balance a check book unassisted, born, 1831.

19 Tu "Dixie" sung for first time by Dan Emmett; everybody applauds, 1859. Battle of Chickamauga, 1863. Prominent couple married not "quietly," 1930.

20 W J. C. Clarke, haberdasher of East Lima, Ohio, actually

moves his business after sale based on the statement that he is compelled to move, 1908.

21 Th First daily paper founded in America; word "crisis" appears on front page, 1784. First vaudeville playlet without a gun in it, 1912.

22 F Nathan Hale hanged as spy, 1776. Emancipation Proclamation issued by President Lincoln, 1862. Picture of Suzanne Lenglen appears showing both feet on ground, 1928.

23 Sa Battle of the *Richard* and the *Scrapis,* most famous American naval victory of Revolution, 1779. Major André captured, 1780. First baseball club organized in America; manager announces that the team that beats them out will win the pennant, 1845.

24 Su John Marshall born, 1755. Black Friday, 1869. Man buys new belt as result of demonstration in store window, 1923.

25 M "My, but you're tanned," spoken 25,736,987 times to 2,837,752 returned vacationists, 1922.

26 Tu Balboa discovers the Pacific Ocean, 1513. Photograph of President Harding's double appears in rotogravure section, two and a half years late, 1923.

27 W British Army enters Philadelphia, 1777. Ward case finally ends, 5,726,987 columns behind the World War, 1936.

28 Th First newspaper cartoon of season showing football crowding baseball off the stage, 1922. Cleaned straw hat looks clean, 1960.

29 F Whites settle Kansas, 1810. Kansas tries to settle White, 1922.

30 Sa Matthew Cradle, East Tarvia, Minn., breaks telephone booth scribbling record of drawing 62 fancy diamonds, 43 watch springs, and the number called, with shadings, in four and a half minutes, 1922.

THE GREEN, WHITE AND BLUE

NEW MASSES, *December 17, 1935*

In nineteen hundred and forty-one, which was just a year after the fascists took over America, Dictator Hamilton Fish issued an order prohibiting the use of the color red anywhere in the United States, or even the mention of the word. This was one of several steps aimed at the crushing of a Communist counterattack and was greeted with approval all over the country.

(There had been a previous order commanding that all orders should be greeted with approval.)

One of the first things to go, of course, was the red traffic light. This was accomplished very simply by just keeping all lights green all the time. Naturally this also speeded traffic greatly. True, there were a good many smash-ups and several thousand pedestrians were killed or crippled every day, but it was rightly felt that the state was more important. In addition, it turned out that a good many people who were killed were Communists, so it was all right.

The necessary change in the American flag was handled very neatly. It was turned into the green, white and blue, and the flag manufacturing companies patriotically worked night and day turning out the new emblems. The night work was necessary because Dictator Fish had just issued an order requiring every citizen to purchase one of the new flags, or else.

The publishers of children's books, too, printed anew the story of *Little White Riding Hood,* and on the adult side, there was of course a reprint of Stark Young's *So Yellow the Rose.* The problem of red roses, of course, was rather a perplexing one, but the Florists' Association patriotically solved it by simply cutting off the flowers and selling just the stalks. Naturally this boosted the price a little, owing to the work of cutting off the flowers, but no one complained. Anyhow, not out loud.

Tomato juice and red cabbage were simply colored blue, which, it turned out, poisoned all those who partook of them. The gain to fascism, however, more than balanced these few hundred thousand deaths. Of course no problem at all was presented by the abolition of red ink, since under fascism no corporation could possibly oper-ate at a loss.

(Whenever a corporation showed a losing year, under the fas-cist regime, a benefit performance was given at Madison Square Garden, for which everyone was required to buy a ticket. The United States Steel Corporation benefit, in 1939, was the greatest thing of its kind ever staged.)

In fact the whole move was a complete success and fascism probably never would have been overthrown had it not been for the children of Public School 62, in Lincoln, Nebraska. It was there, in October, 1947, that an epidemic of pink toothbrushes broke out and which, spreading over the country, finally installed a Commu-nist government in the spring of 1950.

PREFACES

by George S. Kaufman and Howard Teichmann

Appeared in the first edition of their play, THE SOLID GOLD CADILLAC, *1954*

PREFACE

by Ralph D. Saylor, General Manager, the Western Union Telegraph Company

It is a theatrical custom to send opening-night telegrams to the cast and the authors—sometimes even the ushers and the producers —of plays opening on Broadway. The value of these good luck messages to the recipients has never been scientifically determined. There are cynics who claim that if on the way into the theatre on the night of a premiere you strike oil in the lobby—that's luck. Nothing else.

But Western Union does not hold with this viewpoint. Opening nights are always lucky for Western Union. On the opening night of *The Solid Gold Cadillac* more than sixteen hundred orchid-bordered telegrams were delivered at the stage door. Consequently, I consider *The Solid Gold Cadillac* a noteworthy drama, a touching and revealing saga of American home life and ideals. *Grandma's Diary,* where we also delivered sixteen hundred telegrams, was equally good.

PREFACE

by Bernhard Gristede, Gristede Bros., Inc.
Quality Retail Food Merchants for over Half a Century

Since the Messrs. Teichmann and Kaufman are both Gristede customers, our credit manager was naturally very happy at the success of *The Solid Gold Cadillac.* One of our speediest delivery boys had rushed copies of the theatrical reviews to us at the cashier's booth of Store No. 14 (our Times Square shop), where, with beating hearts, we sought the verdict.

A look at the papers told us the story. My brothers and I shook hands all around and toasted our good fortune in a Number Five

Size (Large) can of our Gristede Extra Special Fancy Apricot Juice, Unsweetened. Next morning, Mr. Torquemada, in charge of our Credit Department, at once issued orders putting an end to the leberwurst and Ry-Krisp diet on which the authors had been subsisting for a number of years.

The Kaufmans, I am happy to advise, were and still are customers of our Store No. 98, Madison Avenue and Eighty-fifth Street, RE 4–0200, while the Teichmanns patronize Store No. 12, Lexington Avenue and Seventy-seventh Street, RE 4–0112. I trust that I am not being indelicate when I say that prior to the opening of *The Solid Gold Cadillac* we had not received a check from either of them for many months. While I do not wish to imply that Gristede Bros. had anything to do with the writing of *The Solid Gold Cadillac,* I feel that I am on safe ground in saying that without our help there would have been no play. No playwrights, either.

Both the Kaufman cook, a French countess from the Dijon province, as I understand it, and the Teichmann food-stewer, an Alabamian who keeps within constant reach of a water pitcher filled with gin, proved to be most co-operative with our Accounts Receivable Department. Bills marked LONG OVERDUE were rendered by nightfall and were slipped under the playwrights' filet mignons at dinner that evening.

Within six weeks our lawyers concluded negotiations with the Dramatists' Guild. For the remainder of the New York run we are to get five percent of the first five thousand dollars, seven and one half percent of the next two thousand, and ten percent of everything above ten thousand.

This leaves the authors complete freedom from income tax and unlimited credit at all our stores. Nothing is too good for our customers.

PREFACE

by Hon. Walter P. Abbott, Mayor, Natchez, Miss.

Inaccuracy, friends, that's what's ruining the American theatre today. Just plain, old-fashioned American inaccuracy. People write plays, don't bother to check on things, other people go to see those plays, can't believe a word they hear. Take *The Solid Gold Cadillac.* A lot of talk about the fair city of Natchez in that play. "The Jewel of the Swamps." That's what they call the fair Natchez. Now, friends, Natchez is located on a fifty-six-foot bluff overlooking the Mississippi River. No swamps within half a mile of us. Maybe the writers meant Upper Natchez. That's to the north of us. They got swamps, plenty. But if they meant Upper Natchez, why didn't they say so?

Well, if the American theatre wants to go down the sink hole because of inaccuracy, that's their lookout. I don't mind. Besides, they haven't turned out a decent play since Edward Ferber wrote *Showboat.*

PREFACE

by Hon. Robert T. Capeless, Mayor, Pittsfield, Mass.

The high moment of *The Solid Gold Cadillac,* as far as most intelligent people are concerned, comes surprisingly early in the play. In the first quarter, I am certain, of the first act. One of the women on the stage, it doesn't matter which one, turns to another woman who is also on the stage and reads a letter postmarked in the city of Pittsfield, seat of Berkshire County, Massachusetts. This is very interesting. Pittsfield has 56,117 people who can write letters.

It also has excellent power facilities, a strong sewage system, and a fine statue of "The Color Bearer" which, during the tourist season, is disguised by the trees in the park facing West Street. Industries are welcome. Kiwanis meets on Wednesday, Rotary on Thursday.

The climactic letter which brings the audiences of *The Solid Gold Cadillac* to its feet each night concerns itself with a Pittsfield firm called the Apex Electric Clock Company. Actually, there *is* no Apex Electric Clock Company in our city, but what undoubtedly served as the inspiration to the authors was the Terry Clock Company which originally came to Pittsfield from Connecticut in 1880. High taxes probably. In 1886 it was reorganized as the Russell-Jones Clock Company. In 1887, it went out of business. Bankrupt. But this is no reflection on Pittsfield. Nor on my administration, for that matter.

PREFACE

by a Ticket Speculator

The Solid Gold Cadillac is a great play. On December 7th, 1953, two nights after the opening, I sold Seats F-26 and 27, with a fine view of Seats E-26 and 27, for eleven dollars apiece, or a clear profit of six dollars a ticket, less tax, which I did not pay. The producer paid the actors, the authors, theatre rental and office expenses. He got four dollars a ticket, or a clean profit of a cent and a quarter a seat.

You will not find a finer fellow anywhere than a theatrical producer.

PREFACE

by a Stagehand

I can't honestly say I like this *Cadillac* show very much. Too much scenery-changing. I been with it a year now and the same thing happens every night. "Spike" Conover, "Big Dutch" Klupferman and me, we're down in the cellar and almost before we know whose deal it is the goddamn buzzer goes and we got to drop everything and trot upstairs and change the scenery. One time I pick up a four-fifty hand in spades—cold in my hand, without the kitty even—and bang! up we got to go and change the scenery or something. And matinees, if you're on the phone trying to put down a bet at Belmont or some place, the same thing happens.

Now, *Our Town*—there was a show. No scenery at all, the whole evening. I must of held a dozen four-fifty hands that year, and any number of four hundreds. Stage manager come downstairs, we'd just give him the razzberry and go right on playing. Paydays we'd make them bring us down the money.

How about a revival of *Our Town,* somebody?

LINES UPON LOOKING THROUGH A PILE OF OLD CHECKS

THE NEW YORKER, *May 1, 1937*

Time is a guest at no man's house,
  Gone ere it full appears;
Soft as the velvet-footed mouse
  Speed the relentless years . . .
But first they write on the Golden Scroll,
  And wrap it around our necks—
Jeevers, hand me my pipe and bowl,
  And give me those cancelled checks.

Nineteen hundred and twenty-five
(Hardly a man is now alive)—
Sixteen hundred and fifty bucks,
A sheer caprice of Lady Luck's.
"Aces full," said I, with hope;
"Four of a kind," said Herbert Swope.

There are also grounds for thinking
That my bridge was pretty stinking.
Schenken, Culbertson, and Fry
Always took my good right eye.
Lightner, Zedwitz, or Jacoby—
Didn't matter who my foe be.
Baby took it on the chin—
Cripes, didn't I *ever* win?

And now sing ho! the jolly stores
That deal in hats and pinafores . . .
It sort of seems that Mrs. K.
Had nothing much to do all day:

Black and Starr and Frost and Gorham—
God, what haven't I done for 'em?
Yamanaka, Cartier, Marcus,
Everyone but Parkyakarkus.
Checks to Udall & Ballou,
Checks to you, and you, and *you.*
Checks to Mr. Tiffany,
To your uncle, *if* any.

Bloomingdale's did blooming well,
        And Sterns were never sterner;
Slater, Bonwit . . . who the hell
        Was Jesse Franklin Turner?
Lord & Taylor, Altman's, Saks,
        None of them ever missed. . . .
But why did I give eighty smacks
        To Efrem Zimbalist?

When Dolly Trymlym trimmed a limb,
        She lost but very little;
And Hicks were right up in the swim
        At charging for a victual.
Sheets by McCutcheon monogrammed,
        And Sherry's rich collation. . . .
Suppose we say the whole god-dammed
        Fifth Avenue Association.

Pay to the order of Maison Cohn's,
        Sulka, Finchley, Brooks,
Holliday Bookshop, twenty bones
        (*I* never read any *books*).
Telephone, gas, and electric light,
        Un*holy* amounts of kale—
This check? . . . I heard a speech one night
        (But Mooney is still in jail).

And now, descending like an axe,
That little sweet, the Income Tax.
Hello! Another payment due—
"Pay to Internal Revenue."
Where are the aeroplanes they buy?
I never see them in the sky.
It's time some *other* poor schlemiel
Began to pay for the New Deal.

Time is a guest at no man's house,
    Gone ere it full appears;
Soft as the velvet-footed mouse
    Speed the relentless years. . . .
All right, Jeevers, hand 'em here;
    They come to a pretty figure—
And I'm writing the same old checks THIS year,
    Only just a trifle bigger.

IT'S A DIRTY WORD

Saturday Review, *November 15, 1958*

Mr. Brooks Atkinson of *The New York Times,* in his review of *The Pleasure of His Company*, started out by saying that it was "a delightful comedy," which, indeed, seems to be the consensus. This was a great tribute to the play, because Mr. Atkinson, by his own confession, was already tired before the curtain rose. What gave Mr. Atkinson this feeling of weariness was one quick look at the program. I quote from the review: "Those concerned are Samuel Taylor, who wrote the play 'with Cornelia Otis Skinner,' as the program says with tiresome exactitude."

Now it seems proper to ask at this point just what it was about this billing that made Mr. Atkinson tired. Obviously he could not object to the names of the authors—it is an old custom of the theatre to put the authors' names on the program, and Mr. Atkinson must be used to it by now.

All that is left that could have wearied Mr. Atkinson is the word "with." I have had this word assayed by the United States Bureau of Tiresomeness, and they report that it requires just one-hundredth of a second to read it.

So was this really what made Mr. Atkinson tired? As a matter of fact he cannot be so opposed to the word "with," because he used it himself a second later in the phrase "with tiresome exactitude."

No, I think we have to look further. At the top of the program is the familiar phrase, "a new play." There, I think, we have the answer. It's "a." "A" is a dreary word, and is used so much that we are *all* tired of it. The psychiatrists' offices, I find, are filled with people whose basic trouble is the word "a". . . . "a" pain, "a" bill, "a" critic.

Meanwhile, pending a fuller inquiry, we can all be happy that Mr. Taylor did not write the play *"without* Cornelia Otis Skinner." They would have had to carry poor Mr. Atkinson out.

HOLLYWOOD PINAFORE
Left to right: William Gaxton, Mary Wickes, Victor Moore, George Rasley, Annamary Dickey. Below; left to right: William Gaxton, Shirley Booth, Russ Brown.

HOLLYWOOD
PINAFORE
    Above: William
    Gaxton, Victor
    Moore

Right: Victor Moore
surrounded by
showgirls

"The Story Conference." Left to right: George Rasely, Mary Wickes, Victor
Moore, William Gaxton, Russ Brown, Gilbert Russell

THE COCOANUTS
In the center, left to right:
Chico, Zeppo, Groucho,
and Harpo Marx

Below: Showgirls in their
"Monkey Doodle-Doo"
costumes

Margaret Dumont,
Groucho Marx

THE COCOANUTS
Groucho, Zeppo, Chico, Harpo

LIFE'S CALENDAR FOR OCTOBER 1922

1 Su   Southboro, Mass., man discovers that daylight saving stopped a week ago, 1918. Spain cedes Louisiana to France, 1800. Explorers in India find hardware store window not containing radio outfits, 1922.

2 M   Major André hanged, 1780. Pocket flashlight continues to work after third day, 1906.

3 Tu   George Bancroft, historian, born, 1800. Battle of Corinth, Miss., 1862. New York scientist discovers way to distinguish high-priced yellow taxis from low-priced ones without getting inside, 1922.

4 W   Battle of Germantown, 1777. Rutherford B. Hayes born, 1822. Traveler back from Europe fails to tell about the liquor they all drank the day before reaching New York, 1924.

5 Th   Chester A. Arthur born, 1830. Atlanta Exposition, 1881; somebody remembers it, 1922.

6 F   Hurdy-gurdies start South, 1922. Joseph L. Beresford, Jr., makes wager to smoke lady's gold-tipped, perfumed cigarette, 1922.

7 Sa   Bemis Heights, decisive battle of Revolution, fought, 1777. James Whitcomb Riley born; Indiana begins practicing dialect, 1853.

8 Su   Joseph L. Beresford, Jr., wins wager by smoking lady's cigarette, 1922. World's series breaks attendance record, 1917, 1918, 1919, 1920, 1921, 1922.

9 M   Charter for Yale College granted, 1701; movement started to turn William Lyon Phelps into separate university, 1918. Cow kicks over lamp and Chicago's great fire begins, 1871. First annual memorial service for Joseph L. Beresford, Jr., 1923.

10 Tu U. S. Naval Academy at Annapolis opened, 1845; first hazing charge preferred, 1845. Chicago hold-up men resume work, 1845.

11 W World's first steam ferry operated in Hudson River; first ferry orchestra passes the hat, 1811.

12 Th Columbus discovers America, 1492. Margot Asquith tries to do it again, 1921. "Most gigantic spectacle ever filmed" does not appear in advertisement of William Fox movie, 1936.

13 F Molly Pitcher born, 1744. Cornerstone of White House laid, 1792. Herman J. Redlick, last man in America to wear button shoes, born, 1865.

14 Sa William Penn born, 1644. Loser in poker game quits early because he is sleepy, 1889.

15 Su Lincoln monument dedicated at Springfield, 1874. Annual convention of dancing masters does something worth mentioning in newspapers, 1956.

16 M John Brown's insurrection, 1859. Annual report of Coney Island photographers shows four instances where boys and girls did not change hats, 1921.

17 Tu Burgoyne surrenders to Gates, 1777. Last New York delicatessen store begins using colored paper sauerkraut for window decoration, 1922.

18 W U. S. buys Alaska, 1867. First telephone connection between New York and Chicago, 1892; New York resident almost gets call through to local exchange, 1922.

19 Th Cornwallis surrenders at Yorktown, 1781. Phil Sheridan goes horseback riding and Union army wins Battle of Cedar Creek, 1864.

20 F Spain formally cedes Florida to U. S. for $5,000,000, 1819. Hotelkeepers in Florida prepare to get the money back, 1922. Prince of Wales, later Edward VII, sails home after tour of United States, forty years before invention of rotogravure process, 1860.

21 Sa Edison produces first incandescent light; "Don't-blow-out-the-gas" joke begins to fight for its life, 1879.

First composite photograph of presidential timber, 1892.

22 Su First messages by wireless telephone sent across Atlantic, 1915. Bootblack shines pair of low shoes without arguing with other bootblack or polishing customer's ankles, 1919.

23 M First boat on Erie Canal, 1819. Ten-cent tip for ice water becomes obsolete, 1914.

24 Tu First movie theatre to be christened "Bijou Dream" opens, 1907.

25 W New York subway opens; James L. Gleep, 1675 Amsterdam Avenue, being first man to have back broken while being pushed into car, 1904.

26 Th Impromptu quartette doesn't remember "Sweet Adeline," 1909. Photographs of champion girl swimmers missing from three rotogravure sections, 1922.

27 F William Penn lands in America, 1682. Theodore Roosevelt born, 1858. Single anecdote breaks smoking car record by containing three traveling salesmen, two Irishmen, four Englishmen, three Scotchmen, and eight Jews, 1920.

28 Sa Bartholdi's Statue of Liberty unveiled, 1886. Quite a number of persons suggest reveiling ceremony, 1922.

29 Su Society leader commits suicide on learning through paper company's advertisement that she has been using stationery a size too large, 1918.

30 M King William's War ends, 1697. John Adams born, 1735. Bank presidents begin saving money for tickets to next month's Harvard-Yale game, 1922.

31 Tu ALL SAINTS' EVE. Nevada admitted to Union, 1864. Fifteen million men decide their evening clothes will do another year, 1922.

FORKED LIGHTNING

Introduction to SIX PLAYS BY GEORGE S. KAUFMAN AND MOSS HART, *1942*

Some years ago, during a visit to London, Moss Hart found that the nightly round of top hat, Savoy Grill and Quaglione's was beginning to wear him down. There had been about a week of it, uninterrupted, and a good night's sleep was indicated. So at nine o'clock of a dismally foggy night he put aside all temptation, pulled the shades down in his hotel room and settled himself for at least twelve good hours of slumber.

Sure enough, his watch said nine-thirty when he awoke. A bit of fog was still coming through the window cracks, but Moss was enormously refreshed. He bounced out of bed with high vigor, bathed, shaved, and phoned down for toast, eggs, coffee and marmalade. By the time he had stowed this away he was fairly bursting with vitality. Nothing like a good night's sleep!

He would like the morning papers, he told the phone operator. "Yes, sir!" Up they came, and for twenty eager minutes Moss buried himself in the news. And then presently he came across an item that had a vaguely familiar ring. Hadn't he read that yesterday? Yes, he had. And here was another such item. And another. Then he pulled himself together and looked at the date line. It was yesterday's newspaper.

Back on the telephone, he demanded to know how they could do such a thing. "But you must be mistaken, sir—those are this morning's newspapers." "But I tell you they aren't." "But if you'll look at the date, sir—"

Moss looked, and a horrible foreboding took possession of him. "What time is it?" he asked the operator. "Ten o'clock, sir." "Ten o'clock when?" "Ten o'clock Tuesday evening, sir."

The mystery was solved, of course. Moss had slept exactly half an hour.

Now, I don't for a minute say that this could not happen to anybody but Moss, but it is a little bit remarkable that so many similar incidents have managed to crowd themselves into his life.

Nothing happens to Moss in the simple and ordinary terms in which it happens to the average person. The most normal of human experiences is crowded with drama where Moss is concerned.

Nothing, for example, could be more within the simple range of human activity than a visit to the dentist. We have all gone through it, lingered for our unpleasant hour, and gone on our way. But not Moss. When Moss went to the dentist it was at once discovered that a couple of teeth were growing out of his knee, or his elbow, or something. The dentist called in another dentist, and he brought along two more. It seemed it would require quite a course of treatment.

And it did. For something like three months Moss went to the dentist. But he didn't go the way you or I would. Oh, no! Moss would get there at eleven o'clock in the morning, and he would be there until four or five in the afternoon. Then, one epochal day, he arrived at eleven in the morning and stayed until nine o'clock that evening! This was so whimsical a procedure, even for Moss, that he felt I would not possibly believe him. So he brought along an affidavit from the dentists—there were three or four, and they worked on him in relays—testifying to its truth.

There were weeks, then, that Moss could not keep a dinner engagement because he had to be at the dentists'. This was a new reason for breaking dinner dates, and his friends were somewhat perplexed. But he was only building up to the grand climax. On the final day of treatment Moss arrived at the dentists' at ten o'clock in the morning and left at two o'clock the following morning! There were no affidavits this time, because he knew I wouldn't even believe the affidavits. But it was true.

Nor was that all. This was followed by a complete nervous breakdown on the part of the dentists, although Moss felt fine. And as a complete you-can't-top-this finish to the whole business, the dentists gave Moss a beautiful present when it was all finished, and Moss reciprocated by buying them cuff links!

Now, is that going to the dentist or isn't it?

Forked Lightning, I called him. Only I am not sure that it plays around his head. I think his head plays around the lightning, deliberately.

And that is one of the reasons, if you ask me, why he is a good playwright. The prodigality that marks the simplest moments of his life is matched by the prodigality of his mind. Ideas pour forth, and the simplest things of life are highlighted and made interesting. His is an instinctive sense of drama, on and off. Life, like the plays, cuts itself neatly into acts, with climaxes, second-act curtains, and interesting minor characters.

There are times, I think, when he is not completely sure whether the curtain is up or down. There was, for example, that moment when he decided to drive North instead of South. He woke to a day that promised no particular activity of interest—that same trip down to the office to see what was going on. He decided, suddenly, that he would not drive down to the office at all—he would drive in the other direction.

Drama took the wheel of the car at this point, and at the end of about an hour Moss found himself far up in the city, and just around the corner from the school he had attended as a boy. He would drive around and look at it. He remembered the day the school had opened—there had been a terrific ceremony, and they had all paraded from the old building to the new. The principal had headed the procession. Professor Cartwright. Twenty-five years ago, almost. Was he still there, he wondered?

And then, since the story had to have a second act, Moss got out of the car and went in. There was a door marked PRINCIPAL, and he knocked on it. A voice said "Come in!" and there was a little man back of a desk—a man who might very well have been Professor Cartwright, and who, in the manner of good dramatic construction, was indeed he.

"Professor Cartwright?" asked Moss, eagerly.

"What do you want?"

"My name is—Moss Hart." Moss waited hopefully for the minor sensation which this revelation was supposed to bring about, but nothing happened. "I—uh—I used to go to school here when I was a boy. My name is—Moss Hart."

"Well, what do you want?"

"Why—nothing. I just thought I'd—my name is Moss Hart." Still with a shade of hope. "I just happened to be near by, and thought I'd—uh—you know."

"Is that all?"

"Well, is it all right if I just go through the school—look around?"

"All right. Here's a pass."

Moss went up a flight of stairs, and there was Room No. 5. He had sat in that room for many hours, dutifully trying to learn things that would be of no help in the theatre.

A stern-looking woman opened the door. This time drama had sprung one of its surprises—it was not his old teacher.

"My name is—Moss Hart." A little bit of hope still sticking.

"Oh, yes. You're the father of one of the boys, aren't you?"

"No, no. I write—plays. Plays. I used to go to this school, so—"

"Oh, come right in. . . . Boys, this is—what is the name?"

"Moss Hart."

"Yes. He used to go to school here. Sit right down, Mr. Hart."

So for two hours Moss went back to school, and very dull he found it. But there was a curtain coming, of a sort. When it was all over the teacher pulled a manuscript out of her desk drawer.

"Did you say you wrote plays, Mr. Hart? I just happen to have written a play myself. . . ."

I think, on the way out, that Moss opened the door of the principal's room just a crack. Instinctively he felt the need of a finish. Professor Cartwright might be lying dead on the floor, a knife of peculiar design plunged into his heart. But the professor was still sitting at his desk. He looked up just for a second. "What do you want?" he said.

Forked Lightning. Only Moss could have planted thirty-five hundred new trees on his farm in Bucks County, and only Moss, in the midst of plenty, could have failed to find water at the end of three months and the digging of something like seventeen wells. Only Moss could have bought a hundred pigs to give his caretaker enough interest in the place to persuade him to stay on. Only Moss and his family, after *Once in a Lifetime,* could have moved out of their Sheepshead Bay house overnight, leaving every piece of furniture, every shred of clothes and every kitchen utensil right where it was. Only Moss could have written a show that called for four revolving stages, double the number that had ever been used before.

Forked Lightning.

But it makes for awfully good shows.

THE GREAT WARBURTON MYSTERY

by George S. Kaufman and Howard Dietz

First produced in the revue *The Band Wagon*, at the New Amsterdam Theatre, on June 3, 1931, with the following cast:

IVY MEREDITH	ADELE ASTAIRE
INSPECTOR CARTWRIGHT	FRANK MORGAN
MRS. BOULE	HELEN CARRINGTON
MR. BOULE	ED JEROME
MISS HUTTON	ROBERTA ROBINSON
MR. DODD	PETER CHAMBERS
MR. WALLACE	JOHN BARKER
WALKER	PHILIP LOEB
FIRST POLICEMAN	JAY WILSON
SECOND POLICEMAN	LEON ALTON
THE MURDERED MAN	FRANCIS PIERLOT

SCENE: *The library in the home of Hugh Warburton.* MR. WARBUR-TON, *who has been killed before the curtain rises, is found slumped in a chair. On the table beside him is a wine glass, almost empty, together with the revolver with which he has obviously been shot. On the other side of the table is another chair—an easy chair, and so turned that it seems likely that the murderer had been sitting in this chair just before, or perhaps when, he fired the fatal shot. Several men and women, all in evening clothes, stand around in various attitudes of shock and discomfort. In the main they are clustered together at the right side of the stage, as though they had entered the room together and remained almost in a frozen group. Standing near the group, but a bit apart from them, is a butler, named* WALKER. *Also present are two policemen— one of whom stands near the body of the dead man and seems to be in general charge. The other is on guard at the left door.*

MRS. BOULE: I tell you I can't stand it!

MISS HUTTON: And neither can I!

MR. BOULE: *(To the* POLICEMEN*)* Surely something can be done about this. My wife is very nervous. Can't the women go into the other room?

DODD: Yes!

FIRST POLICEMAN: Sorry, sir. No one is allowed to leave until the Inspector comes.

DODD: But when's he going to get here?

FIRST POLICEMAN: He'll be here any minute, sir.

WALLACE: Any minute . . .

MR. BOULE: It's an outrage!

MISS HUTTON: Good heavens.

IVY: *(Detaching herself from the group)* Well, while we're waiting, who wants to shoot a little crap?

MR. BOULE: Ivy!

IVY: Sorry.

(The door bell rings)

MR. BOULE: Here he is!

DODD: At last!

MRS. BOULE: Do you think we can go home now?

MR. BOULE: The Inspector will tell us.

MISS HUTTON: The whole thing is an outrage!

SECOND POLICEMAN: Right in here, sir.

BOULE: Here he is now!

WALLACE: This is our man.

MRS. BOULE: And about time.

(Enter INSPECTOR CARTWRIGHT. *A quick look around, his gaze lands on* WALKER, *who is standing just inside the door)*

CARTWRIGHT: Is this the dead man?

FIRST POLICEMAN: No, here, sir.

CARTWRIGHT: Oh. *(He crosses and examines body)* When did this happen?

FIRST POLICEMAN: About eight o'clock, sir.

CARTWRIGHT: How long have you been here?

FIRST POLICEMAN: *(Looking at watch)* Twenty minutes, sir.

CARTWRIGHT: Nothing has been touched?

FIRST POLICEMAN: No, sir.

CARTWRIGHT: *(A brisk nod; another look around; faces the group)* Good evening. *(There is a scattered response)* My name is Cartwright. Inspector, First District. *(Responses from guests)*

IVY: *(Approaching brightly)* I'm Ivy Meredith. We've had a little trouble here—

CARTWRIGHT: *(Shutting her up)* Good evening.

IVY: *(Taken aback)* Oh, the hell with you.

CARTWRIGHT: Now then, tell me what happened.

MR. BOULE: We were sitting in the D.R.

MRS. BOULE: There's been a man murdered.

WALLACE: I don't know anything about it.

(Several guests start to reply)

CARTWRIGHT: If you please—I would like to hear from the officer.

FIRST POLICEMAN: Well, sir, the late gentlemen here was giving a dinner. The dining room is in there. And, after it was over, the men were sitting in there drinking. The women had gone upstairs.

IVY: If you please!

FIRST POLICEMAN: Mr. Warburton said he wanted to get something and came in here.

MR. BOULE: That's right.

FIRST POLICEMAN: He brought the wine glass with him.

CARTWRIGHT: I see.

FIRST POLICEMAN: A minute later there was a shot, and they found him here.

CARTWRIGHT: Who found him here?

FIRST POLICEMAN: All of them, sir.

MR. BOULE: All of us.

FIRST POLICEMAN: The men came in from the dining room, and the women came downstairs.

CARTWRIGHT: But one of them *might* have come down before that?

FIRST POLICEMAN: Yes, sir.

CARTWRIGHT: And gone up again?

FIRST POLICEMAN: Yes, sir.

CARTWRIGHT: Or one of the men might have left the dining room?

FIRST POLICEMAN: Yes, sir.

IVY: I wouldn't have a mind like that—

CARTWRIGHT: Whose gun is it?

FIRST POLICEMAN: His own, sir. It was on the wall.

CARTWRIGHT: His own, eh? So it might have been—anyone.

FIRST POLICEMAN: Yes, sir. Anyone.

IVY: Maybe we'd better send for the police.

(CARTWRIGHT stands beside chair; reaches toward gun; pretends to point it at dead man's head. Tries same thing from other side)

FIRST POLICEMAN: Sir?

CARTWRIGHT: It can't be done from either side of the chair. The gun was fired from this angle. *(He draws an imaginary line that cuts squarely across the chair)*

FIRST POLICEMAN: That's right, sir.

CARTWRIGHT: He might have stood back of the chair. But he never would have put the gun over there, because he couldn't reach it.

WALLACE: That's what he couldn't.

DODD: No.

MR. BOULE: He's right.

FIRST POLICEMAN: Maybe he sat in the chair, sir.

CARTWRIGHT: Exactly.

MR. BOULE: That's it.

WALLACE: He sat in the chair.

DODD: That's what he did.

CARTWRIGHT: *(Tries it, but does not actually sit)* He sat in the chair. Perfect for the gun. *(Illustrating)* Perfect for the bullet hole.

IVY: Marvelous for the bullet hole.

CARTWRIGHT: *(Straightens up; looks at chair)* He sat in the chair. *(The phrase runs through the crowd, in little hushed whispers)* No one has left this house since the murder was committed?

FIRST POLICEMAN: No, sir.

CARTWRIGHT: You're positive?

FIRST POLICEMAN: Yes, sir.

CARTWRIGHT: *(A second's thought)* You can take the body out. Have this officer stand guard until further notice. *(The POLICEMEN pick it up; there are expressions of relief from several of the women)* I shall ask the ladies to step to this side of the room. If any of you are faint, you may sit down. *(IVY moves to sit in the fatal chair)* Not there, please. *(The POLICEMEN, having removed the body, return as soon as possible)* Ladies and gentlemen, no one has left this house since the murder was committed. I regret very much to inform you that the guilty person is in this room.

MRS. BOULE: Good heavens!

MISS HUTTON: What?

MR. BOULE: Do you mean to insinuate—

CARTWRIGHT: Not at all, sir. I am simply announcing a fact. Someone in this room had a motive for killing H. W. Perhaps a business quarrel. Possibly—who can tell—*(Turning to the women)* some woman he had wronged. *(All four women drop their bags)* Ladies and gentlemen, there can be no guesswork in modern crime detection. It is a matter of cold science. The man or woman who killed Hugh Warburton sat in this chair. No two people in the world, upon sitting in a chair, leave exactly the same impression.

(IVY *looks at cushion*)

DODD: What did he say?

WALLACE: What's he trying to get at?

MR. BOULE: Search me.

CARTWRIGHT: Ladies and gentlemen, the murderer of Hugh Warburton has left his calling card on that cushion, just as plainly as if he had written his name.

DODD: Oh, come now.

WALLACE: What?

MR. BOULE: Absurd!

CARTWRIGHT: On the contrary, a scientific fact. Find the person who fits that cushion, and you will have the murderer of Hugh Warburton.

MISS HUTTON: Good heavens!

MR. BOULE: I don't believe it!

DODD: What an idea!

WALLACE: It's not true!

CARTWRIGHT: But it is true! There are no two exactly alike in the world.

MR. BOULE: Now, really!

IVY: *(After a moment's pause)* I don't know—it's kind of a comfort.

MR. BOULE: What!

IVY: You wouldn't want to have one just like somebody else's.

CARTWRIGHT: And now with your kind permission, ladies and gentlemen, we will proceed with the examination.

IVY: You will do what?

CARTWRIGHT: I will ask you all to take your places in line, please. Officer!

FIRST POLICEMAN: All right—line up, please! Line right up!

MR. BOULE: This is an outrage!

IVY: It certainly is.

CARTWRIGHT: I regret very much that I must ask you to do this—

IVY: You don't regret it at all, you probably get a great kick out of it.

CARTWRIGHT: Are we ready?

DODD: Well, I suppose if we must we must.

(CARTWRIGHT takes out a tape measure; unrolls it with a little zipping sound. He looks at the line, which is facing the audience. He measures the print in the chair, then looks up again. He considers—shall he ask the line to turn around or not? Finally decides to take a trip around the back; goes accompanied by the two POLICEMEN. He conducts his inspection; each person tries to act unconcerned as he or she is reached)

IVY: *(As he comes down the line, CARTWRIGHT comes to her. She sings a bit of song to show her unconcern)* Are you looking for something?
CARTWRIGHT: *(In a low voice, to a POLICEMAN)* Sixty-two.
IVY: You mean across?
CARTWRIGHT: Never mind, madam. *(Clears his throat; comes in front of the line again)* Ladies and gentlemen, there is only one which—interests me—*(To IVY)* I'm sorry to inform you, madam, that—it belongs to you.
IVY: Me?
CARTWRIGHT: That is right.
IVY: What do you want to do now—make a bust of it?
CARTWRIGHT: Officer, will you bring down that chair please.
IVY: You mean you're going to take an impression?
CARTWRIGHT: *(Bowing)* That's the size of it.
IVY: What's the size of it?
CARTWRIGHT: *(Moves to a spot beside the fatal chair)* Won't you— sit down? *(She hesitates)* If the shoe does not fit—I beg your pardon—then I shall have to admit my mistake.

(With great dignity she advances to the cushion. Somewhat timidly, she sits. Bounces immediately up again. CARTWRIGHT peers quickly; the others strain to see)

MR. BOULE: Well?
CARTWRIGHT: *(A tense moment)* No. *(A general sigh)* I seem to have been wrong. There's nobody else in the house?
FIRST POLICEMAN: Only a cook, sir. The kitchen's in the cellar —she couldn't possibly get up.
CARTWRIGHT: *(A long sigh. Takes handkerchief in hand and picks up the gun. Shakes his head; puts it down. Takes up the wine glass; regards it)* You men who were in the dining room with him—do you remember if this glass was full when he left the room?
DODD: I think it was.
MR. BOULE: I'd just filled it.
CARTWRIGHT: It would have taken him at least a minute to drink it.

WALKER: Not quite that long, sir.

CARTWRIGHT: What?

WALKER: The glass doesn't hold very much, sir. It has a false bottom.

CARTWRIGHT: Ah! A false bottom.

WALKER: Yes, sir.

CARTWRIGHT: A false bottom. *(Something about the way that he says it makes* WALKER *suspicious. He makes a bolt for it)* Catch him, you men! *(The* POLICEMEN *grab him.* CARTWRIGHT *strides over and pulls a pillow out of the rear of his trousers)* I thought so. Aha! Put him down there! *(The* POLICEMEN *put him on the cushion; pull him up. Cartwright quickly compares the print)* Exactly! There is your man, Officer! Arrest him!

WALKER: I'm glad I did it! He wronged my sister!

IVY: *(Looking at the print)* Good heavens! *(Cries from the guests—"What is it?" "What's the trouble?" etc.)* He's my father! *(To* WALKER*)* Daddy!

BLACKOUT

MUSICAL COMEDY—OR MUSICAL SERIOUS?

THE NEW YORK TIMES, *November 3, 1957*

A funny thing happened to a musical comedy on its way to the theatre the other night. It met a joke. Then, before it realized the audacity of such behavior, it took it along to the theatre, and presently there it was in the show.

Well, sir, the audience was pretty surprised, I can tell you that. Conditioned to musical versions of O'Neill and to teen-agers fighting each other with switch-blade knives—and killing the hero, to boot—they were naturally taken aback. Most of them, embarrassed, had the good taste to look the other way and pretend it never had happened. Quite a number broke down and cried, having grown accustomed to crying at musical comedies in recent seasons.

But a few people with long memories had the temerity to laugh. Admittedly, they didn't feel comfortable about it. Laughing at a musical comedy!—whoever heard of such a thing?

Time was, of course, back before musical comedy became musical serious, when the musical shows were just full of jokes. True, the jokes were frequently something less than Grade A—for several seasons it was enough to have the comedian pull out his cigarette lighter, strike it into flame with a quick movement, and say to the audience: "It worked!" (But at least they had comedians.)

Even the plots were something of a joke in those days—there were long years when the outcome of the romance depended on which lad won the big football game, or the foot race, or the automobile race, or the boat race, or the airplane race. Naturally, the fellow who won the race was given permanent possession of the ingenue. This was known as Dillingham's Law—no other qualifications were considered necessary. For the next thirty or forty years, presumably, the winner would wile away the long winter evenings telling and retelling his bride how he had emerged victorious despite the heavy's dastardly attempts to sabotage him by

191

removing a wheel from the auto, or poisoning the football, or moving the centerfield fence farther back so that he couldn't hit that home run.

You may well have felt that the successful outcome of the boat-automobile-airplane-foot race was hardly a foundation for a happy and enduring marriage, but by that time you were either safely at home or else sitting in front of another musical comedy—the one in which the whole thing was resolved at 11:10 when the heroine said: "You mean it was your sister you were kissing all the time?" And there you were, with a reprise of the love song, a bit of hoofing, and curtain. No drama, no tragedy, no deep thoughts.

I am not writing this out of a nostalgic longing for the past—I realize fully that those shows would be hooted off the stage these days, and rightly. But surely the playgoer who wants a musical comedy should know at least what kind of show he is going to see. And just as surely there are still those who want a musical show that has gaiety and fun and lightheartedness in it—yes, and tunes, if I am not asking too much—a show that makes no attempts to delve into either psychological or sociological depths.

Perhaps some such designation as musical drama, or even musical tragedy, would help to guide the questing entertainment seeker. As things stand now, the innocent musical-comedygoer is likely to find himself up to his elbows in problems. Both of the shows to which I have obliquely referred—*New Girl in Town* and *West Side Story,* not to make too big a secret of it—are excellent entertainments and highly successful. But where will the trend end?

I read, for example, that *The Jest* is to be made into a musical show. Now, I remember *The Jest* moderately well and I seem to recall that the protagonist spent most of the evening chained to a pillar —a pillar, moreover, about six feet across and forty feet high. This will certainly hold the dancing to a minimum, to say the least. Speaking of dancing, a friend of mine who greatly admires Gwen Verdon as a dancer went to *New Girl in Town* and waited an hour and twelve minutes before Miss Verdon danced a single step. She finally twinkled a foot or two in the first-act finale. This is fine if you want it that way, but a lot of people, impressed by the show's success, are going to try doing that sort of thing *without* Gwen Verdon, and the results will almost certainly not be happy. (I am sure that at this moment producers are combing the other O'Neill plays, trying to find one sufficiently grim and unhappy to form the basis of a musical show. Will *Long Day's Journey Into Night* be next on the list?)

"Of Human Bondage," I'm told, is also to be made into a musical comedy. Yes, I said musical comedy. *Of Human Bondage,* you will recall, is set against a hospital medical student background, and has a clubfooted hero just for good measure. I have not yet read that it is going to be called *Gimpy,* but nothing would surprise me. However, *Of Human Bondage* is in expert musical comedy hands, and will probably emerge as a hit. I can see that big dance number now:
>It's easy if—
>You keep your right leg stiff—
>Doing the rig-or mor-tis!

Looking back, I am not sure how it all started, but I suspect that it began with Noel Coward. In *Bitter Sweet,* along about 1930, Mr. Coward killed off his hero at the penultimate curtain. In *Carousel,* of course, Billy Bigelow was killed in the first act, but at least he came back later as a ghost—better, of course, than an altogether dead hero, but not exactly conducive to belly laughs. Again, in *Allegro,* Rodgers and Hammerstein, unless my memory is faulty, killed off the hero's mother early in the proceedings, but as things wound up she had one of the biggest parts of the show (more ghosting, of course).

What next? As matters are now going I would say that mental health is a highly promising theme for the musical comedy theatre. The scene will be a sanitarium, naturally, and it will begin with the hero insane and the heroine perfectly sane. Then, as he slowly recovers his sanity, she starts to lose hers. The romantic problem is clear: will they meet midway on a happy plateau? The big love song? "I'm Just Crazy About You," natch.

Or will there be a return to gayer and lighter musical fare? The theatre is a law unto itself, of course, existing from show to show, and reasonably independent of economic or any other kind of trends. Presumably, if enough good musical dramas are written, people will go to them. Just as certainly, there will always be those who want the lighter and more amusing variety.

Vote for one.

LIFE'S CALENDAR FOR NOVEMBER 1922

1 W Stamp Act passed; invitations extended for Boston Tea Party, 1765. Only three out of five get pyorrhea, 1922.

2 Th James K. Polk born, 1795. Warren G. Harding born, 1865. Kansas goes dry; new uses found for cyclone cellars, 1880.

3 F Continental Army disbanded, 1783. William Cullen Bryant born, 1794. First actress photographed getting into Packard, 1902. Maid-of-all-work takes telephone message correctly, 1919.

4 Sa Gatling gun invented, 1862. Evanston, Illinois, resident, while packing trunk, discovers method of refolding sleeves of fresh shirt, 1922.

5 Su Chinese Restriction Act passed, 1892. Woman suffrage adopted by Kansas, Oregon, and Arizona, 1912. Palm trees begin blooming in rotogravure sections, 1922.

6 M United States recognizes Republic of Panama, 1903. Woman suffrage adopted by New York, 1917. Female character in Oriental play is not referred to as somebody's Lotus Flower, 1937.

7 Tu ELECTION DAY; Republican, Democrat and Socialist leaders highly pleased with results, 1922. New York evening papers, printed at seven A.M., announce heavy early vote, 1922.

8 W Lewis and Clark reach the Pacific and are shown over the studio district, 1805.

9 Th Montana admitted to Union, 1889. Paul T. Saddle, only man to refrain from remarking about the three-mile limit when seeing friend off for Europe, born, 1890.

10 F First English settlement in Connecticut; N. Y., N. H. and

H. wrecks begin, 1635. "A" bets "D" instead of "B" in letter to newspaper, 1919.

11 Sa Cherry Valley massacre, 1778. Washington admitted to Union, 1889. Lettuce sandwiches first regarded as sandwiches, 1912.

12 Su Montreal surrendered to American Army, 1775. "Home, Sweet Home" first sung publicly, 1823. Last New York cabaret taken over by colored entertainers, 1923.

13 M Edwin Booth born, 1833. First vacant lot next to skyscraper set aside for measuring transatlantic liners, 1902.

14 Tu Treaty of Commerce signed between Great Britain and Republic of Texas, 1840. Man with black dinner tie folded under collar is shot while passing office of "Vanity Fair," 1924.

15 W Charles Mason and Jeremiah Dixon arrive from England and start well-known line firm, 1763. Articles of Confederation adopted, 1777. Zebulon M. Pike discovers Pike's Peak, one of the greatest coincidences in the history of civilization, 1806.

16 Th Sherman restarts his march through Georgia, 1864; Savannah banks remain open, 1922.

17 F Congress meets for first time in Capitol at Washington, 1800; one hundred and ten million people begin to think it would have been just as well if it hadn't, 1922.

18 Sa Standard time established, 1883; legislators begin to knock the daylight into it, 1918. Turkish baths introduced into Turkey, 1936.

19 Su James A. Garfield born, 1831. Lincoln delivers Gettysburg address, 1863. First piece of hotel soap engraved, 1897.

20 M David L. Fairchild, Topic, W. Va., decides that if cuffs are turned and a new collar put on it will do nicely for another winter, 1922.

21 Tu Napoleon issues "Berlin Decree," 1806. John Meredith, born of obscure parents, discovers new method of arranging oranges and apples in dairy lunch, 1921.

22 W First anecdote about poker game in heaven, 473. Nineteen Russian actors discovered still in Russia, 1923.

23 Th Franklin Pierce born, 1804. Battle of Chattanooga, 1863. Joseph Urban invents Neapolitan ice cream, 1901.

24 F Zachary Taylor born, 1784. Emil J. Scanlan, East Liverpool, Ohio, finds he has rubber band when he needs it, 1918.

25 Sa British evacuate New York; Corn Exchange Banks and Schulte's cigar stores take possession, 1783. Labor Day in Louisiana, but only Nov. 25 elsewhere, 1922.

26 Su First street railway, running between New York and Harlem, begins operation; Mayor Hylan insists on five-cent fare, 1823. First hat band run in and out of soft hat by college student, 1856.

27 M U. S. and Germany sign arbitration treaty, 1904; strong evidence that they must have been joking about it, 1917. Collar button dropped in comic strip fails to roll under bureau, 1967.

28 Tu Jeremiah Castor, inventor of famous oil, born, 1801. Citizens, in nation-wide uprising, voice demand for better blotters, 1923.

29 W Detroit surrendered to the English, 1760; Henry Ford gets first news of it, 1922. W. J. Messner, Little Falls, Ark., uses grape scissors instead of just pulling a handful from the bunch, 1925.

30 Th Mark Twain born, 1835. THANKSGIVING DAY, strangely coinciding with end of twelfth month of LIFE'S CALENDAR, 1922.

THE TRYOUT BLUES (OR COOS)*

THE NEW YORK HERALD TRIBUNE, *September 29, 1957*

BOSTON

It is customary, on Sundays preceding a premiere, for the dramatic pages to print, for the benefit of the playgoer, extensive explanations of the psychological meaning and deeper implications of the play in question. You will get no such nonsense from me. Moreover, I will wager doughnuts to dollars—doughnuts now being more valuable than dollars, thus shifting the odds—that Peter Ustinov is not thus spreading himself in any of the other and equally voluminous Sunday publications. Mr. Ustinov, to clear matters up, is the author and star of the play that I'm talking about—its name is *Romanoff and Juliet.* As for me, I am only the director, and very little of that.

Not that I don't know what the play is about, mind you. It is about the best play that I have come into contact with these many years, and Mr. Ustinov is a gay and highly companionable fellow, charmingly resistant to cuts. Incidentally, he solemnly assures me that he did not write *Romanoff and Juliet* with himself in mind as its star, and I have solemnly believed him. So it is just a coincidence that the eventual production of the play finds Mr. Ustinov in the leading part. And a good job that he is, too.

These notes are being typed in Boston, where the play is about to have its first night—after only about 600 nights in London, and a good lot of them in Germany and environs, too. We open in Boston, and go from here to Philadelphia. Boston and Philadelphia are fine, but too comfortable and pleasant. Somehow that's not show business. I am a veteran of too many of these pre-New York trips, and I am used to New Haven and Wilmington, where the

*This article was first published on a Sunday prior to the New York opening of *Romanoff and Juliet,* a play by Peter Ustinov, which George S. Kaufman directed. It premiered at the Plymouth Theatre on October 10, 1957.—*ed.*

suffering is keener. In those towns things loom up in their proper proportions, and the matter of fixing the second act curtain takes second place to whether you can get room service after eleven o'clock at night. (The answer is simple: you can't.)

New Haven is a charming town, as I understand it, but so far as I'm concerned after you've seen the Yale campus you're through for the week. Once, back when Marc Connelly had a weekly dramatic class at Yale, Max Gordon and I showed up at the college and spent a pleasant hour telling the boys and girls all about show business. Since we had a juicy flop in town at the moment, I can't imagine why the class paid any attention to us. Maybe they didn't, and are happy and successful today.

It was Joe Fields who, standing one day in the lobby of New Haven's leading hostelry, looked about him with a baleful eye and observed: "You know, they opened this hotel in New Haven twenty years ago, and never did bring it in."

My own fondest memory of that hotel has to do with my attempt to go out the front door one day. That was all I wanted to do—go out the front door. But I didn't quite make it. As it happened, it was a Friday afternoon, and the Wisconsin football team was due in town to play Yale the following day. Just as I was going through the door, or trying to, the team arrived—forty-seven bruisers averaging six-foot-six and each weighing about 296 pounds. Since they beat Yale 26 to 0 the next day you can imagine what they did to me. It was not quite an equal contest. The more I plunged the line, or whatever it's called, the farther back I was pushed. They finally scored a touchdown with me somewhere out in the garbage patch, behind the kitchen.

As for Wilmington, I can't explain it, but somehow you always have a bad last act in that town. I know it's not the fault of the authors, so it just must be Wilmington. In Boston the test of a play is simple. If the play is bad the pigeons snarl at you as you walk across the Common. Today, as I sit typing, I can hear them softly cooing in the distance. All is well.

MEMOIR

THE NEW YORKER, *June 11, 1960*

A good many years ago, Irving Berlin and I went to Atlantic City together to work on a musical show for the Marx Brothers—all seventeen of them. We had adjoining rooms at the hotel, and along about the second week Irving woke me up at five o'clock one morning to sing me a song he had just finished. Now, Irving has a pure but hardly a strong voice, and, since I am not very strong myself at five o'clock in the morning, I could not catch a word of it. Moving to the edge of the bed, he sat down and sang it again, and again I failed to get it. Just when it looked as though he would have to get into my bed before I could hear it, he managed, on the third try, to put it across. The song was the little number called "Always," and its easygoing rhythms were just up my street. I learned it quickly, and as dawn broke we leaned out of the window and sang it to the Atlantic Ocean—its first performance in any hotel. It was destined to be sung millions of times after that, and invariably better.

That task done, we then talked about it. At the time, I was woefully ignorant of music, and by dint of hard work over the years I have managed to keep myself in the same innocent state. To this day, I do not quite know the difference between Handel's "Largo" and—well, Largo's "Handel." But I have always felt that I knew a little something about lyrics, and I was presumptuous enough then to question Irving's first line, "I'll be loving you, always." "Always," I pointed out, was a long time for romance. There were almost daily stories to that effect in the newspapers—stories about middle-aged husbands who had bricked their wives up in the cellar wall and left for Toledo with the maid. I suggested, therefore, that the opening line be just a little more in accord with reality—something like "I'll be loving you Thursday." But Irving would have none of it. He was, he said, an incurable romanticist—as opposed to my being an obviously curable romanticist. So he went his own way and celebrated the permanent nature of love, and the history of the song business will show that he was darned right.

My interest in lyrics, mistaken though it was in that instance and discouraged though it was by Irving, did not lag. Not long before turning out "Always," Irving had written the song bearing the somewhat implausible title of "When the Midnight Choo-Choo Leaves for Alabam'." Like "Always," it swept the country. Irving's lyric glorified the enchanted moment when that choo-choo pulled out of the station for Alabam'. With a view to checking up on the facts of the situation, so that I'd be able to make suggestions to Irving about the realism of this lyric, I turned up in Pennsylvania Station at a quarter to twelve one night for that wonderful and glorious departure.

The first thing I found out was that there *was* no midnight choo-choo for Alabam'; the choo-choo for Alabam' left at twelve-nineteen. Well, I was not too worried about that. Clearly, Irving could not have written a song entitled "When the Twelve-nineteen A.M. Choo-Choo Leaves for Alabam'." Next I discovered that the platform was crowded with songwriters, slapping each other on the back and uttering shrill cries in praise of Alabam', "where the rhyming is easy." Between times, they were bidding tearful farewells to their dear old mothers, who had moved up from Alabam' twenty-five years before and were living contentedly on West Seventy-second Street. Some of the poorer songwriters, who had not yet had a big hit, were sad to behold. Getting a piano into an upper berth is, at best, a difficult job. But I did learn one thing about it—always get the stool up first, so you'll have someplace to sit while you're waiting for the piano to get there. The moment of departure was noisy and gay. The happy songwriters, jauntily singing their songs, could be observed at every window as the train pulled out. The mothers went happily back to Seventy-second Street. I gave a lusty cheer myself, and was delighted to have witnessed the whole happy scene.

I learned afterward that the songwriters all got off at Newark, took the Hudson Tube back to Manhattan, and were safely in Lindy's by one-thirty. I never told Irving about that, but ever since then I have not quite believed everything I heard in a song lyric.

THE COCOANUTS*

A Musical Comedy

Book by *George S. Kaufman*
Music and Lyrics by *Irving Berlin*

The Cocoanuts was produced by Sam H. Harris at the Lyric Theatre on December 8, 1925, with the following cast:

JAMISON	ZEPPO MARX
EDDIE	GEORGIE HALE
MRS. POTTER	MARGARET DUMONT
HARVEY YATES	HENRY WITTEMORE
PENELOPE MARTYN	JANET VELIE
POLLY POTTER	MABEL WITHEE
ROBERT ADAMS	JACK BARKER
HENRY W. SCHLEMMER	GROUCHO MARX
WILLIE THE WOP	CHICO MARX
SILENT SAM	HARPO MARX
HENNESSY	BASIL RUYSDAEL
FRANCES WILLIAMS	FRANCES WILLIAMS

*The script that follows was prepared as a documentation of the show as it played on its opening night in New York in 1925. Owing, in part, to the on-stage ad libs and antics of the Marx Brothers, the show changed constantly during its run. One such change was the addition of the now-famous "Viaduct" (or "Why a Duck?") scene between Groucho and Chico. It does not appear in this script because it was not written at the time of the show's opening. Also, Irving Berlin's lyrics are not included along with the text.

The word "business" is used often throughout the following script. In this context, business means stage action, either rehearsed or spontaneous, that is worked out either by the director in collaboration with an actor, or by an actor alone. A piece of business might begin with an actor answering a telephone by speaking into the wrong end of the receiver and could be so extended that the actor winds up becoming tied up in the telephone cable. Essentially non-verbal, business is almost never written down, and is a frequent reference in scripts of this period.—*ed.*

ACT ONE

Scene One

SCENE: *The lobby of The Cocoanuts. Cocoanut Beach, Florida.*

The hotel desk, a concave curve, is large enough to take up nearly all of the right wall. It is equipped with all the usual paraphenalia including a register, bellboys call-bells, phones, pens, etc. There is also on stage the usual assortment of hotel furniture, all good looking.

AT RISE: *Discovered: A number of hotel guests on stage.* JAMISON *and Ensemble go into OPENING NUMBER joined by* BELLBOYS. *At the number's end, the* BELLBOYS *remain on stage.*

JAMISON: Eddie!

EDDIE: Yes, sir?

JAMISON: People are complaining that they don't get any service. How about it? *(*BELLBOYS *start to jabber)*

EDDIE: Shut up! *(To* JAMISON*)* The trouble is they're dissatisfied. *(The* BELLBOYS *start to talk again)* Keep still. *(To* JAMISON*)* Keep still. They haven't been getting their wages.

BELLBOY: No!

BELLBOY: We want our money.

JAMISON: Well, business hasn't been very good so far, but you're sure to get paid soon.

BELLBOY: We want to talk to Mr. Schlemmer.

BELLBOY: Yes! Where is he?

JAMISON: Why, he's—he's not up just yet, but—

BELLBOY: Not up? It's four o'clock.

BELLBOY: That's the trouble with the hotel.

JAMISON: But he's sure to be here soon. He always gets up Wednesdays.

(Enter MRS. POTTER*)*

Now go back to work. As soon as he comes you can talk to him.

(Reprise of OPENING NUMBER. Exit EDDIE *and* BELLBOYS.*)*

MRS. POTTER: Oh, Mr. Jamison!

JAMISON: Yes, Mrs. Potter?

MRS. POTTER: Have you seen my daughter around the hotel recently?

JAMISON: Your daughter? No ma'am. I think she went out early in the afternoon.

MRS. POTTER: I see. And, Mr.—what's-his-name? Is not here either?

JAMISON: How's that?

MRS. POTTER: The other clerk. I forget his name.

JAMISON: You mean Mr. Adams?

MRS. POTTER: Yes—Mr. Adams, did he also go out early in the afternoon?

JAMISON: Well, I—I'm not exactly sure. You see, I didn't get here until—that is—

MRS. POTTER: I see.

(Enter HARVEY*)*

HARVEY: Oh, Mrs. Potter, I don't seem to be able to find Miss Polly.

MRS. POTTER: Oh, thank you, Mr. Yates. I've just learned that she's gone out with Mr. Adams.

HARVEY: I thought maybe that was it. I hope you won't mind my saying so, but people are beginning to talk.

MRS. POTTER: Yes, I suppose so. It's not a matter that I would speak about ordinarily, but with you it's different. I know that you've spoken to Polly *(HARVEY looks up quickly)* She told me. And there's nothing that will please me more, Mr. Yates.

HARVEY: Thank you.

(Enter PENELOPE*)*

MRS. POTTER: I've known your family for a great many years.

(HARVEY gives a nod of acknowledgement)

PENELOPE: Good afternoon.
HARVEY: Miss Martyn.
MRS. POTTER: Oh, Penelope, you'll excuse me.
PENELOPE: Not leaving already?
MRS. POTTER: I'm afraid I must. I'll see you both later.

(MRS. POTTER exits. HARVEY bows, PENELOPE smiles graciously. When MRS. POTTER is gone, she turns to HARVEY, her manner is immediately free and easy)

PENELOPE: Well, that's one way. But it's a little old-fashioned.
HARVEY: What's that?
PENELOPE: Getting solid with mother. It won't work, Harvey. You'll notice he's out with the girl.
HARVEY: Who?
PENELOPE: I think you know, Mr. Robert Adams, Chief Clerk of this hotel.
HARVEY: I'm not worrying about him.
PENELOPE: *(Looking after MRS. POTTER)* Think of all that money, the Potter millions going to a hotel clerk.
HARVEY: He hasn't got them.
PENELOPE: And I feel sure you could use them. You generally could in the old days.
HARVEY: I've told you to lay off that stuff. Suppose somebody came in?
PENELOPE: In fact, if you lose out with Polly, I have an idea you'll be in a pretty bad way.
HARVEY: I can take care of myself.
PENELOPE: Yes? Suppose I happen to have a plan that would take care of both of us?
HARVEY: What do you mean?
PENELOPE: I wonder if I dare tell you.

(She stops as POLLY enters. A bit uncertainly—knowing that BOB is likely to follow on any moment)

Oh, are you Miss Potter?
HARVEY: *(Turning)* Oh, hello Polly.

POLLY: *(Nervously)* Hello.

HARVEY: I was just out looking for you. Your mother wanted you.

POLLY: *(A slight smile)* She generally does.

PENELOPE: Well, I'll see you both some other time.

HARVEY: *(Absently)* What? *(Turns)* Oh.

(With a smile, PENELOPE *exits)*

POLLY: *(Still uneasy)* I imagine I'd better be going too. If mother—

HARVEY: Oh, please don't go. She won't mind if you talk to me awhile.

POLLY: I know, but—I'm afraid I can't just now, because—

(She stops as BOB *enters)*

HARVEY: *(Taking in the situation)* Oh, I understand. I beg your pardon. *(*HARVEY *exits)*

BOB: What's the matter?

POLLY: Why nothing, exactly. He just— *(She hesitates, changes the subject)* He said mother had been looking for me.

BOB: Well, Mr. Schlemmer's probably been looking for me, so we're square.

POLLY: We shouldn't have stayed so long.

BOB: Longer, I thought.

POLLY: It was beautiful.

BOB: Eh?

POLLY: Cocoanut Manor, I mean.

BOB: You needn't have spoiled it.

POLLY: It's too bad that Mr. Schlemmer can't do something with it.

BOB: Would you mind if I told you something about it and about me?

POLLY: I'd love to hear it.

BOB: Did you notice those little hills all through it?

POLLY: Uh huh. I thought they were beautiful.

BOB: They're beautiful all right, but that's why there hasn't been any development there.

POLLY: Oh, couldn't they be cut down?

BOB: *(Shakes his head)* Too expensive. Now here's what happened. John W. Berryman was here to see it last month. You know, from Miami? And he said he wouldn't touch it. And of course when a man like Berryman passes a place up, no one wants it. Do you know anything about architecture?

POLLY: No, but I'd love to learn.

BOB: Well, I made a drawing showing a whole place as a built-up district, without cutting the hills or having them get in the way.

POLLY: Why, you're wonderful.

BOB: I made the hills fit in with the architectural scheme, see? I sent a copy of it to Berryman last week.

POLLY: That's thrilling. Does Mr. Schlemmer know about it?

BOB: Not yet. If Berryman takes it, he may let me design the buildings too. I may be an architect yet.

POLLY: Oh, if he only does take it. I'm sure it'll be the most beautiful place in the world to live.

BOB: Do you think you might ever live there?

(MRS. POTTER enters)

MRS. POTTER: Polly.

BOB: *(Turns to MRS. POTTER none too easily)* How are you, Mrs. Potter?

MRS. POTTER: *(Cooly)* How are you?

BOB: *(Half aloud)* Yes, thank you. *(Exits)*

MRS. POTTER: Polly, I only hope that you will not entirely forget that you're a Potter.

POLLY: *(Sighing)* Sometimes it's awfully hard.

MRS. POTTER: Remember that in two hundred years, the Potters have never been involved in a single scandal.

POLLY: *(As though she has heard this many times)* I know, mother, except for Uncle Dick.

MRS. POTTER: Polly, it is a well known fact that your uncle was drunk at the time. Now listen, dear, I want you to promise me, that you'll give up this clerk.

POLLY: But mother, he's not a clerk. He's an architect.

MRS. POTTER: One who clerks, Polly, is a clerk.

(Enter GIRLS *and* BOYS*)*

And that settles it.

POLLY: But mother, you just won't try to understand.

MRS. POTTER: I understand perfectly, but that a daughter of mine should be seen in the company of a hotel clerk when she has the opportunity of marrying a Yates, that I don't understand.

*(*MRS. POTTER *exits.* POLLY *sits on ottoman)*

GIRLS: Families are an awful nuisance. Aren't they?

POLLY: Especially mine.

(Number—"FAMILY REPUTATION" sung by POLLY*. At cue,* MRS. POTTER *enters)*

MRS. POTTER: Polly, I want to speak to you.

POLLY: Yes, mother.

*(*BOYS *and* GIRLS *and* POLLY *finish singing the last two lines of the Chorus. Then they exit.* BELLBOY *enters)*

BELLBOY: Hey, Mr. Schlemmer is up. He's coming down the stairs. Come on.

(The BELLBOYS *enter talking as they come. The talk slowly changes into a concerted growl. Then* GROUCHO *comes into sight. As he appears, the growling suddenly becomes a roar.* GROUCHO*, never pausing, turns and goes up the stairs again. Disappears. Then after a moment, he cautiously appears again. The discontent is still audible, but lower in tone)*

GROUCHO: There's a lot of static here tonight.

BELLBOY: We want our money.

BELLBOY: Yes, money.

GROUCHO: You want your money?

BELLBOY: We want to be paid.

GROUCHO: Oh! You mean you want my money. Is that fair? Do

I want your money? Suppose George Washington's soldiers had asked for money? Where would this country be today?

BELLBOY: But they did ask.

GROUCHO: And where is it? Where's Washington? Where's Pittsburg? What's the capital of Oklahoma? No, my friends, money is not everything. And everything's not money. *(To the audience)* For all I know that's an epigram.

SEVERAL BELLBOYS: We want our money.

GROUCHO: *(Quiets them with an upraised hand)* Well, I'll make you a promise, if you'll all stick with me and work hard, we'll forget all about money. We'll make a hotel out of this place yet. We'll put in elevators and subways. I'll put three blankets in all your rooms. That is, there'll be no cover charge. Think of the opportunities here in Florida. I came here with a shoe string, and now I've got three pair of buttoned shoes.

BELLBOY: We want our wages.

GROUCHO: Wages? Do you want to be wage slaves? Answer me that.

SEVERAL BELLBOYS: No.

GROUCHO: Well then, what is it that makes wage slaves? Wages. I want you to be free. Strike off your chains. Strike up the band. Strike three, you're out. Remember, there's nothing like liberty. That is, there's nothing like it in this country. Be free. Now and forever, one and indivisible, one for all, and all for me and me for you, and tea for two. Remember, I have only my best interests at heart, and I promise you, that it's only a question of a few years before some woman will swing the English Channel. I thank you.

(BELLBOYS exit cheering. Enter MRS. POTTER)

MRS. POTTER: How do you do, Mr. Schlemmer.

GROUCHO: You're just the woman I'm looking for, and now whether you like it or not, I'm going to tell you about Florida Real Estate. This is the first time it has been mentioned down here today.

MRS. POTTER: I'm sorry, Mr. Schlemmer, but I'm afraid—

GROUCHO: Do you know that property values have increased

1924 since one thousand percent? Do you know that this is the greatest development since Sophie Tucker? Do you know that Florida is the show spot of America, and that Cocoanut is the sore spot of Florida?

MRS. POTTER: But you told me about it yesterday.

GROUCHO: Yes, but I left out a couple of words. Look, tomorrow morning I'm going to hold an auction sale. Cocoanut Manor, the suburb terrible, I mean beautiful. Only forty-two hours from Times Square. Three weeks on the Clyde Line. Cocoanut Manor, glorifying the American sucker. Why it's the most exclusive residential district in Florida. Nobody lives there at all. And the climate. Ask me about the climate, I dare you.

MRS. POTTER: Very well. How is the—

GROUCHO: I'm glad you brought it up. Our motto was "Cocoanut Beach: no snow, no ice and no business." Do you know that Florida is the greatest state in the Union?

MRS. POTTER: Is it?

GROUCHO: It is until you read the California newspaper. Take its climate, no we took that. Take its fruits, take the alligator pear, take all of them and keep them. See if I care. Do you know how alligator pears are made?

MRS. POTTER: I haven't the slightest idea.

GROUCHO: That's because you've never been an alligator, and don't let it happen again. Do you know that it sometimes requires years to bring the pear and the alligator together? They don't like each other. The pear won't associate with the alligator unless he's got his bag with him. Do you know how many alligator pears are sent out of this state every year and told not to come back?

MRS. POTTER: I don't think I do.

GROUCHO: All they can get hold of. Florida feeds the nation, but nobody feeds me. And that's what I wanted to talk to you about. Can you let me have—

MRS. POTTER: Mr. Schlemmer.

GROUCHO: And another thing, take our beef growing. Oh, I don't mean anything personal, but here is—

MRS. POTTER: Mr. Schlemmer, will you let me say something please.

GROUCHO: I doubt it and a—

MRS. POTTER: I think that if I were to buy, I should prefer some place like Palm Beach.

GROUCHO: Palm Beach? The Coney Island of tomorrow. The Edgemere of yesterday. Do you know that the population of Cocoanut Beach has doubled in the past week?

MRS. POTTER: Doubled?

GROUCHO: Three horses were born.

MRS. POTTER: I'm sorry, but I'm afraid I must be going.

GROUCHO: Wait. Let me show you a sample of the sewer pipe we're going to lay. Here, look at it. Nobody can fool you on a sewer, can they? A woman like you. Look at it. Isn't it beautiful? This is an eight inch pipe. But of course, all property owners will be allowed to vote on the size of their pipe, and in case of a tie, it goes to the Supreme Court, and I can let you have a little inside information in advance. Chief Justice Taft likes this size sewer. Here, put it in your pocket. *(Starts to exit)*

MRS. POTTER: Here, what am I going to do with this? Take this, Mr. Schlemmer.

(Ad lib talk and both exit. After they exit BOB *takes his place behind desk. A* GUEST *enters, goes to desk)*

GUEST: 260 please.

BOB: *(Handing key)* Yes ma'am, here you are.

(As GUEST *turns away,* POLLY *enters, crosses to desk.* GUEST *exits)*

POLLY: Well, I was scolded.

BOB: *(Taking her hand across desk)* You were? What did she say?

POLLY: I'm supposed to remember that I'm a Potter.

BOB: But you can't be a Potter all your life. *(*BOYS *enter.* BOB *becomes the clerk again)* Why no, Miss Potter. I'm afraid there's not a thing for you.

POLLY: *(Taking the cue)* Oh! Well, thank you. *(Exits)*

FIRST MAN: Well, you did that pretty well.

BOB: What do you mean?

FIRST MAN: But not well enough to fool anybody.

BOB: I don't know what you're talking about.

FIRST MAN: We're not exactly blind, you know.

(Go into number—"LUCKY BOY." ALL *exit after number—the telephone on the desk rings.* GROUCHO *enters, goes to desk and answers phone)*

GROUCHO: Hello. Ice water in 340? There is? Oh, you want some? That's different. Have you got any ice? No ma'am. This is Cocoanut Beach. No snow and no ice. How are you fixed for coal and wood? You too. *(Hangs up receiver.* JAMISON *enters behind desk)*

JAMISON: Oh, Mr. Schlemmer, Mrs. Thompson wants to know if you'll reserve a table for dinner for her in a nice quiet corner.

GROUCHO: A quiet corner? Tell her if she finds a corner that isn't quiet, I'll give her a thousand dollars. *(*JAMISON *starts off)* Wait. If she finds it the offer don't go.

JAMISON: I think I know what's wrong with the hotel.

GROUCHO: I think I know too. You're fired.

JAMISON: Maybe the season hasn't started yet.

GROUCHO: Maybe the hotel isn't opened yet.

JAMISON: Why don't you sell the hotel?

GROUCHO: I can't find Frank Mumsy.

JAMISON: I think I hear the bus coming.

GROUCHO: The bus? *(Taps bell)* Front! Front! What's the matter, haven't we got any front? *(*TWO BELLHOPS *enter)* Go out and meet the bus.

JAMISON: I hope there's some people on it.

GROUCHO: I hope there's something on it.

JAMISON: *(Handing* GROUCHO *some telegrams)* Did you read these telegrams?

GROUCHO: *(Taking telegrams from* JAMISON*)* No. Did you? *(Opens telegram)* "Arrive this afternoon at four-fifteen. Kindly reserve two floors and three ceilings. If we like your property we will immediately take it over."

JAMISON: Who's it from?

GROUCHO: *(Reads)* No sig. No sig. *(Tears up telegram)* I won't have any Chinese in the house. *(Reads second telegram)* "If there's another hotel in Cocoanut Beach, cancel our reservations. P. S. Aunt Fanny had an eight pound boy. Can you come to the wedding?"

(There is a sound of excited voices off stage)

JAMISON: Here's another telegram.

GROUCHO: I don't want to see any more telegrams.

(Enter TWO GIRLS, TWO BELLBOYS, CHICO *and* HARPO. HARPO *starts upstairs after* GIRLS; *slides down banister)*

CHICO: Hello. We sent you a telegram. We make reservache.

GROUCHO: Oh. Welcome to Cocoanut Manor. *(Business)* What do you boys want? Garage and bath?

CHICO: We go together him.

GROUCHO: You go together him?

CHICO: Sure me.

GROUCHO: Would you mind coming in again and starting all over?

CHICO: We want room and no bath.

GROUCHO: Oh I see. You're just here for the Winter. Step this way. Now if you'll just sign the register. *(Offers pens. Business with* HARPO. GROUCHO *rings bell, gives* HARPO *a cigar)* Now how about signing the book?

CHICO: No, no. We no sign nothing without our lawyer. *(Business with mail)*

GROUCHO: It's too bad the afternoon mail isn't in. *(Enter* BELLBOY *with telegram)*

BELLBOY: Telegram for Mr. Schlemmer. *(*HARPO *takes telegram, tears it up.* BELLBOY *exits)*

GROUCHO: *(To* BELLBOY*)* Tell him there's no answer. *(To* CHICO*)* Now, don't you understand, you'll have to sign the book. If you don't register, you can't vote.

CHICO: You're crazy. Last year I no register and I vote six times.

(Phone bell rings—Business)

GROUCHO: Hello. I can't hear you. Would you mind coming down to the next floor? You don't like your rooms? I don't think much of them either. What's that? Your ceiling is leaking? All right,

I'll be right up. I'll bring you up some ceiling wax. *(Hangs up receiver —starts to exit)* You boys will pardon me. And don't forget, register.

CHICO: *(To* HARPO*)* Hey, don't forget, register.

(Business with register. CHICO *dictates a letter, anvil chorus and quote business with* BOY *and* GIRL. *Phone rings)*

Hello. No no, we got no rooms. All fill up—

(Business with BELLBOYS. *Enter* PENELOPE *and* HARVEY. HARPO *goes toward* PENELOPE. *Umbrella business)*

HARVEY: Come on, Penelope. Let's get away from this bum.

(Business. HARPO, CHICO *and* GROUCHO *exit)*

How'd they get in here? Why I'd just as lief—

PENELOPE: No, wait a minute. I've got an idea. They'll fit right in with the scheme.

HARVEY: What scheme?

PENELOPE: Now, don't get excited about this.

HARVEY: What is it?

PENELOPE: Did you ever notice that necklace of Mrs. Potter's?

HARVEY: Mrs. Potter's?

PENELOPE: Sh-h! *(Looks around)* Her room and mine are right next to each other. Her's is three-eighteen and mine is three-twenty. The door between is unlocked.

HARVEY: Well.

PENELOPE: Well.

HARVEY: What am I supposed to do?

PENELOPE: She keeps everything locked in the jewel case in her dresser. The key is in her bag. That's what you've got to get.

HARVEY: Oh, say.

PENELOPE: It's easy. Ask Polly and Mrs. Potter to have supper with you late tonight in the patio. Say about eleven o'clock. Order a table for four.

HARVEY: Four?

PENELOPE: Mrs. Potter will put her bag on the empty chair.

HARVEY: Yes.

PENELOPE: Then you get hold of it under the table cloth and take out the key. It's the only key in the bag.

HARVEY: But what if we're suspected?

PENELOPE: That's where those two come in.

HARVEY: What?

PENELOPE: Why shouldn't they be the suspected ones?

HARVEY: How do you mean?

PENELOPE: Didn't I tell you that my room is next to Mrs. Potter's?

HARVEY: Yes.

PENELOPE: Suppose I flirt with these two, and they happen to come up in my room. Then what? On the night the necklace disappeared, they were seen near the room—*(There is a sound of voices off stage.* PENELOPE *lays a warning on* HARVEY'S *arm)* Careful. Here's someone coming.

(HARVEY and PENELOPE stroll upstage, talking as they go. GROUCHO and GIRLS enter; ad lib talk)

PENELOPE: Oh, thank you, Mr. Yates. You're so thoughtful.

HARVEY: It's lovely here at this time of day. Don't you think?

PENELOPE: Oh yes. I really prefer it to California.

(Exit HARVEY and PENELOPE)

GROUCHO: No, no girls, you're wrong. And besides, Valentino is much taller than I.

GIRLS: Oh, Mr. Schlemmer, we think you're just marvelous.

GROUCHO: Well, it was always like that.

(Go into number "WHY AM I A HIT WITH THE LADIES?" At finish of number—CHICO and HARPO enter. Business. HENNESSY enters. Walks down stage to CHICO and HARPO. Business)

HENNESSY: Hey.

CHICO: Hello.

HENNESSY: Hello.

CHICO: Goodbye.

HENNESSY: I think you're the two birds I was sent over here to watch, and I'll tell you in a minute. Headquarters sent me some pictures. Let me see your face. *(Business)* Just as I thought. Willie the Wop and Silent Sam. *(Business)* What are you fighting for?

CHICO: Anything you say. Make us an offer.

HENNESSY: *(To HARPO)* What are you fighting for? *(Business)* What's your name? *(Horn business)* Now listen to me, you birds. I know who you are. I haven't got anything on you yet, but I'm going to keep watching. I've got your full record right here in my pocket and it's enough to send you up the minute you start anything. That's all I wanted to tell you. And don't forget it.

(Exits. Badge business. MAN *and* GIRL *enter. Quote business—*MAN *and* GIRL *exit.* CHICO *and* HARPO *exit.* POLLY *enters, goes to desk. Taps bell)*

POLLY: Oh, clerk.

BOB: *(Enters from behind desk)* Hello Polly. Where's your mother? Going out? *(Business)*

POLLY: Bob, she might come in.

BOB: Well, if she does, she's going to have plenty of cause for complaint. Because this time it's serious.

POLLY: Really?

BOB: I still want to know if you think you could live in Cocoanut Manor.

POLLY: I don't think so.

BOB: No?

POLLY: There aren't any houses.

BOB: Well, if I fix that?

POLLY: Oh, that would all depend.

*(Go into number—"A LITTLE BUNGALOW"—*POLLY *and* BOB*)*

END OF SCENE

ACT ONE

Scene Two

SCENE:—*Before the Palms.*

The Scene is in One before the curtain. The "BUNGALOW" refrain is played softly through the entire scene. CHICO *and* PENELOPE *enter first strolling slowly across stage.*

PENELOPE: *(Flirting vigorously)* Do you know you look like the Prince of Wales.

CHICO: Better.

PENELOPE: In fact you have a very distingué appearance.

CHICO: Him I no got.

PENELOPE: Tell me. What are you doing tonight?

CHICO: You got idea?

PENELOPE: Don't you dare come to room three hundred and twenty at eleven o'clock.

CHICO: All right. I'll be there at ten-thirty.

(Both exit. PENELOPE *and* HARPO *enter)*

PENELOPE: Did anyone ever tell you that you look like the Prince of Wales? *(Business)* Tell me, do you know who I am? *(Business)* Do you know where my room is? *(Business)* Well, I'll be there about eleven o'clock, but of course that would not interest you.

(Business. They exit. GROUCHO *and* MRS. POTTER *enter)*

GROUCHO: Did anybody ever tell you that you look like the Prince of Wales? Of course, I don't mean this Prince of Wales. One of the old Wales. And believe me when I say Wales, I mean Wales. I know a whale when I see one. That reminds me, did you say your room was three hundred and eighteen? No, you didn't. You know, I'm the proprietor of this hotel, and I have a pass key for every room in it.

MRS. POTTER: Pass key?

GROUCHO: That's Russian for pass. *(He motions to bench)* Won't you lie down. *(They sit)* Ah, if we could find a little bungalow. Of course, I know we could find one, but the people might not move out. But if there was a bungalow, and you and me, and maybe a couple of other fellows, what do you say? Does that strike you as being A.K.?

MRS. POTTER: How's that?

GROUCHO: I said if there was some B's and apples and maybe a little room—

MRS. POTTER: Little room?

GROUCHO: Not too little. Say, the Hippodrome, and you would be in the middle of it, and I'd be on the outside trying to get in, or maybe I'd be inside trying to get out; or maybe I'd be inside out. I don't know, maybe I wouldn't be there at all. I'll tell you what I'll do, if I don't come home I'll call you up.

MRS. POTTER: I don't think I understand.

GROUCHO: What I mean was your eyes. They shine like the pants of a blue serge suit. And then we'd have some birds and sparrows and—are you sure your husband's dead?

MRS. POTTER: Quite sure.

GROUCHO: I feel better. I guess he does too. What I was going to say was, here I am and you're going to be here all Winter, and I'm stuck with the hotel anyhow. Why don't you grab me until you could do better?

MRS. POTTER: My dear Mr. Schlemmer, I would never get married before my daughter.

GROUCHO: You did once. Don't forget, I love you. I love. I'm mad around you. *(Business)* Oh, I'm not myself tonight. I don't know who I am. God pity the poor sailors at sea on a night like this. But don't be mad. I love you anyhow, in spite of yourself.

MRS. POTTER: I don't think you'd love me if I were poor.

GROUCHO: I might, but I'd keep my mouth shut.

MRS. POTTER: Really, I'm afraid I must be going. *(Starts to exit)*

GROUCHO: Don't go away and leave me here alone. You stay here and I'll go away.

MRS. POTTER: I don't know what to say.

GROUCHO: Well say that you'll be truly mine, or truly yours, or yours truly, and that tonight when the moon is sneaking around the clouds, I'll be sneaking around you. I'll meet you tonight by the bungalow, under the moon. You and the moon. I hope I can tell you apart. You wear a red necktie so I'll know you. I'll meet you tonight by the bungalow under the moon.

MRS. POTTER: But suppose the moon is not out.

GROUCHO: Then I'll meet you under the bungalow.

(Into reprise of "BUNGALOW" number. He sings. They exit)

End of Scene

ACT ONE

Scene Three

SCENE:— *Two Rooms In The Hotel.*

No. 318 and 320 with connecting door. Room 320 at the left is PENEL-OPE'S. It has a door at the rear, leading into the hall. It has a French-window at the Left wall and a desk against the Right wall with a telephone. There are a bed, chair, and various things that go with bedrooms. Room 318 which is MRS. POTTER'S is approximately the same room reversed. Instead of a window, there is a wardrobe closet in the Right wall. Her dresser stands against the Center wall near the bed. There is also a table on which is a telephone.

AT RISE:—PENELOPE enters her room, looks about suspiciously, goes to connecting door, opens it, starts across MRS. POTTER'S room toward the dresser in which is a jewel case. As PENELOPE enters MRS. POTTER'S room, HARPO enters PENELOPE'S room and immediately goes under the bed. PENELOPE hears a noise and becomes frightened and immediately goes back into her own room and closes the connecting door. She then goes to the telephone.

PENELOPE: Hello. Ice water, please. *(Hangs up receiver just as a knock comes on her door. She opens it quickly. It is HARVEY. He comes in and closes the door)* Well.

HARVEY: Here's the key.

PENELOPE: Good work. Now look here, we can't take any chances on this job.

HARVEY: How do you mean?

PENELOPE: There's sure to be a fuss when she misses the necklace.

HARVEY: Well . . .

PENELOPE: Well. We don't want it found on us, do we?

HARVEY: I should say not.

PENELOPE: Then we've got to play safe and hide it somewhere.

HARVEY: Hide it?

PENELOPE: Just for a few days.

HARVEY: But where?

PENELOPE: Anywhere, except in here.

HARVEY: I know. I know just the place. There's a hollow tree stump about a mile from here. Will that do?

PENELOPE: Fine. How do I get there.

HARVEY: It's Cocoanut Manor. You've been out there.

PENELOPE: Well, I'm not sure.

HARVEY: (Drawing diagram on paper) Here, I'll show you. You go right out Cocoanut Road, then there's Augustine Road, but instead you take Grenada Road, then suddenly you come to a clearing with a fringe of trees around it. That's Cocoanut Manor, where the stump is. That's where you put the jewels. It's lot number twenty-six. You can't miss it. It's about twenty feet from the edge of the clearing. There it is. (He hands her the diagram) You take it out there, see. I've got to go back downstairs, or Mrs. Potter will be suspicious.

PENELOPE: All right.

HARVEY: And for Heaven sake, be careful.

(Exits. PENELOPE crumples up diagram and drops it into waste basket at foot of bed. She starts towards MRS. POTTER's room again and as she does, HARPO crawls from under bed, takes paper out of waste basket and exits through window. As PENELOPE opens connecting door leading to MRS. POTTER's room, GROUCHO opens MRS. POTTER's door from hallway. PENELOPE, seeing that someone is entering MRS. POTTER's room, closes the connecting door. Just then CHICO enters PENELOPE's room and GROUCHO enters MRS. POTTER's room. In her own room PENELOPE is facing CHICO)

CHICO: You know me? Prince of Wales?

PENELOPE: (Nervously) Yes, yes, of course.

(At that second, GROUCHO *suddenly throws open the connecting door and enters* PENELOPE'S *room.* CHICO, *as the door starts to open, escapes into the hall. At the same instant* HARPO *enters* MRS. POTTER'S *room from the hall. This leaves* HARPO *in* MRS. POTTER'S *room and* GROUCHO *and* PENELOPE *in the latter's room.)*

I beg your pardon, Mr. Schlemmer?

GROUCHO: Madam, rooms occupied by two people—five dollars extra.

(There is a noise in MRS. POTTER'S *room)*

PENELOPE: Who's in there?

GROUCHO: I am.

*(*HARPO *is whistling in* MRS. POTTER'S *room)*

That isn't me. I can't whistle.

(There is a knock on PENELOPE'S *door.* HARPO *goes into the hall.* GROUCHO *into* MRS. POTTER'S *room and* CHICO *into* PENELOPE'S *room)*

CHICO: Has he gone?

PENELOPE: Who?

CHICO: Anybody.

(There is a knock on PENELOPE'S *door.* GROUCHO *into the hall,* CHICO *into* MRS. POTTER'S *room and* HARPO *enters* PENELOPE'S *room.* PENELOPE *is startled and whirls around facing* HARPO*)*

PENELOPE: Oh, how you've frightened me.

(There is a knock on the connecting door. This drives HARPO *into the hall.* CHICO *into* PENELOPE'S *room and* GROUCHO *into* MRS. POTTER'S *room)*

GROUCHO: This hotel not only has running water, but running guests.

CHICO: I'm back again, the Prince of Wales.

(GROUCHO knocks on PENELOPE'S door from MRS. POTTER'S room)

PENELOPE: Who is it?
GROUCHO: It's me, the King of England.
CHICO: My father.

(CHICO exits into hall. GROUCHO into PENELOPE'S room and HARPO into MRS. POTTER'S room. They reverse again. HARPO into the hall, GROUCHO into MRS. POTTER'S room and CHICO into PENELOPE'S room)

GROUCHO: It's a grand slam.
CHICO: I come back for my horse.

(CHICO goes under PENELOPE'S bed, HARPO enters PENELOPE'S room; he knocks on her door from the inside. PENELOPE speaks)

PENELOPE: Come in.

(HARPO exits into the hall. GROUCHO enters PENELOPE'S room. MRS. POTTER enters her own room)

GROUCHO: This is like working for A. H. Woods.

(There is a knock on PENELOPE'S door. GROUCHO joins CHICO under the bed. PENELOPE opens door. EDDIE enters with ice water. He puts it on table and exits)

PENELOPE: Thank you.
GROUCHO: *(From under the bed)* Thank you. Why don't you give him a dime?

(CHICO exits through window. There is a knock on MRS. POTTER'S door)

MRS. POTTER: Come in.

(HARPO enters MRS. POTTER'S room with ice-water. He walks directly to the bed)

No, no, put it down, there.

(HARPO puts water on dresser)

Now go.

(HARPO exits. He immediately knocks on door again)

Come in.

(He opens door and takes water from dresser and exits. He immediately goes from MRS. POTTER'S room to PENELOPE'S room, while GROUCHO who has emerged from under PENELOPE'S bed goes into MRS. POTTER'S room)

Mr. Schlemmer, please leave my room.

(GROUCHO opens and slams door, but instead of going out, he goes into MRS. POTTER'S closet)

Thank goodness, he's gone.

(There is a knock on MRS. POTTER'S door)

Come in.

(HENNESSY enters)

Who are you?

HENNESSY: Oh, that's all right. *(He looks all over the room but not in the closet)* Well, I guess there's nobody in here.

GROUCHO: *(From behind closet door)* You don't know where to look.

HENNESSY: *(To MRS. POTTER, thinking it was she who answered him)* What's that you said?

MRS. POTTER: Why I—

(During the above dialogue CHICO and HARPO have entered PENELOPE'S room and have gone under PENELOPE'S bed. HENNESSY knocks on PENELOPE'S door)

PENELOPE: What is it?

(HENNESSY enters PENELOPE'S room. GROUCHO comes out from closet in MRS. POTTER'S room and GROUCHO ducks under the bed)

MRS. POTTER: This is awful. When you've finished, let me know.

(MRS. POTTER exits)

GROUCHO: Send up my nightgown.

(HENNESSY enters PENELOPE'S room, looks around the room and exits into the hall. Simultaneously GROUCHO enters PENELOPE'S room)

PENELOPE: What is it you want?
GROUCHO: It's all right, I know where to go.

(GROUCHO ducks under bed. HENNESSY re-enters PENELOPE'S room and PENELOPE enters MRS. POTTER'S room)

HENNESSY: Let me see, three-eighteen—three-twenty—
CHICO: Three-thirty.
GROUCHO: Three-forty.
HENNESSY: *(Thoughtfully)* Three-twenty? Oh yes.

(HENNESSY goes to door and stands in doorway. GROUCHO and CHICO come out from under bed and crawl through HENNESSY'S legs out into the hall. HENNESSY turns into the room again. It is during the above business that PENELOPE, who is in MRS. POTTER'S room, opens the jewel case in the dresser, takes out a necklace and secrets it in the bosom of her dress)

HENNESSY: Believe me, there's nobody putting anything over on me.

(He enters MRS. POTTER'S room and PENELOPE exits into the hall. HENNESSY looks around MRS. POTTER'S room and then exits into the hall. At the same time PENELOPE enters her own room through the hall door)

PENELOPE: Alone at last.

(HARPO sticks his head through center of bed)

BLACKOUT

END OF SCENE

ACT ONE

Scene Four

SCENE: *Before the Palms*

Scene opens with "FLORIDA" number. At finish, GROUCHO *and* CHICO *enter.*

GROUCHO: Now about this red-headed fellow. I can't have him running around the lobby. You'll have to put him in the cellar and check out.

CHICO: That's all right, I'll keep him up in the room.

GROUCHO: Well, if you do you'll have to get a box for him. Who is he?

CHICO: He's my partner. He no speak.

GROUCHO: He isn't Coolidge, is he? Now about these lots you were speaking of. I can let you have three lots for fifteen thousand dollars that cost me almost nine.

CHICO: No, no, we don't want to buy anything. We have no money.

GROUCHO: No money? How do you expect to pay for your room?

CHICO: Well, that's your lookout.

GROUCHO: Oh, I see. You're just an idle roomer.

CHICO: You see, we come here to make money.

GROUCHO: Oh, you want to make money? That's a new idea.

CHICO: Yes. We come here to make money. We hear you got big boom here, so we come too. We coupla big booms.

GROUCHO: Well, I think I can show you how to make some money. Tomorrow morning, I'm holding an auction sale at Cocoanut Manor. You know what an auction is?

CHICO: Sure. I come to this country on Atlantic Auction.

GROUCHO: I'm sorry the matter ever came up. Now as I said before, I'm holding an auction at Cocoanut Manor, and I want you to mingle among the crowds and stimulate the bidding. If they bid two hundred, you say three. If they say three, you say four. If nobody says anything, you start it.

CHICO: How will I know if nobody says anything.

GROUCHO: Well maybe they'll tell you. Now, if you're successful in selling these lots, I'll see that you get a good commission.

CHICO: Well, that's all right, but how about some money.

GROUCHO: Well, that's something else again. Now here's a blueprint of Cocoanut Manor. Of course, you know what a blueprint is.

CHICO: Sure, I had him for dinner last night. Blueprint oysters.

GROUCHO: Well, I'll never say that again. You know what a lot is?

CHICO: Sure. When you got a whole lot, too much.

GROUCHO: Well this conversation is a lot. Now here's a map and diagram of the whole Cocoanut section. Here's Cocoanut Manor and over here is Cocoanut Heights. That's the swamp. Down here is Cocoanut Junction.

CHICO: Where you got Cocoanut Custard?

GROUCHO: That's in the kitchen. Now right over here's the road leading out of Cocoanut Manor. That's the road I wish you were on, and over here is the river front. All along there, those are levies.

CHICO: That's the Jewish Neighborhood.

GROUCHO: Now here are lots fifteen, sixteen and seventeen. Right over there is the Chocolate Factory. Now if you don't like the smell from the Chocolate Factory, you can move down here, where the Fertilizer Works are. That is, providing the fertilizing people do not object.

CHICO: What's that out there?

GROUCHO: That's the cemetery. If you'll walk over here, I'll show it to you. I have a waiting list of fifty people, but I like you and I'm going to try to slip you in ahead of all of them.

(Both exit)

END OF SCENE

ACT ONE

Scene Five

SCENE: *Cocoanut Manor*

Scene opens with number—"THE MONKEY-DOODLE-DOO." At finish of number business of HARPO *finding the necklace.* POLLY *and* BOB *enter.* HARPO *exits.*

BOB: Here it is. This is the place. Remember?
POLLY: Why yes.
BOB: There's the lots we were looking at yesterday. The one with the trees on it. That's where we're going to live.
POLLY: But, Bob, dear, can you afford it?
BOB: Well, I've a little bit saved. I can make a first payment anyhow.

(Noise off stage)

Here they come.
GROUCHO: *(To* CHICO*)* Now don't forget, bid em up. *(To the* CROWD*)* All ye suckers, right this way. This way for the big auction.

*(*GIRLS *and* BOYS *enter and sing a chorus of "FLORIDA")*

JAMISON: That's Florida folks. Sunshine all the time.
GROUCHO: Let's hurry up for the auction before it starts raining. You are now in Cocoanut Manor. One of the finest cities in Florida.

Of course, we still need a few finishing touches, but who doesn't. This is the heart of the residential district. Every lot is a stone's throw from the station. The only reason we haven't got any station is because we haven't got any stones. Eight hundred beautiful residences will be built right here. They are as good as up. Better. You can have any kind of house you want to. You can even get stucco. Oh, how you can get stucco. Now is the time to buy while the new boom is on. Remember a new boom sweeps clean, and don't forget the guarantee. If these lots don't double themselves in a year, I don't know what you can do about it. Now then, take that beautiful lot behind you, lot number twenty, right at the corner of De Sota Avenue. Of course, you all know who De Sota was? He discovered a body of water; you all heard of the water that they've named after him: De Sota water. This lot has a twenty foot frontage, a fourteen foot backage and a nice garbage. Now then, what am I offered for lot number twenty. Anything at all, to start it. *(He starts looking for* HARPO*)* Anything at all? Ah—

CHICO: Two hundred dollars.

GROUCHO: Two hundred dollars. Do I hear three?

CHICO: Three hundred dollars.

GROUCHO: Well, the auction is almost over. I'm bid three hundred dollars. Do I hear four?

CHICO: Four hundred dollars.

GROUCHO: Don't let the folks on this side do all the bidding. Who'll say five?

CHICO: Five hundred dollars.

GROUCHO: Five hundred. Do I hear six?

CHICO: Six hundred dollars.

GROUCHO: Sold for six hundred dollars. *(To* JAMISON*)* Wrap up that lot for the gentleman and put some poison ivy on it. Now, folks, we'll take lot number twenty-one. Right over there, where that cocoanut tree is. What am I offered for lot number twenty-one?

CHICO: Two hundred dollars.

GROUCHO: Two hundred dollars? Why there's over two hundred dollars worth of milk in those cocoanuts, and what milk. Milk from contented cowcoanuts. Two hundred dollars. Who'll say three?

GIRL: Three hundred.

CHICO: Four hundred dollars.

JUDGE: Five hundred.

CHICO: Six hundred, seven hundred, eight hundred. What the hell I care.

GROUCHO: What the hell you care? But how about me? Sold for eight hundred dollars. I hope all your teeth have cavities. Now folks, we'll take lot number twenty-two. This is one of the finest lots in America. If this lot was at Forty-second Street and Broadway, it would bring twice as much money. Who'll start the bidding on lot number twenty-one.

HARVEY: One hundred dollars.

CHICO: Two hundred.

GROUCHO: Sold for a hundred dollars. Now then, we'll take lot number twenty-three. What am I offered for lot number twenty-three?

CHICO: Two hundred dollars.

GROUCHO: What are you going to do with all these lots? Play lottos? I'm offered two hundred dollars for lot number twenty-three. Why this lot is worth twice as much as any of the others.

CHICO: Four hundred dollars.

GROUCHO: Four hundred dollars. Do I hear five?

BOY: Five hundred.

GROUCHO: Sold to you for five hundred—

CHICO: Six hundred dollars.

GROUCHO: Six hundred dollars. Will anybody say seven?

JUDGE: Seven hundred.

GROUCHO: Sold to you for seven hundred—

CHICO: Eight hundred dollars.

GROUCHO: Eight hundred dollars. Do I hear nine? Will the gentleman who said seven, say nine? Will the gentleman who said seven, say seven again? Will he say six?

CHICO: He say six, I say seven.

GROUCHO: Will he say five?

CHICO: He say five, I say six. He say eight, I say nine. He say ten, I say eleven. I no stop for nothing. I bid 'em up. I go higher, higher, higher.

GROUCHO: You'll go higher when I get a hold of you. Sold for eight hundred dollars. I'll see you later. *(Whispering)* What am I offered for lot number—*(*CHICO *looks around and* GROUCHO *stops talking* *until* CHICO *turns away again)* What am I offered for lot number twenty-four?

BOY: Fifty dollars.

GROUCHO: Fifty? Sold to you for fifty dollars.

CHICO: Two hundred dollars.

GROUCHO: Now folks, we'll take lot number twenty-five. Right over there where you're standing. Say, would you people mind taking your feet off of that lot. You're getting it all dirty. Now here is a lot, I know it doesn't look very big on top, but it's yours as far down as you want to go. Now then, what am I offered for lot number twenty-five? Anything at all to start it. Anything at all. Where did Joseph P. Day go to? What am I offered for lot number twenty-five? What am I offered for lot number twenty-five and a set of O'Henry? What am I offered for the O'Henry alone? What am I offered for anything? Does anybody want to buy a set of dishes? I'll wrestle anybody in the crowd for five bucks. *(Enter* HARPO*)* Anybody but Red Grange. Well, folks, if there's not going to be any bidding, we might as well quit. But before I quit, I'm going to try one more lot: lot number twenty-six. Right over there, where the stump of that tree is. What am I offered for lot number twenty-six?

BOB: Two hundred dollars.

GROUCHO: Two hundred dollars. Who'll say three?

HARVEY: Four hundred dollars.

GROUCHO: Four hundred dollars. There's a gentleman with vision. Who'll say five hundred?

BOB: Five hundred.

GROUCHO: Five hundred dollars. There's a gentleman with double vision. Will anybody say six?

HARVEY: Eight hundred dollars.

GROUCHO: Eight hundred dollars. There's a gentleman with stigmatism.

BOB: One thousand dollars.

GROUCHO: A thousand dollars. Will anybody say eleven hundred?

HARVEY: Eleven hundred dollars.

GROUCHO: Eleven hundred dollars. Do I hear twelve.

BOB: Twelve hundred dollars.

GROUCHO: Twelve hundred dollars. Who'll say thirteen?

(HARVEY starts to say thirteen hundred and HARPO hits him with black jack)

Do I hear thirteen hundred? Twelve hundred once, twelve hundred twice, sold for twelve hundred dollars.

POLLY: Bob, you've got it.

HARVEY: What? What happened? *(To HARPO)* You did that. He hit me. I protest against that. I wasn't allowed to bid.

GROUCHO: Hello. Where have you been?

HARVEY: This—This person—That wasn't fair, I tell you. I wasn't—

(Enter MRS. POTTER terrifically agitated)

MRS. POTTER: Mr. Schlemmer, Mr. Schlemmer.

(Everything stops. All give attention)

GROUCHO: Don't worry, there are still some lots left.

MRS. POTTER: I've been robbed. My necklace; in your hotel. My diamond necklace. It's worth a hundred thousand dollars.

GROUCHO: A hundred thousand dollars?

MRS. POTTER: I'll give a thousand dollars reward for its return.

GROUCHO: Ladies and gentlemen, Mrs. Potter has lost a diamond necklace, worth a hundred thousand dollars and she offers a thousand dollars reward for its return.

CHICO: Two thousand.

HENNESSY: *(Pushing to the front)* Here. Let me handle this.

MRS. POTTER: Oh dear. *(HARPO comes to her, taps her on the shoulder; winks and motions for her to follow him)* What is it? *(Business)* What's the matter?

GROUCHO: He wants to know if you object if he hangs himself.

(HARPO is persistent, finally clears a path to the hollow stump, reaches down and brings out a snake. He reaches down again and triumphantly brings up the necklace. Naturally the entire procedure brings reactions from PENELOPE and HARVEY, but they dare not say anything)

MRS. POTTER: *(As the necklace appears)* Why yes, that's it. That's it. *(She kisses* HARPO *on the cheek)* Oh, I'm so happy. I must give you another kiss.

*(*HARPO *refuses to let her kiss him again)*

GROUCHO: No wonder the lot brought twelve hundred dollars.

HENNESSY: So that's it, eh? I saw you in that room last night. Grabbing off stuff for the reward, eh? Now then you, come clean. How'd you know the necklace was in there?

HARVEY: Officer, may I make a suggestion?

HENNESSY: What is it?

HARVEY: Isn't it possible that the gentleman who just bought this lot might know something about it? Why was he so anxious to buy it?

HENNESSY: How about it, you? Why did you buy this lot?

BOB: None of your business.

MRS. POTTER: He's a desperate character.

POLLY: Mother, he isn't.

HENNESSY: Whenever a young fellow shuts up and won't say anything, I've noticed it's generally on account of a woman. Now, who is she?

BOB: I told you before, it's none of your business. I won't say a word.

*(*HARVEY *whispers a few words to* PENELOPE*)*

HENNESSY: You won't say anything. *(Indicating* HARPO*)* This guy is letting on to be a dummy and—*(Indicates* CHICO*)*—this bird you can't understand when he does talk. Is there anybody here who will talk?

GROUCHO: I'll say a few words about Cocoanut Manor.

HENNESSY: *(to* BOB*)* Well, if you won't tell me about it, you'll have to tell somebody else.

BOB: Now just a minute—

*(*PENELOPE *approaches* HENNESSY*)*

PENELOPE: No, no. Please don't take him away. Please don't.

(Naturally everyone is surprised. Principally BOB. *Addressing herself to* BOB)

I didn't want you to steal it, Bob. I'd no idea you'd do it. I feel terrible.

BOB: What are you talking about?

POLLY: Bob. What does she mean?

MRS. POTTER: Polly.

HENNESSY: Oh, so that's it?

PENELOPE: Oh, it's all my fault. I'd no idea he'd think I meant it. Bob, I didn't mean you to do it, really. I only meant that if you ever could give me one like it—

BOB: Wait a minute. Are you accusing me of taking Mrs. Potter's necklace?

PENELOPE: I'm taking all the blame myself. I was just joking and you—you took me seriously. When you told me last night that you'd taken it, I felt—

BOB: Told you I've taken what? Why, Polly, she's out of her mind.

MRS. POTTER: It sounds quite plausible to me.

PENELOPE: He didn't know what he was doing. I begged him to put it back—

BOB: I won't stand for any more of this. The whole thing's a plant. *(Addressing all the people)* Why do you people seriously believe for one second that—Oh, I don't care what you think. Any of you. *(To* POLLY) Polly, you know it's a lie, don't you?

PENELOPE: It was only a harmless flirtation, and then he—he lost his head.

BOB: *(To* POLLY) Don't you know it's a lie?

POLLY: Of course I do. You don't think I'd believe a story like that, do you?

MRS. POTTER: Polly.

POLLY: But I don't believe it, mother.

MRS. POTTER: Mr. Adams, I must ask you never to speak to my daughter again.

BOB: But Mrs. Potter—

HENNESSY: Come on young fellow.

(BOB hesitates for a second, turns to go)

POLLY: *(Following)* I'm going with you.

MRS. POTTER: Polly, come here.

BOB: *(As* POLLY *hesitates)* Yes. You stay here, Polly. It's only for a little while. The whole thing is ridiculous.

HENNESSY: All ready.

BOB: All right. *(Starts to go)*

PENELOPE: *(Taking his arm)* I'm terribly sorry, Bob.

BOB: *(Shaking her off)* Oh, don't keep it up any longer. *(To* HENNESSY*)* I'm ready.

HENNESSY: I'll have a confession out of him, in half an hour.

*(*HENNESSY *and* BOB *exit)*

POLLY: Bob.

(She starts after BOB, *but* MRS. POTTER *takes her arm and stops her.* POLLY *covers her face and turns upstage)*

GROUCHO: Now, then, we'll take lot number twenty-seven.

MRS. POTTER: *(To* POLLY*)* There is only one way to wipe out this disgrace. We must make people forget that you ever knew this young man.

POLLY: Mother, what are you saying?

MRS. POTTER: You see what's come of your way. Now I'm going to have mine. Mr. Yates.

HARVEY: Yes, Mrs. Potter.

MRS. POTTER: My daughter has reconsidered her answer to you.

POLLY: Mother.

MRS. POTTER: Your engagement will be announced tonight.

HARVEY: I'm so happy, Polly.

MRS. POTTER: I shall give a dinner at the hotel.

GROUCHO: Do you want the sixty or the seventy-five cent dinner?

MRS. POTTER: *(To* GROUCHO*)* You may invite everyone.

GROUCHO: Don't worry, I will.

MRS. POTTER: In honor of the engagement of my daughter to Mr. Harvey Yates.

(CHORUS goes into reprise of "LUCKY BOY" sung to HARVEY. This carries all off except POLLY. HARVEY returns at the end of the chorus)

HARVEY: Coming, Polly?
POLLY: In a minute. Please go ahead.
HARVEY: Why, what's the matter?
POLLY: Nothing. Please go on ahead.
HARVEY: All right. I'll wait for you.

(HARVEY exits. POLLY looks at lot number twenty-six—goes into a reprise of "BUNGALOW." HARPO enters as the chorus is still being softly played. He crosses to POLLY, puts an arm around her to comfort her. Brings her closer, finally drops her head onto his shoulder. As the ORCHESTRA starts the final phrase of the chorus, the curtain starts slowly down. HARPO looks toward the audience and winks)

THE CURTAIN FALLS

ACT TWO

Scene 1

SCENE: *The Lounge of the Hotel*

Scene opens with number—"FIVE O'CLOCK TEA"—sung by PENELOPE *and* COMPANY. *After Number,* BELLBOY *starts to cross.* GROUCHO *enters.*

GROUCHO: Boy, it's been reported to me that there's a poker game going on in room four-twenty. You go up there and knock on the door and see if you can get me a seat.

*(*BELLBOY *exits. Enter* POLLY *and* CHICO. POLLY *is apparently absorbed in thought and is about to start to cry.* CHICO *is consoling her)*

CHICO: That's all right, don't cry. Don't worry, we get boy out of jail.
POLLY: *(To* GROUCHO*)* Mr. Schlemmer, you know that Bob didn't steal that necklace.
GROUCHO: Don't worry, everything will turn out all wrong.
POLLY: I've just been down to the jail. They're holding Bob at two thousand dollars bail.
GROUCHO: Congratulations. That's a swell bail for a young fellow his age.
POLLY: *(To* CHICO*)* Could you lend me two thousand dollars?
CHICO: Goodbye. *(Starts off)*
POLLY: Mr. Schlemmer, will you lend me two thousand dollars?
GROUCHO: I haven't even got a raccoon coat.
POLLY: Oh, but to think of him being in jail.
GROUCHO: Don't worry. Stone walls do not a Jackson make.
POLLY: Oh, I've just got to find someone to help me. I've got to get two thousand dollars. *(Starts crying and exits)*
CHICO: We got to get boy out of jail. Where we get two thousand dollars?

(Enter HARPO*)*

GROUCHO: That's the question. Where are we going to get two thousand dollars. I'll tell you, if you boys will each put up a thousand, I'll put up the balance.

CHICO: *(To* HARPO*)* You get two thousand, you give me one thousand.

GROUCHO: Then we'd have three thousand. That's too much. Now the question is, how are we going to get rid of the extra thousand? I knew we'd have trouble with this thing.

CHICO: Maybe we could raise the bail to three thousand dollars.

GROUCHO: I doubt it. They are very particular. *(To* HARPO*)* Have you got two thousand dollars? *(Business)* That must be a Scotch tweed he's got on. *(To* CHICO*)* Have you got anything?

CHICO: I got sixty cents.

GROUCHO: Sixty cents. That still leaves us shy. Each one has got to raise his quota.

CHICO: I got a quota.

GROUCHO: We've got to get two thousand dollars. I could float a loan but I can't float alone.

(Enter MRS. POTTER*)*

MRS. POTTER: Oh, there you are. I've been looking all over for you. Do you know what I'm going to do? Do you, you clever man? I have a big surprise for you. You darling. Isn't he cute. Just a little bear. I'm going to give you a thousand dollars for finding my necklace.

CHICO: *(To* HARPO*)* Two thousand.

GROUCHO: *(To* HARPO*)* Match her. Double or nothing.

MRS. POTTER: *(Offering the check)* Here you are. You won't take it? *(Business)* You mean you won't take anything? *(Business)* Then what will you take? *(Business)* Two dollars?

CHICO: He means two thousand.

GROUCHO: Two million.

MRS. POTTER: Two thousand? But I only promised a thousand.

GROUCHO: Only a thousand dollars, for finding a beautiful necklace like that? Why that's chicken feed. A poultry thousand dollars.

CHICO: He never finds necklaces for less than two thousand dollars.

GROUCHO: That's the standard price all over.

MRS. POTTER: I'm sorry but that was the offer. I've already written the check. Or would you prefer cash?

CHICO: Oh, you got both?

GROUCHO: You got two kinds of money?

(Business. HARPO steals bag)

MRS. POTTER: Please. Please. My bag, my bag. I've lost my bag. You saw it, the bag, I just had it on my wrist. I just had it a moment ago.

GROUCHO: You lost your bag?

CHICO: Lost bag?

(They all begin searching for bag. A movement from HARPO tips them off)

GROUCHO: Why don't you offer a reward for it? That's how you got your necklace.

MRS. POTTER: I'm afraid I'll have to. It's a very valuable bag. I'll give five hundred dollars for its return.

CHICO: You couldn't make it a thousand?

MRS. POTTER: I don't think so.

CHICO: You get it back much quicker.

MRS. POTTER: I think five hundred is quite enough.

GROUCHO: It is, but you won't get it for five hundred.

(Business—HARPO whistles—then produces the bag from his sleeve)

MRS. POTTER: Why yes, that's it. Thank you so much. Now how could I have dropped it in there.

GROUCHO: You can do it every time.

CHICO: Now you owe him fifteen hundred.

MRS. POTTER: Yes, and I'm going to give it to him. *(Opens bag)* Here's a thousand dollars for finding the necklace and five hundred for finding the bag. Oh, you've been so wonderful that I must give you another great big kiss.

GROUCHO: That'll be five hundred war tax.

MRS. POTTER: Thank you ever so much. You've been absolutely

marvelous. I want to compliment you on your honesty and always remember boys, honesty is the best policy. *(Exits)*

GROUCHO: No—twenty years endowment. Say, we were suckers to let her get away with that. We'll never get another customer like that.

CHICO: Now we got fifteen hundred.

(HARPO whistles. GROUCHO and CHICO walk toward him. He hands CHICO check, then the five hundred dollars and then produces MRS. POTTER'S bag again)

He found it again.

(They all exit. Into number—"THEY'RE BLAMING THE CHARLES-TON." After "CHARLESTON" number stage is clear and PENELOPE enters. She is rather flustered—peers off stage. A BELLBOY enters)

PENELOPE: Oh, boy?

BOY: Yes, Miss Martyn.

PENELOPE: Will you ask Mr. Yates to step in here. He's right outside.

(With a nod the BELLBOY exits. PENELOPE is left alone for another nervous moment, then HARVEY enters)

HARVEY: Did you want to see me?

PENELOPE: I just happen to remember something. *(She comes closer to him)* What ever became of that diagram that you drew up in my room.

HARVEY: What diagram?

PENELOPE: Showing how to get to that tree stump. Remember? It had written on it "Hollow Stump." "Jewels."

HARVEY: Well.

PENELOPE: Well. It might be a nasty bit of evidence if it happened to be found.

HARVEY: It hasn't been found.

PENELOPE: How do we know that?

HARVEY: What?

PENELOPE: How did that dummy know the necklace was in the tree? *(HARVEY looks at her)* Did it ever occur to you that he might have picked up that diagram?

HARVEY: By jove. You're right. I never thought of that. I—

PENELOPE: And suppose he still has it and it happens to get into the wrong hands?

HARVEY: *(Nervously)* That's all right. They couldn't prove I wrote it.

PENELOPE: How do you know they couldn't? What we've got to do—

(HARVEY waves her to silence as he sees HARPO entering)

HARVEY: *(Uneasily)* Oh, hello there. *(Business)*

PENELOPE: *(Sweetly)* We—we haven't been seeing anything of you lately.

HARVEY: Why no.

(HARPO perks up—begins to enjoy his popularity)

PENELOPE: Are you—are you feeling all right? *(Business)* Oh, you're not.

PENELOPE: *(Business)* Oh, you are. Well that's fine.

HARVEY: By the way, we wanted to ask you something. Did you happen to see a paper anywhere around the hotel? You know what I mean.

(HARPO nods yes)

PENELOPE: You did see it?

(HARPO nods yes)

HARVEY: Did you pick it up?

(HARPO nods yes)

Oh, that's fine.

(HARPO starts to leave. PENELOPE and HARVEY start after him)

No, no, wait a minute. Now a—this paper—have you got it with you?

(HARPO nods yes)

PENELOPE: Will you give it to us?

(HARPO nods no)

HARVEY: Well, will you sell it to us?

(HARPO nods yes)

Now, supposing I were to give you a hundred dollars—would you give it to us?

(HARPO nods yes)

All right, here is the hundred.

(Business—HARVEY and PENELOPE exit. Enter BOB and GROUCHO. Business)

GROUCHO: *(To HARPO)* Say I wish you'd decide where you're hurt. *(Business)* Well here he is. I got him out of jail for nineteen hundred. They had a sale.

BOB: I'm ever so much obliged to you, Mr. Schlemmer. *(To HARPO)* And to you too. *(To GROUCHO)* It was nice of you to bail me out.

GROUCHO: That's all right. I expect you to do the same for me some day. But a jail is no place for a young fellow. There is no advancement. The highest you could ever get to be is Warden.

BOB: Mr. Schlemmer, you know that story of Penelope's was all a lie, don't you?

GROUCHO: I wouldn't let that worry me. Remember you're here today and there tomorrow.

BOB: But Mr. Schlemmer, I've got to prove it was a lie and how am I going to do it?

(HARPO whistles to attract attention)

What is it?

(HARPO produces a crumpled piece of paper—BOB takes it and spreads it out —GROUCHO looks over his shoulder)

GROUCHO: *(Reading it)* Wanted for murder—Silent Sam.

(HARPO quickly grabs the paper—puts it back in his pocket. Business with knives and jewelry. GROUCHO reads the engravings on the knives)

Hotel Astor, New York, Hotel Blackstone, Chicago. Those are mine.

(HARPO whistles again and produces another piece of paper)

BOB: *(Unfolding it)* It's a map of part of Cocoanut Manor. Grenada Road, Cocoanut Road, Hollow Stump, Jewels. Where'd you find this?

GROUCHO: That's a good guy you picked to ask.

BOB: Whoever drew this must have been mixed up in that—

(POLLY enters)

POLLY: Bob.

BOB: Polly.

(They embrace. HARPO stands fascinated, watching)

GROUCHO: *(Starting off)* Well, I've got to wash the dishes. *(To HARPO)* Come on, you dry them. Say, two is company—three is a quartet.

(Business of GROUCHO *blindfolding* HARPO. GIRL *crossing and* HARPO *after her)*

That guy must be a police dog. *(To* BOB *and* POLLY*)* Say, young folks, you can't make love in this room. You'll have to go in the mushroom. *(*GROUCHO *exits)*

POLLY: Bob, do you know what mother's done? She's announced my engagement to Harvey Yates.

BOB: To Yates?

POLLY: She's giving an engagement supper tonight, but I won't go through with it.

BOB: Yes you must. That's just what I want. Will Mr. Yates be there?

POLLY: Well, it's customary.

BOB: Well, I have an idea. I don't know how to do it yet. But I'll let you know before evening. Until I get it all worked out, don't say a word about it.

POLLY: I can't. I don't know what it is.

BOB: But you do trust me.

POLLY: You know I do.

BOB: Then what's the difference what happens? We should care.

*(Go into number—"WE SHOULD CARE"—*POLLY *and* BOB. *After number—*GROUCHO *and* MRS. POTTER *enter)*

GROUCHO: And I'd advise you to use paper napkins, because the dinner will probably end up in a brawl anyhow. Then we will serve supper in the patio at ten o'clock, F.O.B. in kitchen?

MRS. POTTER: If you please.

GROUCHO: Jamison.

*(*JAMISON *enters)*

Supper at ten o'clock and bicarbonated soda at nine. *(Turns to* MRS. POTTER*)* How about starting with some nice leg of caviar stuffed?

MRS. POTTER: I don't think I ever heard of that.

GROUCHO: Me either, but it's a good idea. *(To* JAMISON*)* One hundred and fifty portions of leg of caviar.

MRS. POTTER: But I haven't asked that many guests.

GROUCHO: They'll be here. I sent out circulars. Then comes bread and butter under glass and breast of goldfish. Solid goldfish. How about some quail on toast?

MRS. POTTER: I'm a little afraid of quail.

GROUCHO: That's all right, I'll get you a shot gun. *(To* JAMISON*)* Bring in one of those new quail and pull his teeth out.

JAMISON: Yes, sir. *(Exits)*

GROUCHO: Champagne?

MRS. POTTER: That would depend on how old it is.

GROUCHO: Made this morning. You don't think I'd try to work off any old champagne on you, do you?

MRS. POTTER: Have you a nice pre-war vintage?

GROUCHO: What war? Civil? Revolutionary? Oh, you want the spirits of seventy-six. Do you want glasses or drink it out of the bottles?

MRS. POTTER: Glasses, if you please.

GROUCHO: I prefer it. They're fifty cents a crack.

MRS. POTTER: A crack?

GROUCHO: I mean a hunk, apiece. *(Starts to figure with pencil and paper)* One dollar each for knives and forks; three hundred shares at fifty cents apiece.

MRS. POTTER: Three hundred, but you said there were one hundred and fifty guests.

GROUCHO: They may want to sit down twice. Do you want seats in the chairs?

MRS. POTTER: Yes, please.

GROUCHO: One dollar extra. By the time this dinner is over, you may be willing to marry me for my money. Do you want finger bowls or chicken broth?

MRS. POTTER: Finger bowls are customary, are they not?

GROUCHO: Not necessary. There's a sink in the hall.

MRS. POTTER: Let me see, I might want some favors.

GROUCHO: Not so loud. I'll see you later. Do you want music, or would you prefer a jazz band?

MRS. POTTER: I think I'd like some Spanish music. All my guests are coming in Spanish costumes.

GROUCHO: All right, I'll get you a German band. No, I'll get you a Spanish band. I'll get you a half a dozen of King Alfonso's assorted musicians. In fact, I might get you the King himself. He's looking for a job.

MRS. POTTER: May I hear them play first?

GROUCHO: I'll let you hear them rehearse right before dinner.

MRS. POTTER: But suppose they're not satisfactory?

GROUCHO: What makes you think they will be?

(Enter JAMISON *carrying a cat on a tray)*

Ah, here we are. *(Takes cat)* You see all our quail are perfectly fresh. We kill 'em to order. They turn red when they're boiled. You'd probably do the same thing yourself.

MRS. POTTER: Quail? But that's a cat, my dear man. A cat.

GROUCHO: Isn't that funny. Everybody thinks that's a cat. That's an Australian quail. The only fur-bearing quail in the world. He carries his own kitty car. I know it looks like a cat, but if you could see it on a piece of toast, you'd immediately know the difference. Here, we'll say this book is a piece of toast. *(Business)* No, he won't stay on there. If I had a catalogue, he'd lie there. Anyhow by the time we serve them, he'll lie perfectly flat and so will you. *(To* JAMISON*)* Here, put him back in the ice box.

(Enter HENNESSY*)*

HENNESSY: Ah ha.

GROUCHO: Put him too.

HENNESSY: You're just the people I'm looking for. Now get this, you people. I've just dug up some new evidence on that necklace robbery.

GROUCHO: That's Hamlet in modern clothes.

HENNESSY: And I'm going to conduct a little investigation. I'm going to hold a probe right here and now. Come on in, you people.

(They all enter)

Everybody take their places.

GROUCHO: Select your partners for the big probe.

(Everybody takes their places. Ad lib talk from HENNESSY*)*

HENNESSY: Ladies and gentlemen, be seated.

(As they all sit the ORCHESTRA *strikes up a chord. They all put on collars and hats)*

Now then, I saw all of you fellows up in Mrs. Potter's room last night. Didn't I?

GROUCHO: I object to the object.

HENNESSY: Well, what was that room I saw you in?

GROUCHO: That was no room, that was a hallway. *(He stands)* Mr. Leander Honeywhistle our silver-throated tenor will now render that popular ballad, "I Love You Always." *(He starts to sing)*

HENNESSY: Stop that singing.

GROUCHO: Thanks for the compliment.

HENNESSY: *(To* HARPO*)* Cut that out. *(To* CHICO*)* Were you in this lady's room last night? *(He indicates* MRS. POTTER*)*

CHICO: I don't know, I meet so many people.

HENNESSY: *(To* GROUCHO*)* Were you in Mrs. Potter's room last night?

GROUCHO: No, but it's not a bad idea.

HENNESSY: *(To* CHICO*)* Did you see him there? *(Meaning* HARPO*)*

CHICO: I don't know. He was under the bed.

HENNESSY: *(To* HARPO*)* Were you in anybody's room last night? Shut up. *(To* CHICO*)* Are you two related?

CHICO: I am, but not him.

HENNESSY: Is he your brother?

CHICO: I don't know. Papa say one thing, another man say something else.

GROUCHO: So far, it's a regular probe. He hasn't found out anything yet.

HENNESSY: *(To* GROUCHO*)* Don't forget you're in on this, too. Didn't I see you with a lady last night?

GROUCHO: That was no lady. That was the night before last. *(To* CHICO*)* Well, Mr. Bones, and how are you feeling this evening?

CHICO: Not so good. I lose my dog.

GROUCHO: You lost your dog? And how did you come to lose him?

CHICO: I shoot him.

GROUCHO: You shot him? Was he mad?

CHICO: He not very damned pleased.

HENNESSY: Look here, you two.

GROUCHO: There you are. His dog got mad and he shot him. *(To* HENNESSY) Let that be a lesson to you.

HENNESSY: This nonsense has got to stop. Now you answer me this question. Why did you cross from Miss Martyn's room into Mrs. Potter's room?

GROUCHO: That's an old one. To get on the other side.

HENNESSY: *(To* HARPO) Cut that out. Now everybody has got to stop this. We're going to get back at this probe.

GROUCHO: We ought to have a probe. To see where the probe has gone.

HENNESSY: *(To* MRS. POTTER) Now then, Mrs. Potter, that jewel case was opened with your key. Is that right?

MRS. POTTER: Yes sir.

END MAN: That's my baby.

HENNESSY: And that key has not been returned.

MRS. POTTER: No sir.

END MAN: Don't mean maybe.

HENNESSY: It was stolen from your bag.

MRS. POTTER: Yes sir.

ALL: That's my baby doll.

(GROUCHO starts to dance)

HENNESSY: *(To* GROUCHO) Stop that. *(To* HARPO) Cut that out. Now then, there is one important witness who hasn't said anything else.

(HARPO stands)

We will now hear from Miss Penelope Martyn.

GROUCHO: You bet you will. Miss Penelope Martyn, Dixie's darling songbird, will now render that popular song success—"Minstrel Days."

*(Number—"MINSTREL DAYS"—*PENELOPE *and* OTHERS. *After num-*

ber—HENNESSY, *who is very much perturbed, proceeds to get back into the probe)*

HENNESSY: This nonsense has got to stop. We are now going to get back into this probe. If we find the person with the key, we will be pretty close to someone who is implicated in this robbery.

GROUCHO: Hennessy, you're a genius.

HENNESSY: A man isn't a detective for twenty years for nothing.

GROUCHO: He'd be a sucker if he was.

(HARPO makes a quick movement as though passing something to CHICO who is beside him. HENNESSY sees it)

HENNESSY: What's that you gave him?

CHICO: Who me?

HENNESSY: Yes you. Give me that key.

(Shirt business)

Who got my shirt? Where is my shirt? I want my shirt.

GROUCHO: Ah, now we have something to have a probe about. Describe this shirt.

HENNESSY: What's that?

GROUCHO: When did you first find out it was missing? Did you have it with you when you came into the room?

HENNESSY: I certainly did.

GROUCHO: Did you buy the shirt in Brooklyn, or was it a Manhattan shirt?

HENNESSY: I want my shirt. I can't go around this way.

GROUCHO: Did you ever lose a shirt before?

HENNESSY: No, I didn't.

GROUCHO: You don't say? Didn't you ever play poker?

HENNESSY: Never mind about that.

CHICO: Maybe it's hereditary.

GROUCHO: Did your father or mother ever lose a shirt?

HENNESSY: *(Bellowing)* No.

GROUCHO: Did your father or mother ever have a shirt?

CHICO: A very mysterious case. Did you get the shirt from your wife or did you get it from a bosom friend?

GROUCHO: We have got to find this shirt before shirty days. We'll go at it scientifically. Jamison.

(JAMISON crosses to GROUCHO and proceeds to take notes. GROUCHO takes a piece of crayon from his pocket and makes a cross on HENNESSY's undershirt)

Now then, X marks the spot where the shirt was last seen.

HENNESSY: Hey, stop that.

GROUCHO: There are only two possible exits. *(To CHICO)* Am I right?

CHICO: *(Examining HENNESSY. He lays his head against HENNESSY)* Say ah.

HENNESSY: *(Angrily)* Ah.

GROUCHO: It isn't down there. *(GROUCHO takes tape measure and begins measuring HENNESSY)* Thirty-seven and a half.

JAMISON: *(Repeating as he jots down the figures)* Thirty-seven and a half.

GROUCHO: Twelve and a quarter.

JAMISON: Twelve and a quarter.

GROUCHO: Turned up cuff.

JAMISON: Turned up cuff.

GROUCHO: Big seat. Long neck and no brains.

JAMISON: Big seat. Long neck and no brains.

CHICO: And no shirt.

JAMISON: And no shirt.

GROUCHO: Do you need any socks?

HENNESSY: All I want is my shirt.

GROUCHO: We've got a special sale on socks today. Silk lisle. You'll be all right. Just cut out all red meat. Jamison, take that dummy out of the window and put Hennessy in.

HENNESSY: Just as I thought. You boys are all in on this and you're all trying to keep me from finding that shirt. I'm not going to stand for any more of this. Now listen to me, you people. I'm going to count three. And when I say three, I want absolute silence. Do you understand. Absolute silence. There is somebody else mixed up in this. Where is that little red-headed fellow. *(Business)* Now then—one—two—three.

("TAMBOURINE DRILL" by the ENTIRE COMPANY. HENNESSY *exits)*

END OF SCENE.

ACT TWO

Scene Two

SCENE:—*Before the Palms.*

GROUCHO *enters.*

GROUCHO: *(Calling off stage)* Oh, Manuel.

(Enter MUSICIAN*)*

And Manuel.

(Enter SECOND MUSICIAN*)*

And a—Manuel.

(Enter THIRD MUSICIAN*)*

And you too Manuel.

(Enter FOURTH MUSICIAN*)*

A—Manuel.

(Enter FIFTH MUSICIAN*)*

And Manuel.

(Enter SIXTH MUSICIAN*)*

I got these boys from Emanuel Training School. They're Spaniards. That is, they're not real Spaniards, they're fake Spaniards. They are Spaniards like the Marx Brothers. They're Spaniards but the accent is on the last syllable. They're Span—yids.

(Exit GROUCHO. MUSICIANS *play)*

END OF SCENE.

ACT TWO

Scene Three

SCENE:—*The Patios*.

Scene opens with number "A TANGO MELODY" by PENELOPE. *After the number enter* GROUCHO *and* POLLY.

POLLY: Oh, Mr. Schlemmer, you look wonderful. Your costume is marvelous. I just love the color scheme.
GROUCHO: That isn't a scheme, that's a conspiracy.

(Enter BOB*)*

BOB: Oh, Mr. Schlemmer.
GROUCHO: Oh, hello there.
BOB: Would you mind if I talk to Polly for a second?
GROUCHO: No, I'd like to hear you. All right, I'll see you later. Be sure to stay for dinner. We got chocolate ice cream and woman's fingers. *(Exits)*
POLLY: Bob, suppose mother sees you.
BOB: I can't help it. Now is the time. You can call him.
POLLY: All right. But what if it doesn't work?
BOB: It must work. But remember, you've got to make him draw a duplicate diagram.
POLLY: All right.

(Exit BOB. POLLY *calls off stage)*

Oh, Harvey.

HARVEY: *(Answering off stage)* Yes. What is it?

(HARVEY enters)

POLLY: Why, I just wanted to talk to you.

HARVEY: Did you really, Polly? *(He reaches for her hand)*

POLLY: Don't you think we ought to go somewhere alone? We've never been alone.

HARVEY: Where will we go?

POLLY: Any where that there aren't a lot of people around and— *(She pretends to get a sudden idea)* Harvey!

HARVEY: Well?

POLLY: Why shouldn't we just elope?

HARVEY: You would? You mean it? When?

POLLY: The sooner the better. Say, tonight.

HARVEY: *(A quick look around)* How will we do it?

POLLY: *(A second's thought)* Let's make it really romantic. And meet at Cocoanut Manor, where we became engaged.

HARVEY: *(Taking her hand)* Polly, you're marvelous. What time?

POLLY: Say, twelve o'clock.

HARVEY: All right. Twelve o'clock at Cocoanut Manor. Oh, Polly. *(He tries to embrace her)*

POLLY: No, no, not now.

HARVEY: Then— *(A second's pause)* Until Cocoanut Manor.

POLLY: *(A brief pause)* Oh—I'm not sure I know how to get there in the dark. You'd better tell me.

HARVEY: You can't miss it. You go right out Grenada Road—

POLLY: I'll never remember it. Maybe we'd better not do it.

HARVEY: Here, I'll show you. *(Takes paper and pencil from pocket)* You go right up Cocoanut Road, see? *(Plays scene exactly as with PENELOPE)* Then there's Augustine Road. But instead you take Grenada Road, then suddenly you come on a clearing with a fringe of trees around it. That's Cocoanut Manor. Remember Polly, twelve o'clock at Cocoanut Manor.

(He starts to embrace her but is interrupted when MRS. POTTER and PENEL-OPE and OTHERS enter)

LACKEY: *(Announcing the guests as they arrive)* Senior Chico, Joseph, Maria, Acounia, Count de Elisinore.

GROUCHO: On track twenty-five.

(Enter CHICO)

CHICO: Bella Señora. Bella Señora. Ah, Mrs. Potter, for a little while I no think I be able to come, but I know you get very much disappoint, so I come anyhow.

GROUCHO: Say, when you get through strutting around here, you can take out the ashes.

LACKEY: His Excellency, the Spanish Ambassador, Senior Don Hose, Harpano.

(Enter HARPO—business)

GROUCHO: When you get through with my slippers, put them back under the bed. *(Business)* They're toasted.

MRS. POTTER: Let me see. I think every one is here.

(Enter HENNESSY without his shirt)

GROUCHO: Ah, the nights of Pythias. Hennessy, you look like a red hot bun. You can't walk around this way. There are ladies present.

HENNESSY: I want my shirt.

GROUCHO: He wants his shirt.

HENNESSY: I want my shirt.

ALL: He wants his shirt.

(Go into number "THE TALE OF A SHIRT")

GROUCHO: Now that we've found Hennessy's shirt, would you all mind looking for a collar button that I lost about three weeks ago. Size fifteen and a quarter.

MRS. POTTER: Now if you'll find places, we'll have a short program.

GROUCHO: I'm going home if you're going to have a program.

(GROUCHO *starts to exit*)

MRS. POTTER: You come right back here. Mr. Schlemmer will act as master of ceremonies.

GROUCHO: Ladies and gentlemen.

CHICO: Two hundred dollars.

GROUCHO: In behalf of the Rotary Club of Minneapolis, I want to take this occasion of welcoming you to San Diego. No, I mean in recognition of my years with the railroad, you have presented me with this travelling bag. Am I right?

MRS. POTTER: Yes, yes.

GROUCHO: Well, where is the bag? This is indeed a happy occasion. It reminds me of the day my mother and father were married. I'll never forget it as long as I live. Everybody should be happy here tonight. Even the bride.

(HARPO *exits*)

They're dropping out early. When this Irishman died and he went to heaven and on the way to heaven—he met a Scotchman and a Swede and there wasn't room for all of them to get in bed so they had to stop over night at a farm house and little Willie had to stay up late. Well you can bet that the Minister never asked that question again. Well ten minutes later when the lady came back in the sleeping car, there was a foot sticking out of every berth. This went on for a good many of years. So St. Peter said you can't come in here and the Irishman said, why not? Now stop me if you've heard it. So the Captain lifted up his car and he went wham. You go down and come up right. This is no time for fooling. Well the result was that my mother and father had to move to New York. So they took a little house in the Bronx. And it was in that very house that Abraham Lincoln was born. Much to my father's surprise. And ladies and gentlemen, now that her daughter's engagement party is being held here tonight, I deem it no more than fitting that we should have a few words from her mother. I am now going to call for a speech from Mrs. Potter, and keep it clean.

(Enter HARPO*)*

MRS. POTTER: My good, good friends, if I could only tell you how rosy–hued everything seems to me tonight.

*(*HARPO *exits)*

As I look into your faces, they are all lit with gay-hearted laughter. The whole world and everything in it is bathed in a soft, glowing luminous haze.

GROUCHO: I think the old girl's got a snootful.

MRS. POTTER: What a wonderful night it is for all of us, especially this happy couple at my side. Posed hand in hand upon the threshold of life.

CHICO: Let's drink a toast.

MRS. POTTER: You're a little premature.

CHICO: So's your old man.

GROUCHO: Well, that's a question.

MRS. POTTER: As I was about to say, what a wonderful occasion it is for all of us.

GROUCHO: Why don't you slink off to bed?

MRS. POTTER: How happy they should be, these two, for their honeymoon they will take a long motor trip. I am giving them a Chevrolet sedan. Just think, this time tomorrow night, they will be many many miles from here.

GROUCHO: Not in a Chevrolet, they won't. I doubt if they get out of the garage.

MRS. POTTER: And now I want to wish you all a most enjoyable evening. I am too overcome to say more.

GROUCHO: Hurrah, she's overcome. And now folks, even on a happy occasion like this, there comes some moments that are quite pastrami. We are now going to have a few words from the groom. I am now going to call on Mr. Harvey Yates, of Yates, Yates, Yates, Yates, Hammacher, Schlemmer and Yates. *(*HARVEY *stands)* And Yates.

HARVEY: My dear dear friends.

*(*HARPO, *who re-entered during previous speeches, exits)*

I really don't know what to say. I feel highly honored that you should call on me, Mr. Schlemmer. I'm not very much of a speech-maker. Nevertheless, it was very nice of you to call on me.

GROUCHO: You must call on me some time.

HARVEY: I really wouldn't dream of taking up too much of your time. Nevertheless I want to thank you all for a most enjoyable evening, and as I said before, I really hadn't intended to make a speech at all.

GROUCHO: Well you certainly succeeded.

*(*HARPO *re-enters. To* HARPO*)*

Say, you, next time you go out, get me a pimento cheese sandwich. And now folks, the first musical number on the program will be a Piccolo Solo, which we will skip. The second number on the program will be a baseball game between the married men and the single women. Boys toe down the box car. Senior Bordello, Italy's Primiere Virtuoso, will now tickle those Florida keys.

CHICO: You want I should play.

GROUCHO: Yes. I've heard quite a bit about your playing from you.

MRS. POTTER: Senior Bordello, what is the first number?

CHICO: Number one.

(Remarks by GROUCHO *during the Piano Solo and Harp Specialty. After Harp Specialty is over)*

GROUCHO: And now ladies and gentlemen, you can have your choice of two things. You can either have a recitation of Gunga Din, or you can have Gunga Din without the recitation. I will now distribute the ballots.

(Enter POLLY *and* BOB*)*

POLLY: Mother. Bob has something to show you.

MRS. POTTER: Polly, Mr. Adams.

BOB: Mrs. Potter, may I show you this diagram?

MRS. POTTER: I don't wish to see it.

BOB: It shows you how to get to Cocoanut Manor and that tree stump, and it has written on it, "Hollow Stump," "Jewels."

MRS. POTTER: Really, I don't see what all this proves.

BOB: Here's another diagram of Cocoanut Manor, drawn by Harvey Yates.

MRS. POTTER: Mr. Yates?

HENNESSY: Mr. Yates?

BOB: Yes, this is Mr. Yates's diagram.

GROUCHO: Yates's diaphragm?

BOB: And the handwriting is exactly the same.

HENNESSY: Say, Yates and the girl have gone.

GROUCHO: Yates gone? And I gave him a hundred dollars this morning. It's a good thing it was counterfeit.

(HARPO enters—wearing HARVEY's hat and cloak)

Mrs. Fiske.

BOB: *(To GROUCHO)* Mr. Schlemmer, who do you think is downstairs?

GROUCHO: The Sheriff.

BOB: No—Berryman from Miami. He's going to take another look at the property and says he's going to buy it. It looks like you're going to be a millionaire.

GROUCHO: I don't want to be a millionaire. Then I'll have to read the morning's *Times.*

POLLY: Mother, you must admit you were mistaken.

MRS. POTTER: Mr. Adams, how can you ever forgive me?

(BOB and MRS. POTTER start to embrace)

GROUCHO: Just a minute. There's three ahead of you.

MRS. POTTER: I will now make an announcement.

(Business of HARPO throwing cape over his shoulders and falling)

GROUCHO: Why, Minnie Madern Fiske. You get right up there. Wallowing around the floor in your good cloak.

(Business of HARPO *spreading cloak on floor for* GIRL *to walk on)*

That's Sir Walter Levy.

MRS. POTTER: I merely want to say that you are all invited to the wedding of my daughter. It will be held exactly as planned with the exception of a slight change. She will be married to Mr. Robert Adams.

GROUCHO: And in honor of the event, I am going to give you all a free dinner. Admission four dollars.

MRS. POTTER: And for a wedding present, shall we say the house in Newport?

GROUCHO: Oh no, we're going to have the house in Newport. *(Indicating* MRS. POTTER *and himself)* Well you can have it. *(Embracing* POLLY*)* We've made our plans.

("BUNGALOW" Reprise)

E N D   O F   S C E N E .

C U R T A I N .

E N D   O F   P L A Y .

NEW YORK: A PRAYER

THE NEW YORKER, *September 3, 1955*

When at last the city's finished—
   When the final nail is driven
   And the final rivet given
   Its eternal niche in space,
   When the men who dig the streets up
   Sound a gentle note of grace,
   And when the final garbage can
   Is clattered by the hand of man,
   The final motorcycle stilled,
   The final berry vender killed,
   The one remaining jet plane
   Soars above the azure deep—
Then, Lord, let me again be born,
And on that still and happy morn,
      I'll sleep.

ABOUT GEORGE S. KAUFMAN

George S. Kaufman was born in Pittsburgh, Pa. in 1889. During his early career as a reporter and drama critic (and eventually drama editor of *The New York Times*), he began to write for the theater. After 1921, when *Dulcy,* his first collaboration with Marc Connelly appeared, there was rarely a year (until his death in 1961) without a Kaufman play—usually in collaboration. His only full-length plays written alone were *The Butter And Egg Man, The Cocoanuts,* and *Hollywood Pinafore.* A master craftsman of the theater with a brilliant eye for comedy and satire, Kaufman was frequently brought in by the producer to transform the script of a promising play into that of a successful one. He was equally adept in almost all varieties of theatrical art—expressionistic satire, as in *Beggar On Horseback* (also with Marc Connelly); social satire, as in *Dulcy,* and *Dinner At Eight* (the latter written with Edna Ferber); revues, as in *The Band Wagon* (written with Howard Dietz and Arthur Schwartz); musicals, as in the 1931 Pulitzer Prize-winning *Of Thee I Sing* (with Morrie Ryskind, George and Ira Gershwin); and comedies, some of the greatest of the twentieth century theater: *Once In a Lifetime, The Man Who Came to Dinner,* and *You Can't Take It With You* (another Pulitzer Prize-winner in 1936—and all three written with Moss Hart), *The Royal Family* (also with Edna Ferber), and *The Solid Gold Cadillac* (with Howard Teichmann). With Morrie Ryskind, he also wrote the screenplays for the Marx Brothers' films: *The Cocoanuts, Animal Crackers,* and *A Night at the Opera.* Mr. Kaufman also directed some two dozen of his own plays plus such other hits as *The Front Page, Of Mice and Men, My Sister Eileen,* and *Guys and Dolls.*

ACKNOWLEDGMENTS

ADVICE TO WORRIERS, Copyright 1922, *Life.* Reprinted by permission.

SCHOOL FOR WAITERS, Copyright 1947, *The New Yorker Magazine, Inc.* Reprinted by permission.

HOW I BECAME A GREAT ACTOR, Originally published in *Theatre.*

ANNOY KAUFMAN, INC., Copyright © 1957, *The New Yorker Magazine, Inc.* Reprinted by permission.

BARBERSHOP "WHY'S", Copyright 1921, *Life.* Reprinted by permission.

DEPARTMENT OF AMPLIFICATION, Copyright 1946, *The New Yorker Magazine, Inc.* Reprinted by permission.

LIFE'S CALENDAR FOR DECEMBER 1921 and JANUARY 1922, Copyright 1921, *Life.* Reprinted by permission.

EINSTEIN IN HOLLYWOOD, Copyright 1938, *The Nation Associates.* Reprinted by permission.

MEET THE AUDIENCE, Copyright © 1979, Anne Kaufman Schneider. Reprinted by permission.

BY THE WAY, Copyright 1945, *Saturday Review,* Reprinted by permission.

THAT MORNING MAIL, Copyright 1948, *The New York Times.* Reprinted by permission.

WRINGING IN THE NEW YEAR, originally published in *Harper's Weekly.*

MUSIC TO MY EARS, originally published in *Stage.*

CAN YOU FINISH IT, Reprinted from "The Phoenix Nest," Martin Levin's column in *Saturday Review.* Copyright © 1959, *Saturday Review.* Copyright © 1960 by Martin Levin. Reprinted by permission of Martin Levin.

WHEN YOUR HONEY'S ON THE TELEPHONE, Copyright © 1958, *The New Yorker Magazine, Inc.* Reprinted by permission.

A PLAYWRIGHT TELLS ALMOST ALL, Copyright 1944, *The New York Times.* Reprinted by permission.

LIFE'S CALENDAR FOR FEBRUARY 1922—NOVEMBER 1922, Copyright 1922, *Life.* Reprinted by permission.

NOW IT CAN BE TOLD, Originally published in *The New York Herald Tribune.*

HOLLYWOOD PINAFORE, Copyright © 1979, Anne Kaufman Schneider. Reprinted by permission.

NOTES FOR A FILM BIOGRAPHY, Copyright 1945, *The New Yorker Magazine, Inc.* Reprinted by permission.

GOD GETS AN IDEA, Copyright 1938, *The Nation Associates.* Reprinted by permission.

BILLING, SCHMILLING . . . , Reprinted from "The Phoenix Nest," Martin Levin's column in *Saturday Review.* Copyright © 1959, *Saturday Review.* Copyright © 1960, Martin Levin. Reprinted by permission of Martin Levin.

BALLADE OF THE UNFORTUNATE FISHERMAN, Copyright 1922, *Life.* Reprinted by permission.

IN ADMIRATION, Copyright 1942, Reprinted by permission of Doubleday, Doran & Co.

IF MEN PLAYED CARDS AS WOMEN DO, Copyright 1923 by George S. Kaufman. Copyright 1950 (In Renewal) by George S. Kaufman. Copyright 1926 by Samuel French. Copyright 1954 (In Renewal) by George S. Kaufman. CAUTION: Professionals and amateurs are hereby warned that IF MEN PLAYED CARDS AS WOMEN DO, being fully protected under the copyright laws of the United States of America, the British Commonwealth countries, including Canada, and all other countries of the Copyright Union, is subject to a royalty. All rights, including professional, amateur, motion pictures, recitation, public reading, radio and television broadcasting, and the rights of translation into foreign languages are strictly reserved. Amateurs may give stage production of this play upon payment of a royalty of Five Dollars ($5.00) for each performance one week before the play is to be given to Samuel French, Inc., at 25 West 45th Street, New York, N.Y. 10036, or 7623 Sunset Blvd., Hollywood, Calif. 90046, or if in Canada to Samuel French (Canada)